Professor Moneera Al-Ghadeer received her Ph.D. in Comparative Literature from the University of California at Berkeley and is now an Associate Professor in the Department of African Languages and Literature at the University of Wisconsin, Madison. Her research is highly interdisciplinary and includes postcolonial studies, feminist philosophy, literary theory and literary translation. She has received a number of fellowships and awards from the University of California at Berkeley and the University of Wisconsin, Madison along with a postdoctoral fellowship from Emory University.

Library of Modern Middle East Studies

Selected titles: for a full list of titles see www.ibtauris.com/LMMES

25. *Religion, Culture and Politics in Iran: From the Qajars to Khomeini*
Joanna de Groot
978 1 86064 571 6

39. *Tormented Births: Passages to Modernity in Europe and the Middle East*
Isam Al-Khafaji
978 1 86064 976 9

41. *Women and Media in the Middle East: Power through Self-Expression*
Naomi Sakr
978 1 85043 485 6

44. *Human Rights in Arab Thought: A Reader*
Salma K. Jayyusi (ed.)
978 1 85043 707 9

51. *Reading Iraq: Culture and Power in Conflict*
Muhsin al-Musawi
978 1 84511 070 3

52. *Monarchies and Nations: Globalisation and Identity in the Arab States of the Gulf*
Paul Dresch and James Piscatori (eds)
978 1 85043 971 4

57. *Filming the Modern Middle East: Politics in the Cinemas of Hollywood and the Arab World*
Lina Khatib
978 1 84511 192 2

58. *Negotiating Change: The New Politics of the Middle East*
Jeremy Jones
978 1 84511 269 1

61. *The Making of Jordan: Tribes, Colonialism and the Modern State*
Yoav Alon
978 1 84511 138 0

62. *Identity Politics in the Middle East: Liberal Thought and Islamic Challenge in Egypt*
Meir Hatina
978 1 84511 135 9

63. *The New Voices of Islam: Reforming Politics and Modernity – A Reader*
Mehran Kamrava (ed.)
978 1 84511 274 5

68. *Arab Media and Political Renewal: Community, Legitimacy and Public Life*
Naomi Sakr (ed.)
978 1 84511 433 6

69. *Imagining the Arab Other: How Arabs and Non-Arabs View Each Other*
Tahar Labib
978 1 84511 384 1

71. *The Zaza Kurds of Turkey: A Middle Eastern Minority in a Globalised Society*
Mehmed S. Kaya
978 1 84511 875 4

73. *The Arab-Israeli Conflict in the Media: Producing Shared Memory and National Identity in the Global Television Era*
Tamar Ashuri
978 1 84511 814 3

74. *Desert Voices: Bedouin Women's Poetry in Saudi Arabia*
Moneera Al-Ghadeer
978 1 84511 666 8

76. *Satellite Realms: Transnational Television, Globalization and the Middle East*
Naomi Sakr
978 1 86064 688 1

78. *Israeli Cinema: East/West and the Politics of Representation*
Ella Shohat
978 1 84511 312 4

79. *Occidentalism in Turkey: Questions of Modernity and National Identity in Turkish Radio Broadcasting*
Meltem Ahiska
978 1 84511 653 8

80. *Narrating Islam: Interpretations of the Muslim World in European Texts*
Gerdien Jonker and Shiraz Thobani (eds)
978 1 84511 978 2

83. *The Emergence of Modern Istanbul: Transformation and Modernisation of a City*
Murat Gül
978 1 84511 935 5

84. *Beyond Islam: A New Understanding of the Middle East*
Sami Zubaida
978 1 84885 069 9

85. *The New Arab Journalist: Mission and Identity in a Time of Change*
Jeremy Ginges and Laurence Pintak
978 1 84885 098 9

86. *Reclaiming Women's Rights in Islam: The Challenge to Muslim Patriarchy*
Hanaan Balala
978 1 84885 118 4

DESERT VOICES

Bedouin Women's Poetry in Saudi Arabia

MONEERA AL-GHADEER

I.B.TAURIS

LONDON • NEW YORK • OXFORD • NEW DELHI • SYDNEY

I.B. TAURIS
Bloomsbury Publishing Plc
50 Bedford Square, London, WC1B 3DP, UK
1385 Broadway, New York, NY 10018, USA
29 Earlsfort Terrace, Dublin 2, Ireland

Desert Voices: Bedouin Women's Poetry in Saudi Arabia was first published in 2009 by Tauris Academic Studies, an imprint of I.B. Tauris & Co Ltd

BLOOMSBURY, I.B. TAURIS and the I.B. Tauris logo are trademarks of Bloomsbury Publishing Plc

First published 2009
This paperback edition published by I.B Tauris in 2024

A catalogue record for this book is available from the British Library.

A catalog record for this book is available from the Library of Congress.

ISBN: HB: 978-1-8451-1666-8
PB: 978-0-7556-5299-0
ePDF: 978-0-8577-1196-0

Contents

Acknowledgements

My memory travels in time and space and gathers many debts as I attempt to remember, acknowledge and express thanks for every gesture of generosity. Recalling the early stages of this project at the Department of Comparative Literature at UC-Berkeley, I am grateful to James Monroe, who provoked my research, propelling me to explore whether Bedouin women's poetry does not actually exist and to destabilize the prevalent assumptions. As a patient and attentive mentor, he inspired and guided my earlier research and continued to offer indefatigable support during the writing of this book. I also wish to thank Ann Smock for her eloquent and astute remarks on the draft of Chapter 1. The encouraging words of Richard Hutson awakened my motivation when there was none.

For the generous institutional support of this project, I would like to thank the Fox Center for Humanistic Inquiry and its director, Martine Watson Brownley, at Emory University for providing me with a Mellon postdoctoral fellowship during the academic year 2003–2004. I gratefully acknowledge the graduate school research fellowship at the University of Wisconsin-Madison for summer research funding in 2005.

My debts are enormous and weigh heavy in this fleeting recollection. I am grateful for Leila Abu Lughod's invigorating comments and intellectual questions after a meticulous reading of the first draft of this manuscript. Her vital remarks guided my revision. I must also thank Mary Layoun, whose intellectual and affirmative conversations made it possible to complete this book; Harold Scheub for his generous reading of various drafts; Muhsin al-Musawi for his enthusiastic support of this study; and Gilles Bousquet for providing institutional support and collaborating with the College of Letters and

Science at UW-Madison to provide me with a semester off to finish the manuscript.

Parts of Chapters 2 and 3 appeared in a special issue of *symploke* titled 'Cinema without Borders' (volume 15, nos 1 and 2, Summer 2008). Also, I gratefully acknowledge my colleagues who invited me to present different chapters of this book at MEALAC, Columbia University; the Department of African Languages and Literature, UW-Madison; the Department of Middle Eastern and South Asian Studies, Emory University; and the Department of Comparative Literature, University of Michigan.

My numerous conversations with Tarek El-Ariss helped me rethink and rewrite my argument. Karen McLaughlin's careful and positive comments on Chapter 2 were greatly appreciated. Tejumola Olaniyan's comments provided the allusive nuance to explore some of the chapters' enquiries. I thank Shireen R. K. Patell for her insightful and rigorous remarks on the first draft of Chapter 1. In my constant nomadic voyages, I learnt from numerous insights, stimulating reflections, sincere excitement and sometimes disquieting fascination about Bedouin women's lyrics. The forceful enthusiasm I encountered urged me to send off this manuscript.

In translating the poems, I faced a number of lyrical, cultural and vernacular challenges that I could not have overcome without the eloquent and sensitive suggestions provided by James Monroe, Michael Sells, Meriam Cooke, Kevin Barrett, Christopher Larkosh, Deirdre Flynn and Jeff Fort, among many readers. I am deeply grateful and indebted to them for their valuable suggestions and fine-tuning of the translation.

I am immensely grateful to my mother, who sang the desert's prosody and captured traces of its tones. She endured my absence and watched over my solitude during a long nomadic experience in America.

Note on Transliterations

The transliteration of Arabic words follows the Library of Congress transliteration system, with several important exceptions. To maintain the aural integrity of the Bedouin poetry, I have transliterated some of its words and references according to the dialectical pronunciations (for example, 'q' is pronounced 'g' in the local Bedouin dialect). I tried to maintain clarity and systematic approach to transliterating these words without going into other dialectical variations that this poetry exemplifies.

In all cases where I quoted from another author's work, I retained the author's original transliteration. Generally, in cases of place and proper names with commonly accepted spellings in English, I have utilized the standard English spellings.

For my mother who endured my absence

Introduction

In recent scholarship on Arabic literature the poetry of Arab women has been given insignificant consideration and continues to be unappreciated, unlike other genres. This is difficult to acknowledge for several reasons, some of which must remain hypothetical, given the nature of exclusion as unspoken and empty space. Other reasons, ironically, are related to the difficulty of poetry itself, and also to fundamental questions of language and gender. Although literary studies on Arab women's writing are impressive, there is an obvious lack of comparative analysis of oral and written Arab women's poetry.

Desert Voices: Bedouin Women's Poetry in Saudi Arabia is a comparative reading of women's oral poetry from Arabia. As the first English translation of this poetry, it is both a gesture towards preserving the oral poetic tradition of women and a radical critique addressing the exclusion of their poetry from current academic literary studies. Bedouin poetry would provide invaluable material for reflection in the debates around oral culture and women's poetic composition, but so far there is no translation or discussion presenting it to English-language readers. Indeed, this impressive poetic tradition has been systematically marginalized both in Arabic and Euro-American literary studies, to the extent that most English and French literary criticism of Arabic literature presupposes that oral poetry by women in Arabia does not exist.

Desert Voices begins an exploration of Bedouin women's oral poetics and uncovers a substantial and aesthetically impressive tradition. The unearthing of this extraordinary material from what seems to have been a memory eclipse confronts the literary critic with several crucial questions. How should we read oral poetry? How do we explicate its historical and cultural significance more effectively in English? Should our approach differ from the analytical models of canonical Arabic poetry? What theoretical insights may be gained from comparative reflection on an excluded feminine oral genre? Are there political consequences from such a comparative reading? Can Bedouin women's oral poems be read in terms of contemporary literary theory/*al-naẓarīyah al-adabīyah*/*pensée*?

One might also ask to whom an Arab woman has to justify her theoretical critique and why 'Third World women' have to conform to these excruciatingly derivative and predetermined gestures? Surely we can hear the echo of presupposed divisions between West/East, theory/literature, orality/writing, among other binaries. Without justifying my theoretical position (there is always a submissive gesture in trying to formulate a defence of an intellectual activity), I believe that the complex debates and vigorous polemics of literary theory and its relevance to non-Western literary traditions can be summarized quite simply in two approaches.

On the one hand, certain Arabic literary studies in both Arabic and English resist the contamination of literary theory and Western philosophical explorations by assuming that ancient Arab rhetoricians and philosophers examined these theorems and constructed their own a priori knowledge. On the other hand, certain Anglo-Saxon and American scholars of Middle East studies shun literary theory because it is foreign, and contend that non-Western literary traditions must be investigated from within their own traditions. They assume the role of the master who protects the slave from reading the white man's philosophical paradigms to prolong the illusion of the archaic and exotic. This type of scholarship strives to maintain the East as the distant and primitive other, a mere looking glass into which the West can gaze at itself and uphold its narcissistic and civilized image. The rationale of discontinuity and demarcation between, say, Western theory and non-Western literature is a rationale of containment and suppression. In this very division lies the desire to preserve a dichotomy that asserts unequivocal superiority.

If such categories are maintained, it would be unproblematic to impose definitions, judgements, beliefs, classifications and repressive ideals on the East, and especially on its women. But it is facile to appropriate and generalize in this way; this is surely what we have learnt from the rigours of literary theory. To maintain these circumscribed borderlines is to extend the allusions of a transparent and unified theoretical model that is essentially static, undeviating and permanently separate from other traditions. Does not the logic of colonialism promote similar divisions? Instead, one must shift these paradigms of cultural superiority and read literary and philosophical productions side by side. After decades of being ensnared in fantasy and conflict, it is time to recognize the psychosis of power and to create a space for the other in and on the peripheries of literature to be explored not only as an aesthetic, but as a manifestation of philosophical meditations on humanist concerns – language, death, mourning, women's passions, and human and animal bonds.

What is representation? Is there a conclusive goal for critical or literary endeavours? A theoretical mode of reading demonstrates that language and representation complicate and disrupt both the notion of language transparency and the assumptions of a complete, linear, socio-historical discourse. Effectively, literary theory has taught us the limits of metanarratives and discourse. It has contested totalities and demonstrated a constant 'arrest' of representation, while deferring or differing the arrival at the represented and the signified. Also, history has revealed that many centuries of contact and transfer took place between Arabic and Greek philosophical and intellectual traditions. These periods of exchange are historically grounded, especially in the extraordinary translations into Arabic of Greek secular texts on science, philosophy, metaphysics, music and other subjects during the Abbasid era from the eighth to tenth centuries. Greek scientific and philosophical knowledge would have been lost without these remarkable translations that preserved and developed all sorts of texts and transferred them back to Europe in the twelfth century. Traces of influence may often be forgotten or suppressed, but they cannot be wholly erased.

In this book I offer a critical analysis of the aesthetic and socio-historical significance of Bedouin women's poetry during two significant phases of globalization: the integration of medieval Europe's cultural legacy of Arab science and thought under the rubric of Arab-Islamic traditions, and the more recent acceleration of that process via transnational capital under the matrix of technology. Arabic oral poetry was first transcribed and preserved at least 1500 years ago, and consists of the pre-Islamic poetry that takes central place in the Arabic poetic canon. With the expansion of Arab-Islamic civilization, the oral tradition of the *muʿallaqāt* from the Arabian Peninsula was adopted as the model for classical Arabic poetry. But it also reflected the exclusions of that era, and generated the unjustifiable fragmentation and dismissal of women's voices that have characterized Arabic oral poetry. Yet, even though these poetic voices were never fully accepted into the canon, they continued to develop through the centuries. Bedouin poetry of the last decades of the twentieth century retains a symbiosis with the old classical composition with variation on its subject matters.

In this book I translate, present and critically reflect on material that ʿAbd Allāh Ibn Rāddas collected and published as *Shāʿirāt min al-Bādīyah*. Beginning in the 1950s, Ibn Rāddas, a male Arab poet, spent more than a decade gathering Bedouin women's poetry. In doing so, he violated tribal law and received death threats. The material he collected not only provides a rare inside view of Bedouin culture from a subaltern or marginal perspective, but also includes poems of astonishing expressive and aesthetic impact.

Only a careful reading of the language of this poetry and knowledge of its cultural and political specificity will free it from the pervasive stereotypes associated with Arab women's writing. Thus, I take into account the unique context of the literary tropes and motifs deployed and the specificity of the Bedouin language and its registers. If my discussion seems discordant, this is both a deliberate trajectory and an inadvertent mimesis, where the reading follows and disseminates this poetry's rhetorical effects. Indeed, the dynamic of this book cannot help but follow the contours, rifts and ruptures of the poems. A theoretical reading 'always in a certain way falls prey to its own work,' according to Jacques Derrida.[1]

In the six chapters of this book I raise pivotal questions; some address a group of poems and some focus on reading single poems that are frequently quoted in more than one chapter. In the first chapter I address the suppression of Bedouin women's poetry, examine some of the current debates on Arabic popular poetry and discuss the hierarchical relationship between classical Arabic and Bedouin dialects. I situate the poetry in the Bedouin context and highlight its recurring tropes and motifs. In Chapters 2 and 3 I explore different elegies and the rhetoric of mourning and melancholy. Discussion of this has been excluded from Arabic literary studies, even though the question of melancholy is deeply rooted in medieval Arabic philosophical and medical discourses. In Chapter 2 I demonstrate that Bedouin women's poems broaden our understanding of the underpinnings of female melancholia and the poetic articulation of loss in a nomadic setting. In investigating mourning and melancholy, I follow a theoretical and psychoanalytical analysis with particular emphasis on the insights of Sigmund Freud and Judith Butler. The rhetoric of grief and lament, melancholy and loss is often aligned with the mechanism of desire, especially when the speaker declares her longing for an absent beloved. In addition, several poems display grief and gender grievance and embody forms of sexual grievance as social critique.

In Chapter 3 I highlight the importance of elegiac evocations that can be traced back to pre-Islamic odes. I show that the elegy, *al-rithā'*, is fundamental in Bedouin women's poetry, which encompasses elegizing the dead, identifying with grieving animals or birds and expressing loss in relation to the desert. A profound poetic relationship with animals and pastoral landscape is presented. This discourse of species and the fascination with animals have been recurrent in Arabic poetry. But Bedouin women poets identify with grief-stricken animals and birds in expressing their loss, and their elegies present a haunting meditation on death.

In Chapter 4 I discuss how voice, as a figure, is fictionalized in Bedouin women's poetry and, more significantly, how it is generated through the trope of prosopopoeia, which dislocates voice and blurs its origin. Voice is neither subjective nor a fixed presence of a human or authorial voice. In these poems I show that the voice is self-referential, since it refers to the poem itself. The exploration of prosopopoeia is guided by Paul de Man's rhetorical reading of this trope.

In Chapter 5 I examine some poems composed after the discovery of oil, in which women speak of technology in the form of motorcars, railways, aeroplanes and binoculars. These poems illuminate an important and neglected historical moment that is relevant to certain postcolonial and globalization theories about current crises in the Middle East. In particular, how can Arab-Islamic cultures coexist with Western civilization in a global age? By considering the advent of technology in Arabia from a marginal perspective, in this book I contribute to the understanding of a crucial historical period. Even the basics of the history of Arabia's oil-driven transformation are little known in the USA – which, ironically, remains dependent on Arabian oil reserves and extending political and military influence over them. But I offer no simplistic narrative of resistance to Western/technological encroachment. In contrast to the almost silent resistance to modes of Western technology reflected in the post-colonial studies of Frantz Fanon and Abdelrahman Munif, the Bedouin poems demonstrate a radical reformulation of technology: for these women poets the machine is neither alien nor a threat.

In the sixth chapter I demonstrate how this poetry incorporates and presents certain aspects of translation. What happens to the marginal subject and the minor language – dialect or dialects – in translation? How can one translate oral poems composed in a nomadic dialect? When do the theoretical and the cultural converge, to present the untranslatable? The most obvious translation problem in these poems is the exceedingly rich vocabulary of Bedouin ethos and the multi-faceted signification of weather and animal imagery.

After discussing Walter Benjamin, de Man, Derrida and G. C. Spivak on the task of translation, I draw attention to Spivak's caution about certain cultural politics that emerge when addressing Third World women's writing. As she says, 'There is an ethno-cultural agenda, an obliteration of Third World specificity as well as a denial of cultural citizenship,'[2] generated by progressive realism that proliferates in the West, attempting to render otherness in material registers or 'metropolitan materialism'.[3] Spivak stresses that the selected text or texts for translation should be those that undo and dismantle suppositions associated with non-Western women's texts and their mirroring of a cultural majority.

In considering questions of translation and reading, I expand on the concept of the motorcar as a metaphor for modernity. The poems that I argue were composed after the discovery of oil are problematic for translation, since they represent a displacement between two temporal stages – the nomadic and the modern. This rift is manifested in the language used. Interestingly, the different makes of American automobiles, as signifiers, are expressed in English, the 'other' language, a point of theoretical interest for theories of translation and cultural transfer.

Throughout, I attempt to portray what lies beneath the archetypal and static images of Arab women and oral tradition. The poems encapsulate women's lyrics of love, desire, mourning and gender grievance along with Bedouin mores and – most significantly – the unique rendering of a desert that is consistently held to be infinite, evocative, stimulating and with an eternal freedom, transmitted by an inappropriable voice.

Chapter 1
Reading the Nomadic Voices

The Arabian Desert has long been the locus of an ancient history of poetry, beginning with pre-Islamic odes and including an ongoing succession of transmitted and disseminated oral poetic forms.[1] Indeed, this desert has fascinated scholars, who in questions relevant to studies of Bedouin societies and oral traditions identify with its Bedouin ethos and artistic imagination. Recent debates on the transnational cultural scene have often revolved around questions of traditional culture, oral heritage and folklore, even as the urgent necessity of preserving and celebrating outstanding genres and performances from non-canonical traditions has been increasingly recognized.

Literary Sources and the Exclusion of Women's Poetry

Despite the proliferation of attempts to preserve world oral heritage and the surge of interest in previously unknown or marginalized cultural production by women, the remarkable poetic composition of Arabian Bedouin women has so far been ignored and suppressed, largely because little was known about it until ʿAbd Allāh Ibn Rāddas's *Shāʿirāt min al-Bādīyah* was first published in 1969.[2] Modern Western and Arabic literary critics, unlike anthropologists, ethnographers and folklorists, have neglected both Bedouin poetry as a body of work and, more importantly, women's contribution to this tradition.[3] At this juncture, I need to highlight how the literary sources have perpetuated the absence of Bedouin women's poetry. A sketch of the beginning of Bedouin poetry in Arabia and its entry into print culture will offer a historical context relevant to understanding this crucial oversight. Further, I will show how commentators and critics perceive and explain the naming of Bedouin poetry as '*Nabaṭī*'. Given that it is marked by loss, rupture and fragmentation, to which I shall return, what follows is neither a historical survey of Bedouin poetry nor an attempt to produce a complete narrative of this genre.

The history of Arabic poetry is one of unrelenting progression from the pre-Islamic to the modern characterized by a number of literary and epistemological discussions. Other forms of vernacular expression flourished on the peripheries of this literary tradition, instigating ongoing debates, which I address later in this chapter.

This Bedouin poetry has been classified and referred to as *Nabaṭī* poetry. What are the historical and linguistic implications of the word *Nabaṭī*, and what was its trajectory? When compilers and readers contemplate the term, they all speculate on how it can be defined or understood in relation to the beginning of Bedouin poetry. In some cases, it seems as if the word *Nabaṭī* is associated or collapsed with *al-Anbāṭ*, the Nabateans, a tribal group who migrated from Arabia around the sixth century BC and established a thriving empire in the Fertile Crescent. Well-known Petra, in Jordan, was their capital in the fourth century BC. In the beginning, they spoke a dialect of Arabic; they then turned to Aramaic as their official language.[4] The compilers and commentators of *Nabaṭī* poetry fail to offer a persuasive reading of its name and its relevance to this poetic genre. In fact, one of their shortcomings stems from their inability to explain the appropriation of the term, the plausible beginning of its deployment, and its echo of the Nabateans. As a result, most of the commentators' explanations of *Nabaṭī* and its significance either turn directly to recalling Ibn Khaldūn's reference to Bedouin poetry, which I address later in this discussion, or duplicate one another, indicating that even though the term *Nabaṭī* recalls Nabateans, it does not relate to this historical reference. The Arabic word *Nabaṭī* is derived from the verb *nabaṭa*, which implies 'to gush out' and 'stream forth'. The tenth form of the verb, *istanbaṭa*, means 'to find' and 'to discover' as well as 'to derive'.

Ibn Khamīs, however, thinks that the quest to explain adequately the linguistic and poetic associations of *Nabaṭī* poetry as well as the way it has been categorized must rely not only on the linguistic definition of the term but also on an examination of its relation to the Nabateans.

Ibn Khamīs emphasizes the various definitions of the term and then offers a persuasive explanation, stating that the poet Dhu al-Rummah (died 735) satirizes Imru' al-Qays's tribe by declaring that 'the people of al-Qays are *Anbāṭ* [Nabateans],' which suggests that they are not genuine Arabs.[5] In *Maqamāt al-Ḥarīrī* (1054–1122), we find a pertinent reference: '*al-Anbāṭ* is the plural of nabat and they are "'*ajam*" [foreigners].'[6] Ibn Khamīs concludes his comments by relating that the Nabateans spoke a dialect of Arabic that was mixed with and distorted by foreignness and is detached from the classical Arabic language. This may explain the characterization of Bedouin poetry as '*Nabaṭī*' since it was composed in Arabic dialects.[7] While al-Kamālī aligns his observations with the previous interpretation, he states that 'this naming does not mean that *al-Anbāṭ* are the first to compose [this poetry] but indicates its impure language and its divergence from *fuṣḥā* and therefore it resembles the language of *al-nabaṭ*. And the language of *al-nabaṭ* is removed from clarity and eloquence and accordingly they say *Nabaṭī* poetry.'[8]

According to Sowayan, Abu Ḥamzah al-ʿĀmirī , who lived during the thirteenth century, deployed this term in a manuscript.[9] While arguing with each other about this poetry as they considered canon formation, Ibn Khamīs, al-Kamālī and Sowayan presented value judgements that have continued to influence recent debates. Hence, the term *Nabaṭī* is used to categorize this type of vernacular poetry regardless of the term's historical significance, ultimately aligning it with a poetic genre, composed in Bedouin dialects, that reflects the nomadic lifestyle and cultural mores of the desert Bedouins. In other words, this naming entails describing all kinds of oral Bedouin poetry as *Nabaṭī*, but it may equally imply a kind of accessible dialectical poetry in that it displays the desire to draw on the desert values and expressions of its dwellers and is unlike classical poetic forms composed in classical Arabic.[10]

The Bedouin poetry in Arabia that is available in print extends from the fifteenth century to the early decades of the twentieth century. It was mostly transmitted by various reciters, then collected and published. Long Bedouin poems that sometimes extend to 1500 lines by well-known Arabian poets from the fifteenth and sixteenth centuries incorporate more classical Arabic fragments, dictions and expressions, which show the proximity of this poetry to literate culture and classical poetic forms.[11] In observing the earliest poems, one cannot assume a clear transition from orality to literacy but can highlight that oral Bedouin poetry has found its way into print, allowing the earliest anthologies and collections to produce considerable changes.[12]

The printed anthologies of these male poets gained favourable status and respect from the exponents of this poetic genre, while women poets generated neither credence nor scholarly attention. Moreover, collected works remain exclusively for prominent male poets such as Rāshid al-Khalāwī (who is thought to have lived around 1494), Ḥumīdān al-Shuwayʿir (who died around 1747), Ibn Liʿabūn (1790–1831), Muḥammad al-ʿAlī al-ʿArfaj (died 1842), ʿAbd Allāh Ibn Rashīd (died 1846), ʿUbaydah Ibn Rashīd (died 1865), Muḥammad al-Qāḍī (1809–68), Muḥsin al-Hazzānī (died early 1880s), al-Shaykh Jāsim Ibn Muḥammad al-Thānī (died 1913), Muḥammad al-ʿAwnī (died 1923), ʿAbd Allāh Ibn Subayyil (died 1938), and Ibrahīm al-Jʿaīthīn (died 1943), to name just a few whose reputation and valour populated the Bedouin poetic domain.

These poets were accommodated and some of their poetic lines were recalled, recited and appropriated in other poems. Among the first works of vernacular poetry are single-authored collections composed in the Arabian dialects and published in different intervals of the first half of the twentieth century. According to Sowayan and Ibn Khamīs, *Dīwān al-Nabaṭ* (The Collection of Nabat) in two volumes by Khālid al-Faraj is one of the earliest anthologies of *Nabaṭī* poetry to be published, in 1952.[13] However, I will note that Khālid al-Faraj's *Dīwān 'Abd Allāh al-Faraj* (Poetry Collection of ʿAbd Allāh al-Faraj) was the first to be published in 1920.[14] ʿAbd Allāh al-Ḥātim also contributed an important collection of Bedouin poetry, titled *Khīyār mā yultiqaṭ min al-shi'r al-Nabaṭ* (The Best of What is Collected from Nabaṭī Poetry), in 1952.[15] Subsequently, ʿAbd Allāh Ibn Khamīs published his study, *Al-Adab al-Sha'bī fī Jazīrat al-'Arab* (Popular Literature in the Peninsula), in 1958. It was followed by Shafīq Al-Kamālī's *Al-Sh'ir 'inda Al-Badū* (Poetry among the Bedouin) in 1964, which offers a valuable study, charting out the historical and literary context of Bedouin poetry and citing a number of well-known Arabian male poets. Women poets are almost entirely excluded from these collected works and studies.

ʿAbd Allāh Ibn Khamīs published other books on Bedouin poetry, some of which focus on a single author such as Rāshid al-Khalāwī. Ibn Khamīs was the earliest to publish a monthly page devoted to *Nabaṭī* poetry in the *Al-Jazīrah* newspaper in 1960. Yet, the earliest collected works mixed critical value at several levels ranging from the quality of the poetry, the randomness of the selections and the paucity of biographical information about the poets to the lack of historical background, explanatory material and useful notations. Some books fail to note the publication dates, which adds to the obscurity of the historical context, especially when it is already difficult to assign accurate dates to poets such as Rāshid al-Khalāwī, some of whose compilers estimate that he lived around the fifteenth century while others make no mention of when he lived or died. Indeed, the paucity of historical references complicates scholarly endeavours.

Other collections printed in the 1960s and 1970s followed these earliest publications and these continue to the present day. Some of the most recent studies of Bedouin poetry in Arabic are Ghasān al-Ḥasan's *Al-Sh'ir al-Nabaṭī fī Minṭaqāt al-Khalīj wa-al-Jazīrah al-'Arabīyah* (The Nabaṭī Poetry in the Gulf and the Arabian Peninsula) and Sowayan's *Al-Shi'r Nabaṭī: Dhā'iqat al-Sha'ab wa-Sulṭat al-Naṣ* (Nabati Poetry: The Public Taste and the Power of the Text).[16] These valuable studies do not reflect on women's poetry. While Ghasān al-Ḥasan cites a number of contemporary women poets, he discards the earlier traditional poems by women, most of which have been included in Ibn Rāddas's collection. This discontinuity makes it impossible for the reader to assemble a more comprehensive perspective on women's ongoing contribution to Bedouin poetry. In addition to the several texts in Arabic about the cultural and historical significance of the landscape of Bedouin poetry in the past, many books, collected works, magazines, poetry contests, as well as radio and television programmes focus on contemporary *Nabaṭī* poetry.

Numerous newspapers and magazines in the Arabian Peninsula currently carry weekly sections exclusively dedicated to *Nabaṭī* poetry, and more than 500 Internet sites and blogs publish, discuss and circulate Bedouin poems. These sites are growing by the day, along with satellite programmes and poetry contests. Although one cannot reduce this recent phenomenon to a rising popular acceptance of *Nabaṭī* poetry, it can be attributed to a publicized interest directed at certain audiences of popular culture that appropriates Bedouin poetry as a cultural commodity promoted and manipulated by advertising and competition in the media industry. In these instances, this genre is treated as an object for consumption and fetishism in a rapidly and alarmingly evolving consumer culture in the Gulf region. Conceivably, although there is a reconsideration of this poetic genre, particularly in current media programmes and books by contemporary commentators, Bedouin poetry nonetheless remains outside the lofty literary discourse of modernism.

A number of folklorists and anthropologists explore and research the culture and poetry of Arabian pastoral–nomadic societies. Their published studies in German, Czech and English allow for further consideration of the exclusion of Bedouin women's poetry. One of the earliest studies is by Albert Socin, who travelled to Arabia in 1900/1 and collected Bedouin poetry from various reciters. His *Diwan aus Centralarabien* (Diwan from Central Arabia) offers a metrical analysis of more than one hundred oral poems but fails to point to the contribution of women.[17] Alois Musil, a Czech ethnographer whose *The Manners and Customs of the Rwala Bedouins* was translated into English in

1928, discusses the Rwala nomads in northern Najd. While this text represents a substantial documentation of the social and cultural ethos of Bedouin society in Arabia,[18] poetry is not, however, its primary focus. More recently, Kurpershoek, in *Oral Poetry and Narrative from Central Arabia: The Poetry of Ad-Dindan: A Bedouin Bard in Southern Najd*, presented a detailed study of the poetry of Ad-Dindan. In his discussion, he cited a few poems from Ibn Rāddas's collections but did not present any commentary on feminine poetics.[19]

The publishing of Bedouin poetry presents a radical shift in the oral tradition after it intersects with the emergence of print culture in Arabia starting in 1920. This juxtaposition of oral poetry and writing has gone unquestioned. The publication of oral poetry brings it to the written representation. What might printing and publishing of oral poetry entail in terms of juxtaposing it with writing? How can we not read this visual staging and the semblance between oral models and written texts? These anthologies of Bedouin poetry can be read as written representations of oral poems or even as visual productions of what were both oral performances and auditory practices. They embody a turn to the page instead of the stage. Not only do the poems become written texts, but they also enact the kind of problematical textual and intertexual relations that are addressed in writing.

One important feature that has been established as a result of printing is the notion of the author, since most of these books were devoted to a single poet or a group of well-known oral poets. The poet's historical and poetic persona is for the most part remarkably highlighted and greatly recognized either by an anthologist noting the attributes of a specific poet or through the frequency of inclusion of his poems in different anthologies. For example, poets such as al-Khalāwī, al-Qāḍī, al-Hazzānī and Ibn Subayyil, among others, appear in more than one source, which indicates the circulation and valorization of their poetry. Likewise, the popular recognition of individual authorship is unmistakable. Even though the anxiety of the author's identity and his relation to the work might be lifted momentarily in this visual approximation, it does not prevent modern readers from posing similar literary questions that are the focus of theoretical explorations. From looking at these collected works, some of which are mentioned above, it appears that anonymous poems occur more often in women's poetry, which I highlight in many instances throughout the following chapters.

By and large, these publications have been susceptible to the scorn of the advocates of fine taste and high culture, and one rarely finds a scholar of modern Arabic literature who examines this Bedouin poetry from Arabia. Scholars of modernity and critical theory seem to overlook popular poetic forms, creating a demarcation between high and low literary productions. Accordingly, Bedouin poetry remains the focus of very few studies by anthropologists, folklorists and ethnographers. More significantly, a critical consideration of a number of anthologies demonstrates how even al-Ḥātim , al-Faraj, Ibn Khamīs and others perpetuate the omission of women poets from the all-male list of Bedouin poets, which may only indicate that women cannot be compared with their male counterparts and that what they composed is considered an offshoot or 'bad poetry'. Also, Bedouin women poets are denied a sophisticated lyrical ability.[20] Certain books on Bedouin poetry, such as those of al-Kamālī , Ibn Khamīs and Kurpershoek, refer to fragments of women's poetry without adequate discussion. Further, the absence of feminine voices in most of these anthologies can neither account for the ambivalent relation toward women's Bedouin poetry nor explain the lack of recognition.

A few feminist critics have introduced popular poetry by formulating alternative discussions of the aesthetic discourses to elucidate the articulations of gender and genre as composed by Bedouin women. Most notably, Abu-Lughod has made some landmark contributions to the study of Bedouin women's poetry in a number of important texts. She offers some extraordinary insights into these oral poems and stories and develops new questions about such topics as honour, gender and sexuality in studies of oral poetry in the Middle East. Her focus, however, is on Awlad ʿAli in Egypt, and there is no similar investigation of women's oral poetry in the Arabian Peninsula.[21]

I have chosen Bedouin women's oral poetry from the Arabian Peninsula not only because it has been systematically marginalized both in Arabic and English literary studies but also for its distinctive aesthetic qualities and its imaginative, feminine modes of enunciation. In what follows, I would like to examine or even dispel some of the oversights and beliefs about this feminine oral genre, and to demonstrate how the rhetorical force of Bedouin women's poetry goes far beyond vernacular diction, metres and rhyme schemes. Indeed, it intertwines questions of politics and poiesis, gender and language, and offers a perspective through which we can begin to read all oral poetry theoretically.[22]

Bedouin women's poetry is by no means homogeneous. It consists of women's lyrical and poetic descriptions of love, desire and longing, and their imaginative preoccupation with the desert, whether chanting a dirge or grievance, praising the oppressed, or admiring the noble. After studying these poems closely, I have noticed linguistic and historical differences between those composed before the end of the nineteenth century and those composed after the beginning of the twentieth century.[23] I argue that the old nomadic dialect spoken in some of these poems reflects an era before the discovery of oil in the Arabian Peninsula and the modernization of the desert. Thus, I do not overlook the absence of the modern in some of these poems. Other poems, however, contain technological features suggesting they were composed after oil was discovered (see Chapter 5).

Before the discovery of oil and the technologization and urbanization of the desert, only fragments of poetic compositions by Bedouin women were known. About 60 years ago, however, Ibn Rāddas, himself a poet, travelled throughout the Arabian Desert, listening to different reciters and collecting Bedouin women's oral poetry. He did not date his travels, but it appears that he started recording these poems in the 1950s. They were published as *Shāʿirāt min al-Bādīyah.* It must be highlighted that a few poems are cited or included in other poetry collections or on certain internet sites. For example, Ṭalāl al-Saʿīd included nine women poets in his *Al-Mūswaʿah al-Nabaṭīyah al-Kāmilah*, five of whom are part of Ibn Rāddas's *Shāʿirāt min al-Bādīyah*; al-Saʿīd acknowledges that they are quoted from Ibn Rāddas.[24] In his introduction to *Shāʿirāt min al-Bādīyah* Ibn Rāddas writes:

> I spent more than ten years collecting women's poetry yet gained only a few samples because it is surrounded with secrecy and is concealed. Moreover, most of what women compose, they hide, and as a result, it is often forgotten. If it is remembered, it is often attributed to another composer, especially the poetry of the sentiments.[25]

Ibn Rāddas was the first complier of Bedouin women's poems. He usually includes a few lines before each poem, varying in length and containing an acknowledgement of the poet by name, tribal connection and social status; often there are a few details of the context of the composition; and occasionally there is a comment on the poet's poetic talent. The arrangement of the poems does not follow any linear method since the date of composition is rarely stated. It often appears as if the few mentioned dates are randomly included. He also includes his unyielding comments about the implications of the poems, which I address in more than one instance.

He attempts to arrange the poems by genre, but since some of the poems blur the generic borderlines his approach is neither methodical nor consistent. Accordingly, in his arrangement, he does not establish a coherent order that would allow readers to follow the historical period and the circumstances of the recording or where and how he heard the poem, thus leaving many gaps that challenge scholars of folklore and oral cultures. Hence, the book fails to provide a methodological sequence that can be grasped and commented on without encountering other discrepant features. Such patchiness could have been avoided if the mediator had been aware of this problematic historical context, which he fails to highlight or incorporate. Hence, Ibn Rāddas intervenes as the scribe and editor of the collection in modifying the poems, offering his own comments, explaining the obscure and vernacular phrases, and omitting the names of certain poets of sensual or erotic poems, all of which attest to his authorial role in assembling and arranging the poems. Indeed, there are clear indications that Ibn Rāddas's structural organization of this anthology was intentional.

The language of the poems varies in its obscurity and difficulty. Certain poems are composed in old Bedouin dialects that are inaccessible to modern readers. Also, there are dialectical variations, for this is vernacular poetry; for example, the dialect of a poet from a Shammar or Rwala tribe differs from that of a poet from the ʿUnayzah tribe in northern Najd. These poems embody the first-person speaker, a woman, grounding them in self-exploration as they draw on social and cultural models that belong to tribal and Bedouin everyday life. Most of the poems display a rhetorical force and paradoxical tones that offer antitheses from the cultural paradigms. These Bedouin poems have no titles. Sometimes they are associated with a certain poet; at other times Ibn Rāddas, as mediator, presents them as anonymous. There are more than 200 named women poets in his book. Occasionally, names are related to the name of the tribe, such as Ḥiṣah al-ʿAnayzīyah and Khaḍrāʾ al-Qaḥṭānīyah. Yet this indicates some anonymity because, since there was more than one Ḥiṣah and Khaḍrāʾ in each tribe, these names are insufficient to identify the poet. Even if we try to establish the authenticity of the names, we are dealing with a crucial element in oral tradition: there are always instances in which we have more than one oral poet appropriating a poem.

In mediated oral poetry, there is never an accurate version. On the contrary, there will inevitably be different versions of popular poetry in circulation, and some poetic fragments have been attributed to more than one poet. The intertextuality of oral poetry poses a challenge in discussing the notion of authorship and authenticity for scholars of orality; however, literary critics have theorized these concepts. The effect of the correlation between oral poems needs to be taken into account, but their lyrical, transitory nature cannot be limited to one explanation of this appropriation.

Alois Musil refers to the appropriation of the same poem by more than one poet. He acknowledges that 'if two Bedouins know the same verses of the same poem, they never recite them in exactly the same way but change the original words and often whole verses.'[26] However, we need to remind ourselves that we are dealing, on certain levels, with an anonymous poetry. The question of an authentic oral text is therefore problematic. Paul Zumthor writes: '*La notion de plagiat n'aurait ici pas plus de sens que celle de droit d'auteur: toutes deux, fondatrices de l'Institution littéraire.*'[27] In Bedouin poetry there are references – for example, to historical events and known proper names or places – that might be read as fictional. Zumthor suggests that '*d'autres indices, plus problématiques, sont parfois recherchés dans les allusions qu'est censé contenir le texte à divers événements, et qui nous renverraient à des circonstances impliquant une transmission orale.*'[28] These Bedouin poems incorporate a number of historical events, place names and names of tribal leaders, thereby creating the correlations between the fictional and historical by which oral poetry is often seen as the source of oral history. Jaroslav Stetkevych discusses the poetic implications and referentiality of place names in classical Arabic poetry.

> These words are names: names of mountains, dunes, rivers, wells, stretches of desert, tribal grounds, regions. There are equally unending insistences on motifs of arrivals at abandoned camp sites, of departures from the tribal grounds, of sorrow over such arrivals and departures and over the emptiness that always lies before and after them.[29]

Bedouin poetry bears equivalent temporal and topographical markers while capturing similar sentiments.

Most of the poems in Ibn Rāddas's collection are fairly brief, averaging fewer than 15 lines each, although a few are much longer. The longest is a narrative poem that conveys a 400-year-old historical story. This poem is considered a narration of oral history, hence a number of historians cite and refer to it since it provides a quasi documentation of a significant political event. In this narrative poem, the woman poet addresses her son and recounts the historical conflict between her old tribe, Ziʿb, and the Sharif of Mecca:

> In 1012/1603, the Sharif of Mecca, who was campaigning in the neighborhood of Bishah, imprisoned the chief of Ziʿb, apparently for not sending the annual tribute to the sharif. The dispute with the Sharif of Mecca is also referred to in a boasting poem by a lady of Ziʿb, in which she speaks of her tribe's defiance and wars with the sharifs. She refers to her tribe area as lying 'between the Empty Quarter and the Hijaz'. ... The wide area in which Ziʿb was roaming indicates the power which this tribal group had up to the end of the 11th/17th century. We do not hear much about Ziʿb during the 12th/18th century, by the end of which time it became an inconsequential tribe.[30]

She narrates the detail of the war and depicts the heroism and courage of her tribe. She calls attention to her noble ancestry, since she was the only one left to tell the story. Her poem consists of 67 lines and has been anthologized in several texts.[31] However, the shorter poems could be the residue of longer compositions, or their brevity may be a poetic convention rather than a loss. The anonymous and fragmentary style is related to this poetry's aesthetic strategy, which, as in classic pre-Islamic poetry, involves the progressive unfolding of a succession of evocative images that stand as objective correlatives for the poet's inner states, including desire, melancholy, dispassion, wanderlust and mystical identification with the desert and its human and animal life. The powerful fragments generated in this fashion are available for appropriation. Certain lines from these poems have become proverbial, while others are borrowed, rearranged and refashioned by other poets.

The poems blossom in pastures, rain clouds and patches of lavender. Bedouin women compose poetry in the desert and about the desert, offering vivid images drawn from life around them. Their poetry displays many extraordinary images of animals, in which the speaker usually identifies her emotional pathos and sorrow with grieving like a she camel, crying like a thirsty wolf, or desiring to travel like a bird towards her beloved's camping land. The repository of wildlife includes lizards, snakes and hedgehogs, as well as plants and the weather.

Some poems have a powerful motif of lightning, which usually arouses the woman's longing. When lightning flashes in the sky, memory opens up and silence is interrupted. Ibn Rāddas mentions repeatedly that the poets are moved by lightning: when there is lightning, there is poetry. This poetry is also rich with images of heavenly bodies such as the sun, moon, stars and Pleiades, and it has myriad references to mirages. The imagery of light illuminates the Bedouin woman's space in the desert, and we are reminded of the tent, which as a dim, limited space is juxtaposed with the openness of the desert.

We do not even know whether these women poets recited their poetry publicly or were excluded from performance. There is not even one reference to women's performance or any discussion of their participation in public recitation. It is evident that men recited and performed some of these poems, but no studies focus on the differentiation between performing males' and performing women's poems. We have no sound recording of these poems to demonstrate how they were sung. Sowayan indicates that performing and reciting poetry is a habitual activity that occurs when men gather.[32] Ibn Rāddas, in his introduction, indicates that he had to seek reciters everywhere, appealing to them to recite for him any women's poems they knew:

> Some of these short poems that we transmitted are only fragments from long poems that were lost and we were unsuccessful in finding reciters who memorize them because reciters are unknown and they are not in a specific place. And I used to chase them in *majālis*, social gatherings and at different occasions where I was able to collect what I was able to collect.

> We could find someone who only memorized a few poetic lines that interested him in order to recite them on occasions. Also, some of the names of the poetesses were not passed down to us because their poetry was memorized as anonymous poetry.[33]

Despite the abundant anthologies of popular poetry in the Arabian Peninsula that often held wide appeal, women's poetry is not part of these collections. As indicated, Ibn Rāddas's text remains to this day the only collection of Bedouin women's poetry. Indeed, Ibn Rāddas's *Shāʿirāt min al-Bādīyah* best represents Bedouin women's poetry and is the only book of its kind. Consequently, this collection allows women's oral poetry to be part of print culture, which preserves it and makes its study possible. This poetry must be considered a part of Bedouin oral poetry despite its exclusion from other collections.

Ancient Traces

The Bedouin poetry of the fifteenth century to the early decades of the twentieth century retains a symbiosis with the old composition with variation on its subject matter and diction. Likewise, Bedouin women's poetry carries traces of a leftover pre-Islamic genre, which I highlight in order to show some of the echoes of this ancient genre within women's oral poems. This poetry is composed in Bedouin dialects, which are considered an outcast mode, a different type of speech, prohibited from circulating in the 'pure' paths of classical Arabic. As a popular genre, poetry in Bedouin dialects remains unacknowledged in the mainstream, and a question of 'impurity' is always raised with regard to the linguistic distance between this form of poetry and pre-Islamic odes. Ironically, this oral nomadic poetry shares a number of prevalent traits with the canonical genre. The repertoire of Bedouin oral poetry is haunted by pre-Islamic themes, and there is a residue of something similar to pre-Islamic diction, *topoi*, words, clichés and stylistic aspects. Sowayan confirms the proximity between pre-Islamic poetry and *Nabaṭī* poetry, suggesting that the latter 'presents many linguistic and prosodic divergences from classical Arabic diction'.[34] He writes:

> After a gap of more than two hundred years, we begin to find more poetic examples in a better state of preservation than those given by Ibn Khaldūn. By the end of the sixteenth century, we begin to hear of poets such as Rāshid al-Khalāwī, Abu Ḥamzih al-ʿĀmrī, Gitan ibn Gitan, and others who are still remembered. … The compositions of these and later poets have survived in manuscripts, and some have been recently published in anthologies.[35]

The poetry is replete with funeral dirges, panegyrics, eulogies and descriptions. Traces of previous poems and popular songs are evident. Moreover, Bedouin women's poetry addresses a variety of domestic concerns as well as carnal desire (see Chapter 2). But, unlike pre-Islamic odes, Bedouin poetry stays within its nomadic dialect(s), which preserve few established classical Arabic grammatical rules. These fundamental distinctions create great anxiety and have provoked many polemical debates in the dominant Arabic critical studies. One may well interrogate the categories of classification and canonization. There were, however, many heated debates about popular poetry in its variations in different Arab countries. Some of these debates alluded to the formation and transformation of the Arabic poetic canon. The emphasis on the purity of classical Arabic, and the importance of scholarly resistance to it, are particularly linked to the lofty status of language in Arabic culture, which has been exalted throughout the centuries.

The responses and discussions are of more than historical relevance: several critics have advanced provocative views and formulations about Bedouin poetry *per se*, arguing that it is a threat to pure language and classical high culture. There have been numerous national calls to protect the Arabic language from this type of poetry because it constitutes a threat to the 'purity' of classical Arabic.[36] I do not wish to elaborate on the debates about oral popular poetry during the twentieth century and will limit my discussion to the more interlingustic understanding of popular Arabic poetry that the prominent Arab scholar Ṭāhā Ḥusayn presents. I cite him because his views about language influence and reflect some of the current debates about oral poetry referred to earlier. Also, I show and trace how the Arab philosopher and sociologist Ibn Khaldūn influenced him. Ḥusayn puts forward his comparative views:

> there are two different literatures in the Arabian Peninsula, one of them popular which takes the language of people as a tool for its expression, not in the Arabian Peninsula but in all Arabic deserts: in Syria, Egypt and North Africa. And this literature – *even though its language has been impure* – is strong and alive. It has its exemplary value as it is a clear mirror of the Bedouin's life in their desert. And its themes, meanings and styles resemble to a great degree that of the old Arabic literature which originated in the pre-Islamic era and in the early centuries of Islamic history [my italics].[37]

Ḥusayn points out the basic similarity between canonical Arabic literature and the popular version. He seeks to stabilize similarities by assimilating the thematic concerns, patterns and motifs common to both pre-Islamic and Bedouin poetry. Yet, it is evident that his perception of Arabic popular poetry is marked by exclusion, since he refers to the language of popular literature as 'impure'. The Arabic verb *fasadat* carries many meanings: 'has been corrupted', 'has been made impure' and 'it is impure'. What is the 'impurity' presented here? What is pure or impure language? How can a pre-Islamic literary genre qualify as pure and authentic? I am not attempting to obliterate the distinction between Bedouin and pre-Islamic poetry, but I am addressing the exclusion of oral women's poetry. This implicit assertion in Ḥusayn's account is derived in part from the Arab philosopher and sociologist Ibn Khaldūn, who included and acknowledged popular poetry in his *al-Muqaddimah*. Ibn Khaldūn is the first to have recorded popular poetry, especially the *muwashshaḥāt* and *al-zajal* of Al-Andalus. He writes: 'the languages *fasadat*, after they are mixed and intermingled with foreignness, lead the Arabs to a language that differs entirely from the language of their predecessors from *muḍar* in case ending, in many linguistic subjects and word structure.'[38]

Ibn Khaldūn inscribes the paradigm of a language that is not influenced by other languages or dialects, and distances such dialects from an uncorrupted Arabic, a pure Arabic. The desire for a pure and refined language is the desire for a classical Arabic disassociated from other dialects. Even as Ibn Khaldūn marks the similarities between classical and popular poetry, he glosses over the question of the precursor. That is to say, classical grammatical structures are shown to have a close relationship with the precursor's 'pure' Arabic language. In Ibn Khaldūn's case, the argument is backed up by the view that there is an opposition between the precursor's language and the foreignness and impurity of the successor's language. He also refers to the naming of this poetic genre by indicating, 'The Arab people of the East call this kind of poetry Bedouin.'[39]

These two poetic genres mirror each other, but their language marks their difference. According to both Ibn Khaldūn and Ṭāhā Ḥusayn, the difference embodied in Bedouin poetry is manifested in the use of a corrupted and impure Arabic. But this notion of 'impure' or 'corrupted' language creates hierarchical relations between canonical pre-Islamic poetry and Bedouin poetry. The presupposition of a pure language therefore emerges in the various debates about Arabic Bedouin poetry. As a result, Bedouin poems are treated as unsophisticated, prosaic compositions requiring little theoretical exploration. In fact, unlike its counterpart, pre-Islamic poetry, Arabic literary criticism has scarcely given oral Bedouin poetry any detailed investigation. In discussing the exclusion of Bedouin women's poetry, it is important to emphasize the question of gender and language.

These factors all contributed to a radical exclusion of an entire corpus of poetry from the Arabian Peninsula. Given that these tendencies of anxiety and resistance are often centred on the dialectic between classical Arabic and the vernacular, it is not surprising to find this poetry excluded from theoretical enquiries. Although the prevalence of vernacular poetry can be read in relation to older traditions that extend from the pre-Islamic to the twelfth century, the resistance to it continues to constitute another inextricable semblance. In her illuminating discussion of Andalusian poetic forms, Maria Rosa Menocal underlines the anxiety and rejection of these new genres such as *muwashshaḥāt*. She writes:

> When the new Andalusian poetic form called the *muwashshaḥa* came to be known in the other parts of the Arabic-speaking world, it was promptly rejected. It was not perceived as a legitimate poetic form, because, among other things, it violated the first law of Arabic poetry, that it be written in the standard classical Arabic language. While the principal strophes or stanzas did adhere to this principle, the final strophe, the kharja, did not; it was composed in the Romance vernacular of Al-Andalus, Mozarabic. This incursion of the vernacular made the entire poetic form illegitimate.[40]

More commonly though, only a few scholars, who wrote off the generalized dichotomy and lifted the poetic sanction, considered and studied popular poetry, which the advocates of high culture contested or despised. In the same way, medieval *muwashshaḥāt*, *zajal*, troubadour and lyrics were overlooked by their contemporaries only to be appreciated later by modern readers who uncovered the underlying literariness of popular lyrics and demonstrated that these genres do not necessarily depend on formulaic patterns or majestically composed lines but embody a mixture of classical motifs borrowed and recalled from previous classical poetic genres and interwoven with popular forms.

We can now see more clearly why canonical literary studies reject oral Bedouin poetry and how this rejection has had a definite bearing on its language. The concept of oral poetry cannot be analysed as conventional auditor performance that is continually separated from the context of literary theory and comparative literature. Without focusing on the line of demarcation, I propose another reading, which will bring oral Bedouin women's poetry to a generous space of reflection free of the prevalent dichotomies and cultural subordination of orality over writing. Bringing women's poetry to the critical discourse will eventually reinstate it into the topography of poetic debates and canon formation, while repositioning its historical significance and allowing it to become visible as an invaluable aesthetic form.

Nomadic Voices

The questions I consider are as follows. How can we speak of voice, and what is the voice in a text? Does it come as a murmur in the language, or as a figure of our reading? What is the proximity of voice to song? What is its relationship to alterity? In posing these questions, I am calling for a theoretical examination of the topoi of voice in Bedouin poetry and of Paul de Man's reading of prosopopoeia (see Chapter 4).

Before embarking on this, it is significant to note that the Arabic *kalimah*, 'word', preserves the memory of a wound; it bears the trace of a wound and is linguistically related to the opening of a wound. Adūnīs, a contemporary Arab poet, says:

> The linguistic root of *kalima* gives us other significations. It has been said that *kalama al-rajul* means 'he wounded the man'. And *kalīm* is 'the wounded one'. Note that a poem is called '*kalimah*'. Imru' al-Qays, the pre-Islamic poet, said 'the wound of the tongue is like the wound of the hand' [my translation].[41]

What, then, is 'the voice' in Arabic? According to the *Lisān al-ʿArab*, *ṣawt* (plural *aṣwāt*) means 'sound' or 'tone'. The verb *ṣāta* means 'to sound', 'to call' or 'to raise one's voice'. *Al-ṣawt* is the human voice. 'His *ṣawt* is spread among people' means that he has a good reputation. Also, every kind of singing is regarded as a voice or *ṣawt*.[42] Adūnīs writes further: 'Pre-Islamic poetry was born as a song, it developed as something heard and not read, sung and not written.'[43] The oral poetry we are reading here enjoys a proximity to singing, since it is rhymed in known popular metres and also sung. It has many musical and rhythmical aspects. We find a regularity of tone, rhythmic formulas, alliteration and assonance. The woman poet is especially adept in her skills as lyricist, mastering the poetic use of metres and rhythmical patterns, whether to allude to other known metres or, as I shall demonstrate, to give phonetic repetition and interplay of aural effects. In general, this poetry relies overtly on metrical patterns and the impact of the musical. Typically, there are lyrical dialogues between a woman and her beloved, a woman and her mother, or a woman and her father. The dialogues are usually broken into fragments.[44] In many instances this poetry is referred to as *qawl* 'speech', *kalām* 'speech' and *jawāb* 'response'.

Before the recitation of a poem, the oral poet is introduced as one who will sing, indicating that the poet will recite her poem. We are at the interface between what is sung and what is spoken. It is known that the poet insists on finishing his or her poem before calling it *nashīdah* or *qaṣīdah.* The noun *nashīd* means 'voice' in Arabic; specifically, it signifies raising the voice by a tone. If the poet could sing his or her poem, then he or she would say its creation was complete. The musicality of the poem is thus a condition of its completion. Zumthor writes: '*en toute poésie orale il y a présomption de chant; que tout genre poétique oral est aussi genre musical, même si les usagers ne le reconnaissent pas pour tel.*'[45] There is no recitation of this poetry without singing it. Therefore, these oral poems are constituted in their musicality. For the most part, the words 'here is a voice' preface each poem. This aligns poetry not only with voice, but with song, as mentioned above. In these poems the trope of the voice is self-referential, referring to the poem itself (see Chapter 4).

More specifically, women poets begin their poems with a variety of expressions that usually designate a sound or murmur by which the poet initiates the timbre of the poem. Since we find the same utterances in men's poetry, these sounds are not part of a gendered articulation.[46] I have found that such preparatory sounds mostly characterize oral Bedouin poetry. Several poems open with *yā-wannitī*, 'Ah, my moan'; *yā*, 'oh, o', signifying an exclamation or evocation; *wannitī* is derived from *wanna* 'to hum or buzz', but the dialectical *wannitī* probably connotes the classical Arabic *anna* 'to groan or moan', whereas *anīn* is a plaintive sound or moaning. Another expression is *yā-lajjitī* 'oh, my heart's clamour', from classical Arabic *lajjah* 'clamour or noise'. Often, women poets use *yā-jarr-galbī* 'oh, the pull of my heart', which in classical Arabic is *jarra* 'to pull, tug, drag or draw'. A similar opening is *wā-tall galbī* 'ah, the pull of my heart'; *wā* is 'oh, o' and *tall* means 'to pull' in the Bedouin dialect. A powerful utterance is *yā-ḥann galbī* 'ah, the moaning of my heart', which can be linked with the classical Arabic *ḥanna* 'to long, yearn'. However, in the Bedouin dialect it suggests a moaning sound, and Bedouins refer to the moaning of the camel as *ḥanīn*.

Several poems start with the sound *wāī*, indicating surprise. Other sounds express complaint and astonishment. Some examples show how Bedouin women poets utilize these expressions: 'O hum of my heart/A Mack truck groaning';[47] 'My heart's moan';[48] 'O moans, deepest unearthing of my heart';[49] 'My heart so hard-pulled';[50] 'The pull of my heart/The pull of a bucket';[51] 'O my cries are that of the camp site's dogs';[52] 'O my moaning like the moaning/Of the she camel that lost her calf';[53] 'The moaning of my heart is the hum of a black-wheeled Mack';[54] among many others. Moreover, in some poems the woman speaker utters the 'O' sound; she apostrophizes by addressing a silent entity or a distant interlocutor (see Chapter 4). Interestingly, this 'sound', *ṣawt*, is also 'voice' in Arabic, but when we refer to these openings this voice is voiceless.

When the poet begins a love poem or an elegy with a moaning sound, it sets the tone for what follows. The surge of sound in a fractured voice and the delicate yet impressive openings arrest the listener, attracting attention to what will follow, gesturing to the poem itself. After hearing or reading these sounds, one anticipates that the speaker wishes to express her distress and anguish. It is not the words or syntax that have this effect, but rather the pre-linguistic moment, the flight from signification that is stressed in sounds like *yā*, *wa*, 'ah' or 'oh', and sometimes followed by utterances such as *ḥanna*, *jarra*, or *talla*. All these openings are monosyllabic utterances emitted with a terseness that emphasizes the poem's spoken power. When we read or hear these sounds, we wonder what they refer to. What is unspoken and inferred in these compelling murmurs? If we read these sound effects as hollow, what does the void refer to, or from where is it coming? To utter a fractured sound, to signal the heart's distress, to experience the voice's ruptures as it approaches the spoken word that may explain its anguish, is the poet's unrealized anxiety, moving back and forth between silence and speech, life and death. These sounds, of course, gesture to a void, to the absence and loss of the object of desire, which ultimately points to the signifying order. This void inhabits the signifying system of language (see Chapter 4).

The intricate nature of these expressions and their specificity to Bedouin vernacular poetry and desert life make it challenging to produce equivalent, or rather reciprocal, references in English. How many or which English expressions can capture these sounds? Not only do these vocal traces raise questions of translatability and untranslatability, but they also pose questions about the reading process. If an encounter with a poem begins with vocal effects, how then can we read these oral murmurs or cries of sorrow, and what do they say about reading and about the poem itself?

When a woman composes poetry, however, unlike a man she does not perceive herself as the voice of the tribe but rather sings from within her exclusion. One could say that for women, poetry is not the work of an empirical voice. If a Bedouin woman in the desert fails to identify herself as the voice of the tribe, then what is her relationship to her voice/song/ poem from her stance on the periphery? Despite this poetic oversight, women poets explore in many ways how voice, which male poets have already appropriated as representative of the tribe, breaks and disperses in their fragmented feminine vocal noises and, moreover, how language that tries to represent such configurations has to face postponement and temporal deferral. The clamour of wailing and lamenting the dead or departed, the flow of tears falling like rain or water, the howling like a wolf to express grief, the amorous moans as the groaning of a thirsty herd, all turn the poem into a poignant personal expression. The woman speaker emphasizes her emotional distress in the words *yā galbī* 'my heart', which follow the gushing sound, as the previous examples demonstrate. But what compels the woman speaker to voice her personal feelings instantly after voicing *yā*, a sound devoid of meaning? The poetic expression torments, as well as eluding the voice that tries to grasp it. In many ways, the very act of uttering these opening sounds of the poems first and foremost gestures towards voice.

Moreover, expressing the sound, uttering the cry, exhaling the sigh, whispering the throb of the heart or the moan in the throes of love, all are profoundly bound up with the poetic expression that follows. Indeed, these sounds are significant in setting the scene for the moment of poetry. They are a prelude to the poem, since it is only in this preparation that the poet wishes to recite her poem aloud; it is, after all, a performed piece. If the broken voice precedes the poem, it does not diminish it, but rather calls attention to it and amplifies its rhetorical force. To declaim the poem is to recognize the voice that breaks and delays its presence, and after its fragmentation into an undercurrent of tones and sounds, the poetic image emerges in its most splendid poetic form, as these lines portray: 'My heart's moan, O 'Ali, is the thirsty herd's moan/In front of a spring too shallow to quench them';[55] 'O my moaning like the moaning/ Of the she camel that lost her calf.'[56]

In addition to these openings, Bedouin women perform other pervasive recurrences of sound and oral effects in their poems. In fact, the incorporation of many sound motifs and figures reinforces the poets' receptiveness to the external world, gathering the murmurs of animals from the suckling calf to the crying wolf or singing bird: 'I listen to a calf suckling from its mother after moaning';[57] 'My heart moans like howling/ Of dust-throated wolves';[58] 'O wolf, O you who draws out ululations/ Are yours howls of thirst or of hunger, O wolf?';[59] 'How happy you seem with blissful music, O dove!/O you in the greenery of palm branches singing';[60] 'And hear in the morning the roar of pure horse's hooves/Like thunder from a hail-cloud that flows into the wadi';[61] and 'stallions galloping'.[62]

Sounds of water, rain and thunder are deployed to convey sorrowful moments: 'I weep like a ruptured waterskin/Carried till nightfall on a jittery camel;'[63] 'I heard the sound of the water wheel before sunrise:/ The rising voice of water gushing over wood';[64] 'Pouring forth rain as thunder rumbles';[65] 'As sharp-ringing pestles increase in their clamour'.[66] The feminine sound play emphasizes that the poem itself is the voice/ song, as the nomadic idiom indicates.

Furthermore, the poems do not display a desire for a living or transcendental voice, as exemplified in the Greek formula. For the poet is always a voice, and this desire for an empirical voice grounded in daily life can be traced in old European traditions as well. Certain oral studies distinguish voice from writing and attribute an immediate understanding to oral songs. In fact, multiple renditions or recordings of songs demonstrate constant variations, which suggest that the meaning cannot be conceived as something immediate and present. This binary opposition between voice and writing governs a number of studies of orality, and such a distinction calls for a dismantling of its hierarchical structure.[67]

The broken sound that initiates the poetic moment that surges from the void is the sound that breaks off and changes its thematic direction, generating an ambiguity that poses questions about antecedents and the poem's continuity. In Bedouin women's poems, the speaker expresses her longing, desire or grief, and on the verge of her anguish and tension she swerves and turns towards what may seem another topic. Consequently, the first part of the poem appears to be disjointed and removed from the second part. This rift perplexes the reader, and some may assume that the poem's thematic concern has been disintegrated, but ironically, it has not. In juxtaposing the two parts of the poem, the subterranean and suggestive correlation becomes apparent. The powerful and affecting images succeed one another rapidly, and the connection between them often consists of an abrupt transition that demands theoretical interpretation.

Classical pre-Islamic poets are skilled in creating these poetic rifts, which seem to interrupt, break off and diverge from the thematic continuity, so that the notion of linearity is subverted and altered. These poetic rifts have perplexed and fascinated literary critics and readers of classical Arabic poetry. Bedouin poetry, in its mirroring and echoing of pre-Islamic odes, stages comparable rhetorical shifts, as is shown in the following elegy:

My heart:
A she-falcon
With broken eggs
Whose yolk has vanished:
Nothing left but the shell.
O my companion!
Hunter of the fleet gazelle
With long eyelashes,
This passion of his
Brought on each night.
By God! Were not the desert path
So rugged and impassable
I'd jump like a heedless one
Startled by a slithering snake
Dreading its sharp-toothed sting.[68]

The speaker describes her grief by associating the witnessing of her beloved's death with a she falcon stunned by another loss, figured in the broken eggs. Then she swerves to talk about something different, the rough desert path (see Chapter 3).

The assumed problem is how to read the sudden shift in these poems without misreading what I call a delayed continuity. Subsequently, categories of continuity or rhetorical shift cannot be approached in terms of semblance, linearity or discrepancy, but can only be read in terms of variation, treating the poem as poetic constellations. While the poem is drifting or swerving, it in fact stages a conceptual association with the antecedent. The subsequent part may embody a conceptual moment, as it compels us to reflect on the earlier part of the poem. In its self-reflexivity, the subsequent section of the poem comments on the antecedent and hence is related in a reflective way.

Rhetoric of Love

In *Shāʿirāt min al-Bādīyah* Ibn Rāddas includes love poems that have profoundly altered how people perceive Arab women's oral poetry. The explicit ways in which women articulate their emotions and describe their desire and love are very evident. Their poems display erotic imagery as the poets reveal their sentiments, express their desire for a beloved, and in certain instances name him. Al-Kamālī , in his inspiring discussion, *Al-Shʿir ʿinda Al-Badū* (Poetry for the Bedouin), describes the role of women in the tribe:

> And in the tribe, a woman has the same freedom that the man enjoys and she has a superior status. The woman does not wear the veil and the Bedouin in his unconstrained nature does not see any harm or indignity in allowing his daughter to participate in dancing and singing with other women. And the innocent *gazil* (courtly love poetry), which does not go beyond the boundaries of speech, is a permissible matter; a plethora of love poetry by amorous women who composed it about their beloved without instigating their father's anger still exists.[69]

Love in the nomadic discourse, as well as in classical Arabic poetry, has been associated with insomnia, sickness, madness, loss and dying; it is always a painful affliction that strikes, arrests and captures regardless of intent.

Taking the following love poem as an example, I try to unravel its woven song and to hold one fine thread, trace it to the scene of composition, to the desert, to the creators of songs and tales, to the beads scattered as stars on the sand. Reading this poem should be similar to singing it:

O beloved,
I give you my veil in ransom for you
Although its beads
Are lost.
I remember them when we met
Together,
Behind the camp,
O beloved,
My eyes are watching over you
Like a herdsman
Watching his camels.[70]

In the beginning of the poem we find a veil without its beads. It is sent out in language as a ransom for a beloved. There are three incidents (giving the ransom, talking with the beloved and singing the poem) separated by 'lost beads'. It is the image of the 'lost beads' that opens up a possibility of remembrance and speech. The memory, like the mouth, has to open up and retain the past – a past that cannot be retained. Yet, if the woman, in the blink of an eye, had not noticed something missing, the poem would not have been composed. This indicates that the poem begins with absence: the absent beloved, the missing beads and the past.

The creation of the poem out of loss may bring a notion of death into play here, corresponding to that of the pre-Islamic *muʿallaqāt*.[71] The poem stages another related trope, the veil. If one becomes seduced by reading this as the 'veil' that dominates studies of Arab women in general, then the only way out is to shift focus and read the 'ransom'. Any temptation over the veil faces the fact that the speaker gave it away, revealed her face and used the veil as a ransom for her beloved. In other words, a reading of the veil gets caught in the fact that it is sent away as a ransom. This black veil/ransom as something related to a woman and given by a woman seems to confront the tribal law that dictates moral values. According to this law, women should practise modesty and protect their honour by refraining from any act that will bring shame on their family and tribe. In the poem, the veil is perpetually missing its beads as it is missing its meaning after it has been sent outside the tribal law. The hierarchical relations between man and woman, subject and object, silence and speech are transformed.

Since to read a displaced veil is to relate it to the figuration of face, it is possible to ask if we have a face without a veil? What is a face? Are we reading a transparent face, a non-face – in other words a face that cannot be perceived? I suggest a reading of the veil as a mask, in the sense that it is masking the *visagtée* of the face, namely its facial surface.[72] Therefore, the face is being exposed in speech and must gather its features from a fragmented articulation in language. The voice in the poem affirms its possession of an eye, which guards the space in which the beloved dwells.

Bedouin women's poetry is rich with tropes of seeing, intimately conveying what compels speech. It embodies many references to the roaming feminine gaze, depictions of different ways of seeing and of setting eyes on those who are departing, or who have already left but are coming back, yet the eyes await the departed in vain. The gaze is projected throughout unlimited space – a space similar to the desert. The eye moves endlessly across an open landscape. Indeed, the desert creates the illusion of visibility and the ability to see and be seen, but vision faces the desert void and compels the speaker to return to speech, as shown in the previous poem. The poet concludes affectionately: 'My eyes are watching over you/Like a herdsman/Watching his camels.' There is an interesting displacement from the voice to the eye within the poem, but this displacement can be taken further, from the look to the speech that haunts Bedouin women's poetry.

Chapter 2

Melancholic Desire

The scholarship of Arabic poetry in English has always acknowledged elegiac poetry, but has failed to give Bedouin poetry, and Arab women's writing, the recognition it deserves for contributing to the feminine lament – a longstanding concern of women since the Greeks – and for offering a unique articulation of melancholy and desire.[1] This lacuna in the theoretical and psychoanalytical discourse on melancholy and loss is quite striking. To date, there has been no single theoretical analysis of the profound significance of these tropes in Arab women's poetics. Lila Abu-Lughod accurately observes that 'Lamentation by women is common across Egypt and other parts of the Arab world but the genre has received little scholarly attention.'[2] What has motivated the suppression of melancholy in studies of Arabic literature, and where should we begin the discussion of melancholy in the nomadic context?

Melancholy from Europe to Arabia and Back

For present purposes I discuss the cultural and philosophical displacement and/or exchange of the writings on melancholy without examining the intertextual links between the Greco-Arabic tradition and medieval European discourse on medicine and philosophy. In general, the lack of theoretical analyses of melancholy in relation to Arabic literature suggests an unwillingness to recognize this long comparative history of melancholia. More significantly, it may well indicate an anxiety of influence, which is sometimes accompanied by an antagonistic and reductive reaction to anything related to literary theory, in this case to Freudian texts.[3]

In my view, the failure of Arabic studies to think critically about mourning is symptomatic of a recurring ambivalence – a resistance to the theoretical in relation to its perceived foreign origin, whether that origin is Western philosophy, psychoanalysis or feminist theory. This perception limits Arabic literary studies in English to an empirical treatment of death and mourning, resulting in a conflation of the symbolic and pragmatic aspects of politics and culture. It also, in an uncomplicated way, attempts to demarcate territory, limiting knowledge by imposing linguistic and cultural borders in a process of globalization. At the same time, a desire for anthropocentrism and empiricism circulates in certain Middle Eastern literary studies. I prefer to offer a counter analysis, opening up Bedouin women's poetry to contemporary theory and criticism.

Ironically, many scholars have characterized the medieval Arab philosopher and physician, Avicenna (Ibn Sina), as one of the earliest thinkers after the Greeks to propose an illustration and diagnosis of melancholy or *suwaydā'*, literally 'blackness' in Arabic. In his masterpiece, *Canon of Medicine*, Avicenna explains his theory of the humours, *akhlāṭ*, which in many ways resonates with the ideas presented in Greek scientific and philosophical texts. This can be read as a result of the many translations and borrowings from Greek tradition during two historical eras, the Abbasid period in the ninth century and the Umayyad period in twelfth-century Spain.[4] Al-Mansur, the Abbasid caliph in Baghdad, was the first Arab ruler to encourage the translation of medical, scientific and philosophical texts from Greek into Arabic. In *Al-Muqaddimah*, Ibn Khaldūn underlines this historical point.[5] Later, in AD 830, his brother al-Ma'mun went further in fostering translation projects. He was associated with the foundation of the *bayt al-ḥikmah*, a phrase signifying 'library' in Sasanian and 'house of wisdom' in Arabic, and a place in which translation was encouraged.[6] Philip Hitti summarizes these efforts: 'The Abbasid era of translation lasted about a century after 750. Since most of the translators were Aramaic-speaking, many of the Greek works were first done into Aramaic (Syriac) before their rendition into Arabic.'[7]

Subsequently, this intellectual influence returned to medieval Europe, where many medical and philosophical texts were translated from Arabic into Latin. This double trajectory of an intellectual debt, as it were, marks the articulation of melancholy. A few centuries later Arabic texts were transmitted to medieval Europe. Hitti describes this intellectual exchange in Andalusia:

> Indeed, the current became strong enough in the twelfth century to overflow into Europe. In the transmission of Arab medicine to Europe, north-western Africa and Spain, in particular Toledo, where Gerard of Cremona and Michael Scot worked, played the leading part. The initiator of this significant movement of acquainting the West with the learning of the Arabs by means of Latin translation was Constantine the African (1087) who translated many medical texts. In 1187, Gerard of Cremona translated Avicenna's *Canon of Medicine* among other texts.[8]

This exchange through translation explains the echoing of Avicenna's characterizations of melancholy in medieval European texts, notably by the leader of the medical school of Salerno, Constantine the African, a phenomenon that Walter Benjamin and others in the West noted.[9] Avicenna illustrates the symptoms of black bile and melancholy in his *Canon of Medicine*, as summarized by Jennifer Radden:

> Avicenna proposed that there were four primary fluids or humors whose disposition explained temperament as well as states of health and disease. These were blood, phlegm, (yellow) bile, and black bile, or *sawdā'*, which is literally 'black' or 'blackness' in Arabic. … Normal black bile is defined as the sediment, or heavier constituents, of blood. It is necessary for health. All abnormalities of the black bile, such as those that account for the

> disease of melancholia, result from combustion and a process of sedimentation allowing overheated vapors to interfere with bodily and brain functioning.[10]

In *Stanzas*, Giorgio Agamben is one of a number of contemporary theorists who has called attention to the progression of melancholy from Aristotle to Freud, through medieval Arabic texts. More appropriately, he shows the poetic element in melancholia that Aristotle emphasized, and this link between melancholia and poetics is very relevant to our discussion:

> Nevertheless, an ancient tradition associated the exercise of poetry, philosophy, and the arts with the most wretched of all humors. 'Why is it,' asks one of the most extravagant of the Aristotelian problemata, 'that all men who are outstanding in philosophy, poetry, or the arts are melancholic, and some to such an extent that they are infected by the disease arising from the black bile?'[11]

This unanswered question has continued to haunt theoretical studies to the present day.

Of all psychological afflictions, melancholy is one of the most studied and reflected on by thinkers and literary critics alike. However, it appears to be also the most elusive and undefined of psychic processes.[12] This could suggest that there is an unsettled and even unreadable trace in melancholy that has left its mark on many exploratory efforts. Therefore, rather than seeking definitions, I examine theoretically the melancholic tropes performed and re-enacted in Bedouin women's poetry. Yet, any attempt to understand the melancholic staging in such poetry must also take into consideration the gender and social figurations of melancholia that characterize their aesthetic experience.[13]

By reinstating the discussion of melancholy within a nomadic feminine poetics, I hope to unravel the inadequacies mentioned above.

Once we acknowledge the long route of melancholy throughout Eastern and Western discourses, it becomes possible to explore it in a contemporary context, where I read Bedouin women's poetry along with Freud's essays 'Mourning and Melancholy' and 'The Ego and the Id', and Judith Butler's *The Psychic Life of Power.*[14] These texts help to ground this argument in a more psychoanalytical and philosophical framework. I undertake a close reading of some poems on loss and explore the inscriptions of mourning, melancholic desire and gender.[15] I also retrace the ramifications of melancholic loss in the nomadic context, and the way in which these poems stage the feminine lament as an aesthetic genre that obliquely critiques cultural prohibitions imposed on desire.

From a theoretical and psychoanalytical perspective, understanding the feminine lament, its nomadic and gender workings and the scholarly suppression of elegiac Arabic poetry by women, is more pressing than a cultural account of women's mourning rituals, especially when these rituals do not exist as such in central Arabia, unlike Egypt and Morocco, for instance.[16]

In 'Mourning and Melancholia' Freud differentiates between mourning and melancholy and defines mourning as a reaction to loss that usually lasts a finite period of time, whereas in melancholia the female subject's response to a sorrowful loss confines her in a persistent melancholic state: the subject retains a constant and complicated attachment to the lost object. It is clear that Freud tries to normalize mourning and suggests the pathological nature of melancholia, which he considers a mental disorder:

> Mourning is regularly the reaction to the loss of a loved person, or to the loss of some abstraction which has taken the place of one, such as one's country, liberty, an ideal, and so on. In some people the same influences produce melancholia instead of mourning and we consequently suspect them of a pathological disposition.[17]

Freud illustrates the distinction between mourning and melancholia in pathological terms, and underlines this distinction at the outset of his essay. This, of course, casts a perplexing light on melancholy, since mourning is a response to loss that is usually overcome after a specific period. After the process of mourning, the ego gains its autonomy and 'becomes free and uninhibited again', re-establishing new attachments.[18] In melancholia, however, there is a complicated trajectory to loss, and the subject refuses to mourn. Although mourning and melancholy display similar mental features in their response to a painful loss, the mourning subject recognizes that the loved object is dead and no longer exists, and this is what Freud calls reality testing: 'It proceeds to demand that all the libido shall be withdrawn from its attachments to that object.'[19] Thus, the libido's detachment from the loved object differentiates the working of mourning and melancholy.

Following Freud, then, the same divergence takes place in melancholia, since the subject fails to recognize the loss as loss and continues her attachment to the absent object. Hence, the libido clings to the cherished object in a complex way. Loss masks itself to the extent that it becomes intertwined with a sense of losing an ideal in the lost object. Freud points out that the patient 'knows whom he has lost but not what he has lost in him'.[20] The subject is stuck with her loss, since she can neither distinguish nor identify what has been lost in the loved object; what was lost remains indefinitely in unconscious terrains, initiating a new divergence and identification with the ego.

Because of this divergent course in responding to loss, the subject begins her journey with melancholia. The inability to relinquish the lost object and to realize what was lost in the love object causes the subject to remain in the past, unable to develop new attachments. Freud states: 'In mourning it is the world which has become poor and empty; in melancholia it is the ego itself. The patient represents his ego to us as worthless, incapable of any achievement and morally despicable.'[21] Clearly, the reaction to loss is transmuted in melancholia, given that the subject turns this loss inward, gesturing to something lost in the ego. Eventually, this leads to a sense of emptiness and lack within the ego itself. The ego internalizes the lost object, which is then attacked severely by an outraged and a critical voice, leading to the ego's impoverishment after this loss.

Following Freud's analysis, the ego is split, creating a 'critical agency' that keeps judging the subject and diminishing her self-regard.[22] Thus, the reaction to loss in melancholy takes a different route and whatever was lost in the loved object is incorporated and internalized, manifesting a loss in relation to the ego itself. More importantly, unlike mourning, where the libido detaches itself from the forsaken object and is able to seek a new attachment, in the melancholic person the libido shifts itself from the love object to the ego through a confusing process of identification, internalization and incorporation.[23] The failure of the libido to withdraw from the lost object and its displacement onto the ego complicates the relationship with the lost object because it has been appropriated and integrated through this process of identification. Freud explains: 'In this way an object-loss was transformed into an ego-loss and the conflict between the ego and the loved person into a cleavage between the critical activity of the ego and the ego as altered by identification.'[24] In this sense, the libido could not detach itself from the forsaken object and was unable to find a new attachment, indicating that a violent process occurred when the libido was severed from the lost object and redirected itself into the ego. 'Thus the shadow of the object fell upon the ego,' as Freud suggests.[25] This shadow of the object is a shadow of death, which will haunt the ego, as we see later.

It is significant to observe the mechanism by which the ego gives up the love object, and how it attempts to let go by internalizing and incorporating certain aspects that belong to the forsaken object. Whatever is acquired from the outside object is taken into the internal province of the ego. In this process there is no differentiation between what is part of the self and what belongs to the other. Butler elaborates on Freud's ideas of the identification process and mentions how, in *The Ego and the Id*, he considered identification to be a precondition for this assumed letting go of the forsaken object. She writes:

> Insofar as identification is the psychic preserve of the object and such identifications come to form the ego, the lost object continues to haunt and inhabit the ego as one of its constitutive identifications. The lost object is, in that sense, made coextensive with the ego itself. Indeed, one might conclude that the melancholic identification permits the loss of the object in the external world precisely because it provides a way to *preserve* the object as part of the ego and, hence, to avert the loss as a complete loss. Here we see that letting go means, paradoxically, not full abandonment of the object but transferring the status of the object from the external to internal. Giving up the object becomes possible only on the condition of a melancholic internalization or, what might for our purposes turn out to be even more important, a melancholic incorporation.[26]

Butler explains how identification is crucial if the lost object is to survive inside the ego. At the same time, the ego presumes that it is giving up the lost object. Butler emphasizes that this melancholic internalization is the condition on which the ego can abandon the love object. Hence, incorporation and introjection, which are regressive in nature, help the ego give up the love object. The ego, when it incorporates the object and generates an identificatory relationship with it, presupposes that it is releasing the object and sending it off. However, I argue that this sending-off is a masqueraded mechanism, since the ego has already established its own resemblance with the lost object in order to preserve it internally. Also, it seems as if the ego is merely preserving a reflection in its mirror. We can see another process of clinging onto the lost object, but it is an attachment to reflections and images, a preservation of phantoms and spectres. More precisely, melancholia is the phantasm of being loyal to the lost object and establishing unending love, with all it entails, from a state of waiting, agony and pleasure. In this perspective, the phantasmic relationship with the object is caused by an irretrievable and unnameable loss.

Given the association of melancholy with the ego's vulnerability to loss and the way in which it incorporates into the ego whatever was lost in the object, creating a relationship of familiarity and fixed attachment with the love object, it is pertinent to suggest that in the nomadic context melancholy can be seen to incorporate many losses. This extends the exploration of melancholy beyond the reactions to the death of a loved one to any sorrowful loss that creates an inability to grieve, or to the substitution of the lost object by another. I argue that melancholy, regardless of its origin, can include poems about loss, following Freud, who indicated that the notion of loss involves 'the loss of some abstraction which has taken the place of one, such as one's country, liberty, an ideal, and so on'.[27]

In this chapter and the next, I show how Bedouin women's poetry presents a variety of loss lyrics, reinforcing the idea that these poems are reflections of their speakers' reactions to empirical and spiritual loss. By no means am I suggesting an analysis of the poet's psychological condition, nor do I assume that it is possible to theorize. I intend only to trace the melancholic effects inscribed within the language of these poems and conveyed by the feminine 'I'. Even the pervasive elegizing of the dead often involved figuring it as the melancholic voice of a beloved, a mother, a daughter. It is indisputable that the desert is a fundamental topos of loss that encompasses death, migration, travel, separation, desire and waiting, among other tropes. The poems about 'losing' the desert not only emphasize this point, but repeatedly show that the speaker holds the desert as a loved object that cannot be mourned, or perhaps even acknowledged as lost. They also include an explicit assertion of desiring death if the speaker continued to live in an urban setting, which demonstrates a heightened state of melancholia (see Chapter 3).

The Melancholy of Desire

Bedouin women's poems therefore broaden our understanding of the underpinnings of female melancholia and the poetic articulation of loss in a nomadic setting. The poetic rhetoric of grief and lament, melancholy and loss, is often aligned with the mechanism of desire – precisely when the poets declare their wanting in relation to an absent lover, or long for the desert, or express their grief and gender grievance. The feelings of want and desire are remembered in a moment of separation between the subject and the object. Given the apparent dynamics of desire and melancholic mode in Bedouin women's poetry, it seems imperative to unfold these tropes in tandem with a theoretical reading of melancholy. Feminist philosophy, with its concept of desire, offers a comprehensive analytical model for exploring melancholy.

We have seen that there are residual affinities between Bedouin and pre-Islamic poetic discourses, and it is true that tribal and patriarchal laws have regulated the rhetoric of love and desire since pre-Islamic times, so that the regulatory system can control the individual in the name of polity, modesty and honour. However, poets have not always remained loyal to the guardians of honour and suppressed their desire because of public constraints. On the contrary, since the pre-Islamic era poets have transgressed these conventions. To this day, commentators celebrate Imru' al-Qays, the wandering king, in his pre-Islamic ode and unravel his elaborate description of erotic desire and the female body.[28] Al-Musawi, in his comprehensive study, *Arabic Poetry: Trajectories of Modernity and Tradition*, recalls al-Mutanabbī and comments on his extravagant poetic persona captured in his well-known declaration, 'nobody is better than me, or even my equal.'[29] Al-Musawi continues: 'In practice, however, talent and powerful entrenchment in a masculine tradition make it possible for the poet not only to get away with defiance, but also to legitimize transgression within the dialectic of aggrandizement and supplication.'[30] He elaborates on the legitimization of masculine defiance:

> This order eventually suffered further rupture whenever social and cultural change brought about other tempers with no shared agenda and expectation. Abū Nuwās's (d. 813) transgressions were permissible, not only due to the Caliph al-Amīn's acceptance, a fact that carried a definite legitimizing power, but also because of the vogue with new urban audiences. He was lucky 'that people celebrated his poetry and the notables of his age acclaimed him,' said Ibn Manẓūr.[31]

Desire is by no means either alien to Bedouin women's poetry or a simple allusion to an erotic encounter or experience.[32] Desire is unmistakably stated in many poems. Indeed, forms of self-expression and explorations of desire, wanting and passion proliferate alongside descriptions of the desert and nomadic life. Bedouin women repeatedly explore love and desire in an attempt to articulate their erotic longing for a male beloved, to express their relationship to the desert and sometimes to evaluate social and tribal practices. Expressions of desire are not a theoretical language external to Bedouin women's poetry, but constitute a primary theme: they are inscriptions declared within the vocabulary of the poetry itself.

There are references to women's sensibility, and a number of poems depict a series of utterances such as sighs, moans, sobs, tears, a fast pulse, a heart beat, insomniac nights, nocturnal remembrance, longing and waiting, all conveying an unquestionably erotic overtone, and each connecting a woman with her emotions as the desiring subject. Other examples can be categorized as erotic or sexual. I limit my observations to specific inscriptions in selected poems.

Often a desiring feminine gaze looks for a beloved with anticipation:

'O preserve my eyesight!/The day it swept across sun-livened herds';[33] 'O my people! If you insist you are leaving/Cover my face so I won't see your caravans';[34] 'From all of the glances/I cast toward travellers';[35] 'My springtime is the sight of you';[36] 'O eyes, gaze at his harvest and guard it';[37] 'My gaze fell upon him';[38] 'When my eyes desired your company';[39] and 'I would fill my eyes/With his image.'[40] The following lines capture this yearning:

Sita says, 'O my sleepless eyes'
But my eyes too stray from sleep
My desire is *Surūr*
I have never wished for anyone but he.[41]

The next poem portrays a clear articulation of desire, gaze and separation:

If in the vast desert void you desire me
I too desire you, desire you every day
If you are pouring forth secretive moans,
My moaning means more, damn the womb that bore you!
Your love deprives my eyes of sleep
My springtime is the sight of you
My desire just hearing your name
O that our meeting be unmet, our knowing each other
unknown!
I fear your love has snarled me in the rope of doom.[42]

The list of poetic examples could be longer. It seems that the interplay between the infinite void of the desert and the constantly transitory nomadic world heightens and intensifies this roaming, longing gaze. But the gaze does not see; the object of desire is absent. Furthermore, it is a melancholic gaze, and Freud reminds us that we cannot see what it is that is engrossing the melancholic.[43] The melancholic is withdrawing something from the external world that has been attached to the lost object, but one cannot see this external trace. Butler elucidates this important point:

What cannot be directly spoken is also what is occluded from sight, absent from the visual field that organized melancholia.

> Melancholia is kept from view; it is an absorption by something that cannot be accommodated by vision, that resists being brought into the open, *neither seen or declared* [my emphasis].[44]

My particular concern is the interplay between lack of speech and seeing in melancholia. Butler perceives this crucial dynamic between the inability to describe the loss and the fact that it has been concealed from sight. Other poems help us to elaborate on the boundary of seeing and speech in the melancholic.

Even though desire seems to have an erotic overtone in these poems, it usually displays a woman's wanting and longing for a male lover, juxtaposed with the external forces that women have to navigate while declaring their erotic desire. The ubiquitous 'I' dominates most of the poems of love and desire. The subjective and personal are intertwined with the social and political, pointing toward female–male interactions in a tribal and patriarchal environment. The tribe functions as a moral agency, compelling individuals to limit the articulation of desire. But how do Bedouin women poets manage to articulate desire when they are surrounded by tribal and social codes? What rhetorical strategies do they utilize? There is a certain kind of conversion in their enunciation of desire, a shift from imaginary wanting to real violence, from erotic defiance to ironic articulation of chastity, lending a more recognizably melancholic tone to their words. To read the poems in such a way does not reduce desire and melancholy to the cultural gendered binary of male/female that tends to privilege empirical accounts. But certain potentially misleading issues should first be considered.

In particular, we should not pass a negative judgement on the situation of women in a tribal society. Certainly, there are complex gender roles but my approach is concerned with being attentive to the registers of this poetry. How else can we approach the subject of desire in this context? Focusing only on the restrictions on women in a nomadic society can lead to general assumptions that would entail misreading women's poems. It would be a mistake to force this poetry into supporting the misrepresentative general claims about sexuality in Arabic culture. Further, any approach to the topos of desire will encounter a widespread claim about Arab women and how they are repressed; how their relation to desire is always disguised. I intend to show how these poems undo this alleged perception of Arab women's relation to love and sexuality, which tends to assume that any expression of emotions is stifled before its inception because of a repressive social and political discourse that tries to silence and regulate the articulation of desire. On the contrary, Bedouin women's poems eloquently demonstrate that such presuppositions cannot be taken for granted. We have learnt from Foucault that we cannot reduce the modalities of desire to the binary opposition of repression and emancipation. Butler provides an illuminating critique of Foucault's *History of Sexuality*:[45]

> Desire is not repressed by the juridical law, and neither is it a derivative or sublimated form of that originally repressed instinct. Desire is created by the repressive law itself, and has no other meaning than that which an historically specific form of juridical power inadvertently produces. The law that we may expect to repress some set of desires which could be said to exist prior to the law succeeds, rather, in naming, delimiting and, thereby, giving social meaning and possibility to precisely those desires it intended to eradicate.[46]

Indeed, it is imperative to recognize that juridical power generates and produces desire. More specifically, the repressive force of power creates desire, and one cannot assume that desire is an a priori condition.

To elucidate the dialectic between tribal law and desire and to explain that general claims about Arab women and sexuality are inconsistent, I show how a Bedouin woman poet describes her longing for her beloved. In the poem below, the speaker articulates her desire in explicit, erotic imagery while acknowledging the tribal law, and abruptly withdraws the rhetoric of desire in a melancholic mode. It is ironic to see how Ibn Rāddas conceals this imagery in his introduction by suggesting that sentimental poetry by women is suppressed. In fact, he withheld the names of certain poets later in the collection.[47] Occasionally, he writes 'a poet says' and presents an anonymous poem instead of revealing the woman's name or tribe. Paradoxically, Arabic is a gendered language and *shā'irah* means poetess, indicating that it is a woman who composed the poem. The following is one of these anonymous poems:

By God, I wish that the soft summer wind would blow
And bring the blossoming pastures to nod.
When we settle down on summer nights,
Seeing my lover will fill my eyes.
I swore that I would pour to him my saliva
Even if my family should kill me by the sword,
My lips are pure and never seen,
Never unveiled by lovers.
I say this as a joke and sketch
To amuse the anguished mind.[48]

This wry and minimalist poem displays both the fascination and challenge of a Bedouin woman's life in the desert. Indeed, the poet is an artist of the desert. Embedded in the verse is distinctive visual imagery that privileges the desert. The speaker portrays the landscape, the summer wind, the seasonal change, and its moods and effects on nomadic pastoral journeys and desert caravan transport.[49] She captures tribal practices, above all, the limits put on desire. When spring has arrived and the neighbouring tribes have departed, separating the poet from her beloved, the poet composes her poem to express her feelings. Her evocation discloses the fantasies of an omnipresent speaker: 'I wish that the soft summer wind would blow/And bring the blossoming pastures to nod.' Were the 'blossoming pasture' to sway, the distant travellers would come back to settle down. Desire permeates the text, from 'the blowing wind' and 'blossoming pasture' to more explicit utterances of desire: 'saliva', 'lover', 'lips' and 'lovers'. This setting invites the speaker to imagine what is not there and increases her longing to connect with the object of her desire.

From the outset, the poet invokes the name of God to confirm her earnest longing for the summer wind, signalling the end of the spring when the tribes return to the nomadic camp, allowing her to see her beloved.[50] In the desert, weather regulates nomadic voyages, which continually head towards rainfall, vegetation and grazing land. If the summer would come, seeing her beloved would fill the speaker's eyes, indicating a fulfilment and contentment after emptiness and absence. Ironically, this seeing does not see, since her beloved is absent, but she yearns for him and imagines seeing him. Desire signals the absence of the beloved, or what is missing in the visual field. It points to what lies beyond, what cannot be represented, and therefore gestures to a lack, showing that desire cannot reach its satisfaction, as the poem indicates. The speaker seeks what fills her eyes, but what emerges instead is a vast void.

Furthermore, she confirms her true desire by uttering: 'I swore that I would pour to him my saliva.' She utters an oath, asserting her desire in the most erotic and unequivocal image that stages a fantasy of consummation. She elicits the sensual experience of a passionate kiss, a burning desire that cannot be satisfied, and she offers an articulation of physical intimacy, an imaginary erotic exchange between the speaker and her lover, displayed in the 'saliva'. The risk she is taking is to perform an affirmation of desire in the face of the inhospitable and threatening tribal law is personified in the following line: 'Even if my family should kill me by the sword.' The poem's speaker, the feminine 'I', confronts the reality of this law by articulating and imagining it, attesting to the power of imagination at this climactic point. Her desire defies cultural restrictions that attempt to contain it and treat it as a violation of social norms. She defies the culture that still views women with ambivalence.

By laying out her imagined desire before the reality of the tribal law, the speaker inscribes a feminist grievance about the terrible fate that awaits any woman who transgresses. The threat of the sword is met head on and challenged by uttering her desire. The speaker wants to fantasize about being with her beloved and being passionate, even if she has to undergo death. Her desire forces her to confront the tribal law, to imagine its severity and be willing to endure it – to bear the suffering of death by the sword. Clearly, the poem draws our attention to a number of relations: desire and the tribal law, the poet's relationship with her tribe, her relation to language and our relation to her language, knowing the threats that besiege it. What is striking is the poem's elocutionary power, submitting us to the effects of language.

If we read the poem attentively, we can follow Bedouin women's insights into a multilayered network of cultural and political gender relations. Curiously, the poem recapitulates what a woman wants and what the tribe leaves unspoken. But when a woman speaks out what she wants, she is in fact set up to negotiate with something else that opposes her want, as if language cannot articulate her desire without confronting her with other limits – those of language. What does language withhold and what does the poet attempt to offer? Focusing on the latter part of the poem helps to answer this. In Arabic, the poem consists of five lines, and a clear shift marks the first three from the last two. The poet plays against the tribal law signified by the sword by ending on a satirical note, reappropriating the rhetoric of modesty and politesse. By stating her desire, she almost gives up her position as a 'good' and honourable woman; but in order to retain her position she negates it. So the poet negates what she has stated earlier, by saying: 'My lips are pure and never seen/Never unveiled by lovers/I say this as a joke and sketch/To amuse the anguished mind.' After what we have read earlier, we are suddenly and abruptly withdrawn from the articulation of desire, just like the speaker. Soon after articulating her erotic desire and imagining the tribal sword and potential aggression that await her, she collapses what she imagines with reality.

This tension between power and desire suggests further speculation.

For Foucault, this is the repressive law that disseminates and creates desire discursively, rather than negating its presence.[51] He writes: 'Where there is desire, the power-relation is already present: an allusion, then, to denounce this relation for a repression exerted after the event.'[52] When the poet recalls her desire, she is in fact situated in the power's matrix, since desire cannot be inscribed without this 'power-relation'. Following Foucault, it is an illusion to contemplate the possibility of erasing or removing this power's matrix even if it is denounced in language, for it returns to haunt the subject after the moment of denunciation. The speaker in the poem navigates this paradox adroitly.

However, according to the poem's last lines, the threat is a reality in tribal society and the speaker's desire is just an imagined remark, suggesting that the only way she can renounce the threat is by renouncing her desire. This erotic desire is considered inappropriate and should remain unspoken. Consequently, she conceals her longing by describing the purity of her mouth and then ultimately veiling it, as if she appropriates silence and wears the tribal garment, the veil with its symbolic significations. An understanding of such rhetorical changes in the poem and the language of loss sheds light not only on a woman's grief but also on her grievance. In Butler's words, 'melancholia is a rebellion that has been put down, crushed,'[53] and, I would add, by an idealized vision of what the tribal law dictates about what is acceptable.

The speaker becomes chaste in the last two lines, observing the code of honour. Why does a lover claim chastity? The dialect word *'ashāshīg* suggests both lover and beloved and is analogous to the classical Arabic *'ushāq*, which only means lovers or sexual partners. Both are derived from the triliteral root *'ashaqa*, which indicates 'to love passionately, join together closely or make love'. In the plural the word exerts even more power because it is unusual for Arab men or women to be outspoken about having lovers. The poet uses *'ashīgī* to refer to her lover or beloved at the beginning of the poem; later she repeats the word but in its plural form, *'ashāshīg*. In the opening of the poem the speaker exposes her mouth, and then tries to conceal it at the end. This negation goes further, when she attempts to cancel out what she has said earlier: 'I say this as a joke and sketch/to amuse the anguished mind.' Why does the poet employ this evasive gesture and what does her irony suggest? Does she attempt to relinquish or conceal what she said in the first three lines? Does she try to renounce her words and what they refer to? Butler observes a mode of 'moral reflexivity' that causes this type of split or separation between the ego and the object of desire:

> A form of moral reflexivity is produced in which the ego splits to furnish an internal perspective by which the ego becomes an object for itself turns out to be a withdrawn and transformed … [in] relation to the lost other; in this sense, reflexivity appears to depend upon the prior operation of melancholia. The ego is also figured as having a voice through this process, and it appears imperative within melancholia that self-beratement be voiced, not merely to oneself, but in the presence of others.[54]

After the ego has internalized the lost object, moving it from the external world inward, a moral and judging voice is reproduced. In other words, the ego is split and becomes the object that reflects upon itself. As mentioned above, it looks at itself in its own mirror and torments itself because it could not acknowledge or cope with the loss of the other. This tormenting and ambivalent voice can be loud and shameless, pronounced against the self in front of others. In fact, it is directed against the lost object.

At the end of the poem, desire is interrupted and a didactic and judging voice derails its course from a love poem to an elegiac mode in which the speaker renounces her desire. A structural loss is initiated as a result of this 'moral reflexivity'. Even though desire constitutes a lack, the way in which it is perceived culturally generates a prohibition that has led to another loss. According to Freud, melancholic response extends 'for the most part beyond the clear case of a loss by death, and includes all those situations of being slighted, neglected or disappointed, which can import opposed feelings of love and hate into the relationship or reinforce an already existing ambivalence'.[55]

It seems equally important that we neither reduce the poem to the content of its last two lines nor readily ignore that the renunciation corresponds to the affirmation of the previous lines, regardless of the experience the speaker seeks to convey. In fact, the renunciation mimics the affirmation. The mouth as the site of speech turns from the outset into eroticized desire, signified in the 'saliva'. Subsequently, the mouth emerges in the word 'lips', which represents chastity towards the end of the poem. To sum up, the speaker has announced her desire so eagerly, described her passionate kiss, allowed herself to contemplate death with endurance while the tribal sword hangs in front of her, but then hastens to an ironic renunciation. She has distanced herself from what she described in the first three lines and, above all, she steers away from her oath, inverting her passion to grief. Is the woman sacrificing part of her self in this disavowal, which seeks, as in melancholy, to withhold what it attempts to let go? If the structure of desire is actually a structure of delays and postponements, then the ability to reach satisfaction is mutually deferred. 'Renunciation becomes the aim and vehicle of satisfaction,' as Butler explains.[56] The choice left for the female speaker is to relinquish her desire, which by extension is relinquishing part of the self, because of the social and tribal order.

Moreover, the ever deferred desire and cultural prohibition create a structural loss, showing how the occurrence of desire in Bedouin women's lyrics is aligned with the configuration of melancholic motifs, and the erotic representation is accentuated in an elegiac mode. The poem suggests that withdrawal from the external world into the internal is generated because of social life. But is it possible to read how social realities influence or heighten melancholy? Butler examines the correlation between melancholy and social life, and admits that it is unclear how to begin tracing the social in melancholy. However, she observes that 'the social world appears to be eclipsed in melancholy and an internal world structured in ambivalence emerges as the consequence.'[57] In melancholy, the ego turns inward and assembles a different relationship with the love object that is marked by ambivalence, because the ego cannot be the substitute for the lost object. According to Butler's analysis, the ego's failure to generate a substitute that can fulfil what has been lost and at the same time overcome the fact that it is the surrogate, creates an ambivalent relation with the love object. Thus, following the ego's turn inward can show how the immediacy between social and psychic spheres is produced. Butler states: 'As such, melancholy offers potential insight into how the boundaries of the social are instituted and maintained, not only at the expense of psychic life, but through binding psychic life into forms of melancholic ambivalence.'[58] She highlights that it is precisely the ego's turning that establishes the division between the ego and the love object, and the internal and external domains.[59] Keeping this in mind as we read the poem, we see how this presumed division that the ego undergoes bears witness to the influence of the social realm on the psychic domain. In fact, I agree with Butler that the social regulates psychic life. The poetic turn in the poem exemplifies this division and illustrates the dynamic between the psychic and social worlds.

If we read more carefully, we realize that the poem exists and continues to circulate because of the renunciation. Indeed, it is the ironic tone that causes the speaker's words to revolve steadily in the transmitters' memory and allows her erotic depiction to shun the sharp surveillance of tribal society. If she ultimately embraces her erotic desire ('I swore that I would pour to him my saliva') and did not reclassify it as a 'joke', her poem would not have perhaps existed. Here we observe a significant rhetorical strategy in Bedouin women's poetry, stemming from their insight into the power of language. An attentive reading of melancholic description of desire unfolds a space where erotic longing and its declaration signify risk, even violent retribution, for any woman who transgresses.

Deferring passion, or ironically denying it, is a common lyrical strategy that is both political and a compromise: it destabilizes a woman's relation to her own desire. Another example illustrates this rhetorical strategy of depicting erotic desire and then shifting to an ironic gesture. According to Ibn Rāddas, this poet's name is Ḥiṣah, from the tribe of ʿUnayzah:[60]

O soul, how sweet joining my soul to your soul!
Such intimate melding –
May we not be afflicted! …
I was quoting a proverb, or telling a joke!
I don't have a lover, and we don't walk that path![61]

This poem presents a similar irony after the speaker expresses her desire, staging the union of her soul with that of her lover. The poet employs the word *rūḥī*, which means 'soul' but also indicates the body, suggesting a physical as well as spiritual reunion. Other poets use the same rhetorical strategy: 'My desire is Surūr/I have never wished for anyone but he/My love is too pure for those plagued by blame.'[62] One poet says: 'If not for fear/And knowing humiliation/I'd put him to rest/Between my breasts.'[63] In these examples, we see that immediately after the evocation of erotic desire, conveyed in sexual imagery, the speaker is faced with the threat of immediate cultural conventions, so she initiates a didactic mode that separates her from what she describes. She negates having a lover so that she can reaffirm being a chaste woman. Foucault underlines this paradox: 'We must not think that by saying yes to sex, one says no to power.'[64] I will reverse his statement: we should not think that by saying no to desire, one says yes to power.

From this perspective, we find lyrics about passion, desire and longing marked by the anxiety of overtly uttering passionate and erotic love. I am not trying to cancel the tribal prohibition or to reinforce it. I merely show that it exists, not necessarily in harmony with desire, but as a cultural matrix in which these poems are composed and to which they allude. Hence, each poetic example displays the anxiety of declaring desire in a cultural context that is apprehensive of it, especially when enunciated by a woman. This reality confronts the speaker in each poem and brings her to loss. One might say that femininity and the inscriptions of desire are constructed on the configuration of loss.

The first poem incorporates an extraordinary irony in its conclusion: 'I say this as a joke and sketch/To amuse the anguished mind.' This declaration allows the woman's erotic desire to remain, and at the same time to abide by tribal and social norms. By appropriating the external limits put on her desire, she secures a space for her poem. Moreover, the two parts of the poem are not discrepant with each other or aligned through contradiction, yet they extend unceasingly a displacement of the speaker's desire. It is precisely the rhetorical negation that connects them. The ending of the poem can be read in relation to this poetic shift, which can be attributed not only to the cultural norms that regulate and prohibit feminine desire while shunning its assertion, but also to the relationship of women poets to the language of desire. In fact, in the very act of recognizing the cultural limits on desire, the poet declares her ironic disavowal

The ramifications of this disavowal go further, culminating in a sense of loss. In effect, a melancholic response becomes the substitute for the lost object. Mourning what has not happened, or what the speaker wants to have happen, brings her response to this melancholic terrain because we have a staging of both love and loss; neither is fully acknowledged in its own way. In these examples, we can see that desire is generated through prohibition, yet is given up because of this prohibition. Thus, we can track a topographical site of loss where even though the speaker disavows her desire, she is still withholding the love object. She cannot grieve over the loved object, but brings it inward through a process of sorrowful identification because of the prohibition. I would align these rhetorical strategies with Butler's observation that 'when certain kinds of losses are compelled by a set of culturally prevalent prohibitions, we might expect a culturally prevalent form of melancholy.'[65]

Grief and Gender Grievance

Although tribal legacy imposes sanctions and prohibitions on woman's sexual desire, the image of a Bedouin woman should not be perceived as silent, subservient and passive in the face of social injustice. Rather, she has rightly responded to man and tribal hierarchy, as the previous poem indicates. Other examples show that women in the desert confront the limits of the permissible and acceptable, and challenge codes of silence by laying bare their intimate personal experiences, invoking fantasies of love and passion. These poems might be categorized as nuptial and personal, concerned with divorce, marriage, dispassion, betrayal and private relations. Yet, the poets appropriate these topoi not to convey domestic distress but rather to address sexual politics and conventional views about gender while articulating powerful pathos. They epitomize a certain form of gender grievance as social critique, and subvert the assumption that they are exceptionally subservient women in the desert. Such grievances exemplify the inseparability of poetry from commonplace social matters, juxtaposing the internal world with the external one.

The women utilize poetry to express the domestic narratives of their lives, to cry their outrage, provoke surprise and generate ironies where the imaginative and rhetorical meet the social and the political in a transient poetic instant. Their poems evoke this extraordinary encounter. Denouncing the husband because he is a coward, wanting divorce because he is impotent, relating a new desire and demanding separation with ironic deviance – all are private and intimate concerns that are not only supposed to be concealed but are also not the subject of poetry. By bringing them into the poetic realm, the speakers extend the threshold of the literary and the poetic to include a different articulation of gender relations. How convincingly these poems portray how women articulate their grievance as an unending experience of grief! Intertwined in a melancholic process, the speaker can neither separate herself from the object of love or resentment nor entirely sever her attachment.

The language of desire and transgression can be read in the light of the dramatic staging of grievance, particularly in the way it is intermingled with grief in these poems. In most instances, grievance merges with rage and grief, transforming it into bereaved grievance. What motivates Bedouin women poets to assert their sexual complaints and put forward unanticipated erotic descriptions despite the social prohibition and tribal ideal? Why does grievance incorporate traces of grief and grieving? These poems should be differentiated from the poetic examples in Chapter 3, in which an amplified melancholic state in relation to losing the desert is examined. The death wish is strongly inscribed after the departure from a desert dwelling, and the aggression against the self is certainly different from what will follow.

Freud explains how the melancholic reaches a state of shamelessness and lack of remorse, in a sort of confessional spectacle:

> The melancholic doesn't behave in quite the same way as a person who is crushed by remorse and self-reproach in a normal fashion. Feelings of shame are lacking – or are not prominent – one might emphasize the presence in him of an almost opposite trait of insistent communicativeness which finds satisfaction in self-exposure.[66]

According to Freud, then, the melancholic does not display feelings of remorse or sorrow, which are generally expected to accompany loss, precisely because he or she is going through a complicated psychic circuit and refuses to recognize the forlorn object. Butler observes that 'the melancholic sustains an indirect and deflected relationship to the sociality from which he or she has withdrawn.'[67] It is this paradoxical moment in melancholia where at one point the ability to say what is lost is almost impossible, but is now juxtaposed with a furious speech. Thus, melancholia stages both a lack of address – or what Butler describes as 'I have lost nothing' – and a misdirected angry address.[68] The angry address turns towards the self in a merciless voice, and it is precisely here that one can show how melancholia interconnects with social life.

Reading Freud's and Butler's formulation leads me to argue that women speakers in the following poems cannot name their loss, and utter raging words that clearly get entangled in the moment of address, while the addressee remains unnamed or conflated within the ego. An anonymous poem illustrates this conflation:[69]

By God, what a spring I found!
Grass watered by endless successions of downpours!
You'll admire the lavender meadows as you tread upon them –
So much sweeter than stepping, on hard, barren land.[70]
The husband: God forbid I should enter his house!
No! Not till the sun goes down in the east.
Not till the living call out the dead,
Till the poison of serpents mingles with saliva.
Once I desired him, he desired me
And throngs of suitors never seduced me.
But today's a new day. He dropped me, I dropped him:
Like a wild cow dropped
By a hunter's bullet.[71]

Even though some of these poems are anonymous, their significance and influence is not reduced because they rely on recitation, which maintains poetry's circulation and transmission. Aloof or defiant, limited or constrained – the speaker contests older constructs of tribal and social norms by offering erotic imagery of a newfound desire and by denouncing her husband. Her expressiveness weaves together modes of enunciation and address and evokes a critique of traditional gender relations, eloquently conveying the regrets of long-gone love and passion gone astray. A certain rage, wistfulness, aversion, rebellion and an astonishing candour about sensual and sexual matters can all be traced within the poem and may surprise the reader. The speaker addresses a 'you', but it remains a floating pronoun, since the addressee cannot be identified. Evidently, the poem calls attention to the social and cultural context that attempts to tame and regulate the erotic imagery of women poets, ultimately taming the feminine psyche.

The tribal legacy cannot contain woman's desire in the same way in which it has accepted and tolerated – willingly or unwillingly – man's erotic declarations since the pre-Islamic era, because woman's desire carries threats and could destabilize tribal and social ideals. Honour and modesty are tribal and social inscriptions commonly related to the female body. The poem diverts the notion of sexual desire from the private domain to public social space. It opens with an utterance of amazement: 'What a spring I found!' The speaker's personal disclosure is of finding lush landscape after unwelcoming barren land. The repetition of rain and 'Grass watered by endless successions of downpours' not only indicates the stark contrast between newly discovered spring meadows and the previous desolate, desiccated land, but also reveals the new and overwhelming sensual bliss. Consequently, the speaker's declaration of disbelief is justified. What amuses her is the discrepant configuration of both terrains. Her figurative language articulates very sensual images, which culminate, and are also ironically affirmed by, the rhetorical swerve to what seems another subject matter: 'The husband: God forbid I should enter his house!' The romantic and sensual tone is interrupted, as it were, by sharp reality. As it turns out, the poem is about excess, because the poet articulates both her desire and rage in uncompromising tones. Like the two inverse landscapes, her pathos proliferates alongside a discursive reflexivity divided between irreconcilable emotions: desire and love, loathing and rage. However, this incompatibility extends to other metaphors of impossibility and negation: 'No! Not till the sun goes down in the east./Not till the living call out the dead,/Till the poison of serpents mingles with saliva.' The excessive refusal hinges on the discrepant boundaries or limits of impossibility. In fact, the poetic tone becomes a woman's cry because of the repetition of 'no' and 'not', stressing an unmistakable intent as well as knowledge of her desire. But this disobedient cry renders the impossibility of reconciliation or return.

These metaphors release a passionate fury. As the speaker extends her metaphors of rejection she articulates a scene of death: the language of desire reawakens a sense of loss that was denied its mourning. In vanquishing carnal desire, the speaker describes a scene of finality. The image of the sun setting in the east and the dead rising to call the living creates an apocalyptic tone. The rhetoric of finitude grasps the desperate condition in which the speaker exists; a condition marred by bleakness and great anxiety. But this melancholic tone extends to a clear threat of dying: 'As if she says, even if I would die, I would not return to him.' The rage conspicuously turns into an aggression against the self. The disguised death wish is related to the characteristic of melancholic desire discussed above. It is a death wish, a wish for a grave that ironically diminishes death's force and singularity.

Once more the poem shifts, but to the past, and its tone seems unperturbed and subdued: 'Once I desired him, he desired me/And throngs of suitors never seduced me./But today's a new day. He dropped me, I dropped him:' and it concludes in a sarcastic and aggressive tone: 'Like a wild cow dropped/By a hunter's bullet.' This ironic defiance demonstrates the crucial politics of desire and portrays a gendered form of grievance, while the poem puts forward a private woman's feelings in the public sphere. The word 'desire' carries a melancholic tone; it is the unspoken grief that accompanies a woman's grievance. If in this poem the woman speaker expresses a grievance, objection or contravention in relation to her husband, then her words suggest that she was aggressed by the denial of her choice to end her marriage, by her grief, as it were. She grieves at the same time as she protests and contests domestication. In fact, like other poems, this invokes a number of word associations in relation to grief and grievance. Françoise Lionnet comments on the associations of the word 'grief', allowing us to refine the reading of mourning and grief:

> The French word *grief* (grievance) comes to mind as an interestingly ambiguous term, as one of those '*faux amis*' as

> translators like to call words that are identical in two languages, yet have different meanings in each. To grieve is '*avoir du chagrin, de la peine*', whereas to have a grievance is '*avoir un grief*'. … [This forces] us to bear in mind that grief and grievance are co-constitutive linguistically as well as within the psychic economy of loss. They can never be two opposed concepts. The etymology of the word 'grief' in French implies that both concepts – grief and grievance – are actually contained within one another. This suggests that the work of grief and the articulation of a grievance must go together for freedom to be achieved. These two sides of the same process are, however, in constant and unresolvable tension since each functions according to a different logic, lending to this process the air of an interminable search for freedom from sorrow, and, simultaneously, for material and psychological compensation.[72]

Another poem displays an analogous mode of grievance as a critique of normative social hierarchies converging on gender. This mode is divided between grief and rage, and is a forceful wordplay:

> I wish my husband, like Semiha's, had his throat cut.
> I'll mourn the required four months and ten days.
> I'll patiently mingle with the funeral assembly,
> And I'll wail! I'll dress myself up in sorrow,
> And his separation from me
> Will be heaven.[73]

The woman speaker is prepared to grieve for her husband, but does not disclose why she wishes his death. Like the previous poem, the language is replete with aggressive pitch, and one can argue that the woman speaker has been aggressed even though she does not directly describe this, but suggests it. To be aggressed is to experience a violent loss, and therefore the woman speaker is grieving too. The poem stages the funeral scene where the speaker imagines herself dressed in black, mingling 'with the funeral assembly' to the extent that she captures the temporality of mourning; in Arabic and Islamic traditions the wife/ widow has to dress in black and mourn her husband's death for 'four months and ten days'. The woman speaker is willing to go through the mourning process. Associatively, she imagines a consoling assembly and creates a collective solace. Through this imagined assembly she protests about her condition, but this scene of protest is full of despair and grief. As in the first poem, the speaker mourns the passing of what she had and could not relinquish because of the social and tribal sphere. Furthermore, she is grieving for what she cannot have. Interestingly, the language of the poem does not name this loss, even though there is a staging of an imagined mourning scene. In other words, while the speaker wishes the death of her husband, she cannot declare her loss.

To discuss these grievances is to suggest that Bedouin women's poetry can be read in terms of speaking at risk and of exposing the feminine erotic desire in a social space where it has been constantly contested. Thus, it is not possible to address desire without looking at how the poet confronts power when poetically enunciating her fantasy, when she confesses injustice or wants to break free. An anonymous poet expresses another grievance:

> Regrettable luck brought my husband, Hagāsh
> Of all beauties I am the ill-starred one
> He's ungenerous, no brave warrior
> Learning to ride failed to refine him
> He saw the bed being spread, and he fled
> He wanted to curl up behind his camels
> O mother, I want to leave him and flee
> No one shall return me to his vileness.[74]

By disavowing the conventional tribal limits, the speaker criticizes her husband. What disquiets her is that he is unmanly and unrefined and has qualities she disdains. His actions are far from courageous or chivalrous and she is both aggravated and aggrieved by an unjust marital situation. We can also follow a process in which the woman speaker unravels the cultural construct of masculinity and reverses the desired nomadic ethos of manliness. She wishes to sever herself from a husband who cannot fulfil her desire: 'He saw the bed being spread, and he fled/He wanted to curl up behind his camels.' The woman articulates this social and domestic injustice by revealing her inner, private world not only to illustrate their interdependence, but also to guard against suppositions about feminine desire and sensuality. In a more subtle way, another anonymous poet presents a feminist grievance concealed in a riddle:[75]

> O my brother, springtime
> Of exhausted travellers,
> Leader of horses
> Followed only by their dust,
> I ask you about a man
> With all the tools for making coffee,
> Yet it's been eight long years
> And he hasn't ground a bean!
> He should either brew something in his pot
> Like other men,
> Or else yield the pot
> To someone
> Who cares for it.

The speaker addresses her brother after praising him for his nobleness and heroism. Her address is a riddle that attempts to capture the story of her life and thus advance her grievance. It requires a careful reading and compels the reader to pose a number of questions. What forces the speaker to conceal her complaint and allegorize it? What type of risk does her poetic confession entail? What is her grievance to begin with, and can a reader decipher it? She addresses her brother: 'I ask you about a man/With all the tools for making coffee/Yet it's been eight long years/And he hasn't ground a bean!' However, she treads delicately to convey her grievance, a difficult one to express because her husband is impotent, a fact she has concealed for eight years. This allegory presents a gendered grievance, centred figuratively inside the masculine legacy – the coffee scene (see also Chapter 6). The speaker deploys this spatial configuration to challenge tribal ideals of masculinity and reveal the pitfalls of marriage. Coupled with her grievance is a sense of grief that marks both its articulation and the allegory of desire itself. In the same way, this allegory disguises the grievance rhetorically and postpones its arrival in the moment of address. As Butler explains, 'the unspeakability and unrepresentability of this loss' remains and 'cannot fully be denied' by the melancholic, compelling her to utter something.[76] As in the previous poem, the speaker's complaint gets entangled in another fictional narrative, the allegorical story, and she seizes the opportunity to mourn or grieve the loss she has endured for eight years.

The lines 'O husband, why not divorce me/And I will reward you' and 'O mother, I want to leave him and flee,'[77] are a call for unadulterated freedom and autonomy. These poems are characterized by a strong language that combines passion, discontent, aversion, fantasy and conflict, developing a feminine mode of expression that challenges the tribal ethos. Their emotions can be related to a mourner's plethora of chaotic feelings. Indeed, each poem takes up most of these emotions, but eclipses grief and the ability to grieve, since the speaker is choking on her loss. The life of these women becomes a site of grief, and of the ungrievable life. Similarly, I argue that every unsettled grievance generates unresolved grief, both of which remain inadequately articulated in these poems. In this other form of melancholia, a woman in social or political subjection grieves over lost liberation, freedom and autonomy, all of which external forces have renounced but the ego cannot give up. Butler aptly comments that 'forms of social power emerge that regulate what losses will and will not be grieved; in the social foreclosure of grief we might find what fuels the internal violence of conscience.'[78]

Chapter 3

A Malady of Grief[1]

According to many accounts of pre-Islamic odes, elegiac underpinnings can be seen in the *nasīb* (yearning) expressed in the opening lines of these poems and capturing the speaker's sense of loss when facing the deserted abode. In *The Zephyrs of Najd*, Jaroslav Stetkevych stresses this elegiac tone: 'the poetic time of the *nasīb* becomes once again explicitly that of the past – indeed of the radical past of loss, which takes the poet back to the brooding mood of the poem's beginning.'[2] Likewise, Al-Musawi returns to what he calls 'the elegiac prelude' and comments on its formation of a dialectic relation to the poem itself: 'on the formal level, the elegiac prelude, *nasīb*, motivates the poem through a recollection of loss, as imaged in the camp site.'[3] He notes also the continuity of this trope and its nostalgic mode in Arabic poetry: 'Opening[s] or preludes have other functional and psychological justifications. Poetic tradition resonates with openings and thresholds that are loaded with accumulated nostalgia for the past, along with convincing pronouncements of desires and agonies.'[4]

If we accept these observations, we can read *nasīb* as a referential temporality that operates not only as an indispensable elegiac trope in the Arabic ode, but also as a primary aspect of language and its relation to loss and death. It is within the temporality of *nasīb* that the rhetorical force of endless prosopopoeia should be considered: it represents the precise moment in which the speaker attempts to narrate loss, but this narrative hinges on the speaker's inability to recuperate what has been lost – the abode, the beloved, or the past (see Chapter 4).

Elegies are central to Bedouin women's poetry, especially those lamenting the dead, whether a child, a beloved, a husband or a fallen warrior. After briefly demonstrating that *al-rithā'*, the elegy, has been presupposed as the only genre ascribed to Arab women poets since the pre-Islamic era, I examine Bedouin women's elegiac poetry to show what induces the feminine speaker to deny death by constructing an allegory and recuperating the dead. In doing so, the poet stages a melancholic mode and generates an internalization of the love object through a process of identification. It is important to stress that there is a long tradition of elegiac poetry by Arab women and that Arabic literary history has celebrated their contribution to this prevailing genre.[5]

Male poets were recognized for addressing several thematic concerns, but in the seventh century Al-Khansā' was distinguished only for her elegies and was restricted to this mode even though she also composed praise and love poems. She lamented her brothers, Ṣakhr and Muʿāwiyah, who were killed in tribal battles before the rise of Islam,[6] and her eloquence and poetic language exert rhetorical power to the present day.

What makes the elegy compatible with gender, given that it became prominent in classical Arabic literature? Does the elegiac voice mirror some of the prototypes assigned to women? Does this recognition of the feminine genre of lamentation indicate its detachment from any rhetoric of menace toward the tribal authority? If so, how can we explain relinquishing the threat in these commemorative acts by women? What makes Arab women's laments unthreatening and culturally acceptable to the patriarchal society, whereas other traditions perceived a certain menace in women's lamentations?[7] These questions are beyond the scope of this book, but the discussion of Arabian Bedouin women's elegies suggests further reflection on the enquiries about classical Arab women's elegiac poetry in general.

By most accounts, the elegy is a poem about mourning and

consolation, but it is important to see the divergence of this genre in the nomadic context. In general, poems of loss in the Bedouin tradition incorporate diction similar to that of classical Arabic elegies. Bedouin women's elegiac poetry likewise conveys the main characteristics of the genre, from recounting the attributes of the dead to sorrowful depictions of bereavement, creating an echo of amorous poetry. While Bedouin women's poems contribute to the genre, however, they do not repeat its conventions, but rather participate in and borrow from it, as the poets seek to understand loss. Thus, it is not surprising to find a feminine trace in these laments and a generic difference. Occasionally, there are references to reuniting with the dead in the afterlife. Laments also provoke powerful emotions and sometimes Bedouin women appropriate and manipulate the elegiac pathos to instigate revenge for slain warriors and murder victims.[8] As mentioned, Bedouin women's elegiac poetry does not embody any threatening implication of the female as a mourner.

When an elegy does undertake pathos as its central theme, it provokes the listener's feelings to convey understanding of the demise with which the poet herself is trying to come to terms. This is particularly true when the speaker compares her agony with the pain of an animal by means of a powerful allegory or extended metaphor, turning to a traditional Bedouin reference and denying death. In Bedouin poetry in general, one notices a unique relationship between Bedouins and animals. Hence, it is not surprising to find a few elegies about animals in which the speaker laments the loss of a beloved horse, calf or sheep.[9] Not only do the poems portray the seriousness of the Bedouin attachment to animals and pastoral landscapes, but they also shed more light on feminine grief, particularly when a woman portrays her loss as that experienced by an animal. Indeed, the extended figurative meditations on loss appear to perceive death as a metaphysical and universal event that bonds all living beings together in their experience of suffering and mourning.

I interpret these elegiac moments as melancholic in nature because they can broaden our understanding about the working of mourning, gender and loss in a tribal society. Bedouin women's elegies focus exclusively on the speaker's pathos and on the dead person, and the following example can be read as a topos of melancholy. To trace these melancholic mediations and not the conventional figurations of loss, note how the mourner begins by elegizing the deceased while withholding certain attributes of what has been lost in the love object. Sometimes consolation is transformed into a refusal of death.

Furthermore, women's elegies for the dead and poems about loss in general share psychological features in which the metaphysical, spiritual and moral implications of loss are melancholic. The speakers in these elegies attempt to grasp the meaning of death, but, more importantly, they attempt to remember, preserve and consequently idealize not only the dead, but also what was lost and cannot be identified. As such, a process occurs by which the speaker internalizes and incorporates certain attributes of the dead, ultimately creating an identification with what was lost in the loved object, as the following poems show. The poet composed this elegy after the death of her husband. Ibn Rāddas refers to her as the wife of Zurayyib al-'Utāybīyah:

O highland of the valley, secure the one interred within you
The knight who left his people, climbing high and deep inside you
At first thread of daylight he guarded your slopes,
At the end of the day he lay crouched in your shades.
If you're hungry he'll nourish you generously
And pour coffee if you're thirsty.[10]

As often seen in this Bedouin poetry, the poet is struck by death as a perplexing event and faces her own finitude. Then she attempts to confront it. This poem is preoccupied with loss, as if it begins from loss and absence. How can this be articulated? The elegy attempts to defy death by figuratively resurrecting the dead in allegorical fashion. If we read it word by word, we see that the speaker's remarkable inability to utter 'death' allows her description of the dead beloved to represent life, since he continues doing what he was best known to do. The speaker gazes with desire at the highland where her beloved is buried. The poem appears to be constructed as another genre, a praise poem in which the elegy cannot be formulated in the wake of death, as if loss is excluded. This generic reversal can be traced in the elegiac mode in different literary traditions. The inversion, however, suggests that language cannot fulfil its promise, and instead of an elegy we see the structure of a eulogy. Once more, this generic exchange generates an attempt to defy absence in language, since the elegy cannot describe loss. As Peter Sacks remarks, 'elegies have always questioned the adequacy of their own utterance.'[11]

The opening of the poem shows the rhetorical force of apostrophe: the speaker addresses the highland as a silent entity that 'secures' the dead, and assumes the highland's ability to listen and speak.[12] She beseeches the inanimate highland to care for the dead, as if poetic imagination is able to resurrect this silent world and animate it. This gesture performs the configuration of prosopopoeia (see Chapter 4). As a composer of oral elegy, the speaker substitutes death with travel so that death is overcome, allowing the power of imagination to disseminate life. She perpetuates the life of the deceased so that the act of climbing the slopes denotes existence in a topological sphere where the dead can act and communicate. She focuses exclusively on the deceased as a living being and eliminates any references to death or passing, as noted above.

The speaker refuses death and transforms its static terrain into an animated world of the deceased, staging an external search for the dead. The tone is self-determined to inaugurate the place of burial as a lively dwelling, where the dead man caringly and generously attends to the needs of the highland. He occupies the highland as an attentive and a generous host. In reviving the dead and celebrating him, the speaker refuses to see the void in death and persists in maintaining the love object as animated. The highland is personified as a living being that seems to take the place of the female speaker. The images of 'climbing high and deep', ascending and descending are rapid movements complemented by the dynamic actions of 'guarded your slopes', 'crouched in your shades', 'nourish you' and 'pour coffee'. They not only convey the rapid activities of a vigorous living being, but capture the virtues of an idealized Bedouin ethos. The poem performs at several levels: it shows that the highland is securing the absent beloved, as well as asserting that he is taking care of it, and it creates a reciprocal relation in the figuration of prosopopoeia, turning the highland into a living being. Death as an end becomes life on this lofty land, which suggests that language cannot represent this loss. Likewise, the speaker cannot perceive death as an end, but imagines a continuation of the deceased's life.

Following this allegorical staging, loss ignites the memory and a psychic image of the deceased is assembled from the remains, some of which are idealized and internalized to become memorialized in the melancholic process. The ego continues its attachment to the remains (the beloved's generosity, devotion and humanity) by guarding them and identifying with them so that the lost object is buried, but not forgotten, in this process of internalization – as if the traces of the lost object disguised themselves within the ego after the process of internalization and identification. Judith Butler describes how identification is generated as an effect of unfinished grief: 'melancholy, the unfinished process of grieving, is central to the formation of the identifications that form the ego. Indeed, identifications formed from unfinished grief are the modes in which the lost object is incorporated and phantasmatically preserved in and as the ego.'[13] During the process of identification and internalization the ego assumes that it has overcome loss, but that is the paradox of this inward appropriation. Butler explores this moment in detail:

> If in melancholia a loss is refused, it is not for that reason abolished. Internalization preserves loss in the psyche; more precisely, the internalization of loss is part of the mechanism of its refusal. If the object can no longer exist in the external world,

> it will then exist internally, and that internalization will be a way to disavow the loss, to keep it at bay, to stay or postpone the recognition and suffering of loss.[14]

The melancholic fails in the attempt to refuse and deny loss because it cannot be entirely erased; even if the melancholic imagines and wishes to abolish loss, it is impossible to do so. In fact, the process of internalization attests to this psychic refusal.[15] Internalization thus shields the forsaken object from the external world and delays the realization that it is gone. As such, we can say that melancholy revels in this intricate ironic staging of the response to loss. Clearly, there is an ambivalence and discontent towards the lost object; otherwise the process of grieving would not have been so strenuous and at times immeasurable. That is the ego's ultimate trick, so to speak, in response to unbearable loss and death. By preserving the remains of the lost object, the ego triumphs and continues the fantasy of never ending love, despite loss. It is important for the melancholic to hold onto this illusion of a loyal love, and that the lost object becomes an essential part of the ego.

Perhaps the most striking aspect of the poem, however, is its ending, in which the dead man would pour coffee if his guest wished him to do so. Coffee hospitality is one of the most cherished Bedouin customs,[16] but the deceased pours it for the highland, which has been deployed in prosopopoeia throughout the poem. This not only inscribes one of the traditional elegiac modes but, more significantly, shows the withholding of normative mourning and generates the configuration of a melancholic response. The poem complicates our understanding of the elegiac genre since it does not refer to death or dying but instead creates a powerful prosopopoeia of the highland as a living entity. The speaker negates death at the rhetorical and philosophical levels and holds an idealized image of the deceased as a heroic, attentive, caring and, most importantly, generous warrior.[17] Indeed, the poem does not perform mourning, and we immediately notice how the elegy fits within a description of a melancholic process that cannot perceive the loss of the love object and perpetuates its permanence in the psyche. Following my discussion of Butler, I read the elegy as representing the inability to mourn, staging the working of melancholy. Thus, this poem can be seen as both an elegy in the conventional sense and an example of the melancholic response to death.

Mourning Like Desert Animals

> 'The animal, what a word! The animal is a word; it is an appellation that men have instituted, a name they have given themselves the right and the authority to give to another living creature [*à l'autre vivant*]'
>
> (Jacques Derrida).[18]

The following two poems express some of the most haunting and extraordinary meditations on loss in the Bedouin context. The insurmountable loss and pangs of pain are eloquently expressed in images of grieving animals or birds. And, as we shall see, the unmistakably precise depiction of animals has a long trajectory in the history of Arabic poetry. These elegies can be contextualized within Arabic tradition and its contribution to the animal literary genre, for the word *ḥayawān*, 'animal', invokes a number of classical Arabic texts and treaties. One may argue that Arabic letters encompass a discursive literary and encyclopaedic genre that is devoted to exploring, commenting on or surveying sources on animals.

In recalling the classical Arabic context, ranging from al-Jāḥiẓ, al-Qazwīnī , Ibn Qutaybah, and Ikhwān al-Ṣafā to Al-Damīrī, a clear connection can be seen between animality in Bedouin poetry and pre-Islamic zoopoetics.[19] Indeed, if one compares the configuration of animals in Bedouin women's poems with pre-Islamic poetic discourse, an important insight emerges: what constitutes the beautiful is always aligned with images of wildlife. For instance, in his *mu'allaqah* (ode) the pre-Islamic poet Imru' al-Qays creates a menagerie that incorporates animal imagery, depicting first the deserted encampment, then women and subsequently his horse. For him, the woman can neither be imagined nor become more beautiful unless associated with animal attributes. Even the portrait of his horse is equated with other animals to demonstrate its unrivalled speed, exceptional beauty and distinctiveness: 'His flanks are the flanks of a fawn, his legs like an ostrich's/The springy trot of the wolf he has, the fox's gallop.'[20] In his opening lines Imru' al-Qays shows how the abandoned camp is marked by dung, which stages a picturesque scene of loss with an insignificant, yet evocative trace: 'in the dry hollows/You may see the dung of antelopes scattered like peppercorns.'[21] *Ārām* is the plural of *ri'm*, which means 'white antelope, addax'. According to al-Aṣm'aī, these are the pure white gazelles. It may also refer to the young gazelle, since *ri'm* is derived from *ra'ama*, 'to love tenderly', and suggests maternal tenderness for an infant.[22]

It is common to relate a woman's beauty to the gazelle, and this recurrent configuration shows the mythical implication of this animal in ancient Arabia. Arabs revered and worshipped the gazelle, and archaeological excavations dating back to pre-Islamic Arabia have revealed effigies and carvings of this graceful animal. Likewise, Imru' al-Qays refers to effigies of gazelles sculpted in ancient fortresses of the Yemenite kings.[23] Indeed, this explains their considerable aesthetic and historical relevance. Even after the Umayyad period, a number of communities continued to worship the gazelle and took part in funeral laments and elaborate burial ceremonies for it.

Al-Shanfarā, one of pre-Islamic Arabia's *ṣu'lūk*, 'brigand poets', unravels the exhaustive poetics of animality. In his ode, *Lāmīyat al-'Arab*, Shanfarā not only identifies and describes animals in the desert but also interchanges his natal tribe with the wilderness and its wild beasts, depicting an oppositional world of ethics, responsibility and hospitability. He addresses his tribe:

I have in place of you other kin:
The wolf, unwearying runner,
The darting sand leopard,
The bristle-necked hyena.
These are my clan.

They don't reveal
A secret given in trust
And they don't abandon a man
For his crimes.[24]

Al-Musawi describes the discrepancy between the pre-Islamic ode and Al-Shanfarā 's, especially in its prelude:

> The case is more conspicuous in the poetry of the brigand poets, especially al-Shanfarā . The opening line of his Ode calls on his people to embark on their journey away from him, as he intents to depart, too. The emphasis on separation, not integration, gains impetus through substitution of loyalty to 'another people'. In this instance, the *nasīb* prelude no longer holds.[25]

After his tribe considers him an outcast, a transgressor, Shanfarā criticizes the structures of sociality and constructs a different articulation of subjectivity, in which man or human depends on the relationship with the animal. Yet, it is undeniable that the evocation of animality involves a lament about the vanished tribe in his poem.

At the poetic level, however, this discourse of species and this fascination with animals persist in Arabic poetry. In fact, in the Abbasid era, elegizing the non-human is a prevailing genre.[26] Moreover, al-Jāḥiẓ and Ibn Rashīq have explored how classical Arabic elegies are replete with imagery of animals,[27] and I wish to emphasize the relevance of these poetic and historical configurations of animals to our understanding of similar motifs in Bedouin poetry.[28] But why do Bedouin women poets identify with grief-stricken animals and birds to express their loss? What is to be revealed about this loss, ultimately, other than to suggest that it is unspoken? How can one depict a loss that is by definition indefinable and remains unrepresentable?

It is evident that women poets have to struggle to put into words a narrative about loss that seems to be universal but at the same time is inexpressible. They have to find a language that will express loss and is equivalent to their experience of grief. Walter Benjamin observes that mourning 'is at once the mother of all allegories and their content'.[29] At the limits of representation, the poet constructs a unique allegory of a grieving female animal in order to express her experience of a catastrophic death, which suggests that the speaker's grief exceeds the human condition to engulf creatures of the desert. This ultimately reinforces the idea that death is indescribable and a woman's grief deprives her of words. It is this sense of deprivation that creates identification with mournful desert animals and birds. The poems present images of animals that have just experienced loss, and attempt to stage the moment of their grief.

To return to Derrida's speculative and rhetorical question: 'The animal, what a word!' we are confronted with a word assigned by man to what is deprived of word and language, according to an extensive philosophical discourse in which the animal is made 'a theorem, something seen and not seeing'.[30] For Derrida, depriving the animal of words, language and mimesis is a common presupposition that has been inscribed by philosophers from Aristotle, Descartes, Kant and Heidegger to Levinas and Lacan. Instead of just questioning if the animal responds – 'does it speak?' – and whether it reasons, Derrida carefully addresses the question of pathos.[31] Appropriately, he recalls the British philosopher Jeremy Bentham, who refined the philosophical enquiry about animals with his profound question: 'Can they suffer?'

Following Derrida, this mode of questioning changes how one might think, refine and illuminate the philosophical argument of animality. 'Can they suffer?' conveys a rush of pathos and suggests that the animal can endure pain, sorrow and grief, thus changing the question from an absolute theorem gazed at by philosophers enquiring into the *logos* to one of contemplating 'whether they *can* speak or reason thanks to that *capacity* or that *attribute* implied in the *logos*, the *can-have* (*pouvoir-avoir*) of the *logos*, the aptitude for the *logos* (and logocentrism is first of all a thesis regarding the animal, the animal deprived of the *logos*, deprived of the *can-have-the-logos* ...).'[32]

Thus, the enquiry 'can they suffer?' does not concern the *logos* or the ability to speak; nor does the animal have access to lexis. 'The question is disturbed by a certain *passivity*. It bears witness, manifesting already, as question, the response that testifies to a sufferance, a passion, a not-being-able. The word *can* (*pouvoir*) changes sense and sign here once one asks "can they suffer?"'[33] Derrida unravels the philosophical paradigm by focusing on this latter question, and his insight illuminates my reading of Bedouin women's elegies and their configuration of animals.

The next poem presents a rare exploration of an animal's suffering and sorrow. The desire to capture the temporality of mourning is also explicit. A widow, or a grieving mother, suffers in the same way as a mournful animal, a comparison evident in this elegy by Saʿīdah al-Thaʿalīyah:[34]

O my moaning like the moaning
Of the she camel that lost her calf
Circling around the dried inflated skin

She roams the camp each morning
Turning circles round each dwelling
In her womb she feels the lost warmth of her calf

Alas, his coffeepots
Remain abandoned
After entertaining
Many worthy guests

His house is still ready
For a throng of visitors
But today I don't know
Toward which house he is headed.[35]

This poem begins with an apostrophe, 'O my moaning', dramatically aligning it with loss.[36] The bereaved mother–speaker employs certain emotions interchangeably with animal behaviour. Her experience of grief differs from any human experience and extends to include the animal's response to loss. In comparing her pain with an animal's, the poet establishes the singularity of her loss. Her vulnerability as a mother in mourning matches the anguish and pain of a bereaved mother animal, as she has perceived it in her nomadic landscape. Another poet compares her wailing cries with the animals', 'O my cries are that of the camp site's dogs.'[37] The desert, the animal and the bird have a connection and a distinctiveness that is no different from that of the nomad who relates to them and who cannot imagine life without them. Indeed, the woman's reaction creates a primal moment in which finitude is encountered but cannot be realized. This comparison makes the elegy remarkably powerful, although the loss becomes ungrievable. It immediately draws the listener into the experience of loss because it is unimaginable. From this topography of loss and lamentation, the focus of the poem is to portray maternal grief and sorrow. We note the excessive aspect in a mother's lament; it is singular to the extent that she hastens to compare her bereavement with that of a she camel.

By using the allegorical structure, which extends through two stanzas, the poet is neither drifting nor turning away from loss. On the contrary, she intensifies the meaning of loss by transferring it to the animal world. Grief in the poem depends on what the allegory conveys. This figure renders a woman's grief and the world of loss inaccessible, while the speaker remains deeply attached to the loved object. The sublimity of the image attracts poetically but at the same time produces the fear of finitude.

Here, the speaker is confronted not only with the utter devastation of death's finality and its uncanny qualities but also with her own mortality. Her metaphorical reaction perpetuates loss instead of surmounting it. Benjamin writes: 'The greater the significance, the greater the subjection to death, because death digs most deeply the jagged line of demarcation between physical nature and significance. But if nature has always been subject to the power of death, it is also true that it has always been allegorical.'[38] Once more, the powerful allegorical gesture brings a convergence between the speaker's pathos and that of the she camel: 'O my moaning like the moaning/Of the she camel that lost her calf. … She roams the camp every morning. … In her womb she feels the lost warmth of her calf.'[39]

What is the boundary between human and animal in these poetic lines? Mourning appears as a language of animality or nature, which suggests that the woman speaker and animal cannot be differentiated. In choosing the she camel as a vital part of her elegy, the poet redefines a woman's loss by stripping it to its instinctive state. The profundity of a woman's loss of her child goes to the uttermost sensations of animality. The mother grieves like a beast in the desert, and the mourner assumes knowledge of how the animal displays feelings of loss. However, by claiming this knowledge, the mourner attests to an attentive gaze that observes how animals react to loss. Ironically, this gaze is a melancholic one, which indicates its removal from the visual field. The poem also points out a pivotal relationship between Bedouin women's laments and their connection to animals. The following lines from another poem illustrate this unique identification:

> My heart's moan, O 'Ali, is the thirsty herd's moan
> In front of a spring too shallow to quench them
> When they're driven away, straight back into the desert,
> By a sun-addled fool: My heart moans like howling
> Of dust-throated wolves.[40]

The speaker struggles intensely to convey her feelings through dramatic imagery of animals. Her heart moaning like 'the thirsty herd' indicates that her grief is inconsolable. She also compares her moan with that of the 'howling of dust-throated wolves'. Both analogies embody the torment of grief allegorically, but fail to state what it is.

In the same vein, the female speaker in the previous poem chooses to represent *khalūj*, a term in Bedouin Arabic dialect designating a she camel that has lost its calf. The speaker depicts a very specific and exceptional response to loss in the nomadic setting. The deployment of *khalūj* is common in Bedouin poetry and is not limited to women poets. It is the most compelling image of grief in the Bedouin Arabic dialect. According to many accounts, the she camel is perceived as the animal most vulnerable to loss, displaying its reactions in extended and lingering mourning intervals. Sometimes its extreme mourning leads to death. Commonly, the *khalūj* circles around the place or dwelling where its calf was slaughtered and then lies down moaning, almost guarding the space of death. It will linger and refuse to leave or move until it dies, according to many Bedouin oral narratives.[41] Bedouin tradition embodies several references to *khalūj*, and in particular its anguished and persistent moans haunt Bedouin poetry. The piercing sound of loss produced by desert animals is an echo that torments the Bedouin poetic psyche. After slaughtering the calf, Bedouin tend to inflate its skin to alleviate the mother's loss. In an unforgettable image, this practice cannot satisfy the she camel, which continues to express its suffering. The poem exalts loss by staging how the animal cannot overcome its grief. The death scene, as portrayed by the female speaker, can be viewed as a dramatization of the melancholic affects.

Butler describes how melancholia becomes a gathering space of loss and death:

> In this sense, in melancholia the superego can become a gathering place for the death instincts. As such, it is not necessarily the same as those instincts to the superego, the death instincts being understood as a regressive striving toward organic equilibrium, and the self-beratement of the superego being understood to make use of that regressive striving for its own purpose. Melancholy is both the refusal of grief and the incorporation of loss, a miming of the death it cannot mourn. Yet the incorporation of death draws upon the death instincts to such a degree that we might well wonder whether the two can be separated from one another, whether analytically or phenomenologically.[42]

The superego in melancholia continues to attack the ego. Since the melancholic refuses to mourn and draws loss inward, as the poem illustrates, it 'can become a gathering place for the death instincts'. The ego appropriates the remains of the dead, so to speak, and builds its memorial as the site of identification. The ego is devastated by the immensity of loss and contorts itself to maintain the life of the lost object by defiantly withholding it and refusing to let go. Perhaps the ego does not know how to let go because it forms a complicated identificatory relationship with the lost object. The ego needs to form such an identification so that it can assume its fictional ability of letting go of the love object.

Given the correlation of mourning with the she camel's vulnerability to death in the nomadic context, it is not surprising that the figure of the animal can be employed to accentuate loss and, conversely, show the inability to articulate it. The female animal expresses maternal grief by moving in endless and dizzying circles: 'She roams the camp each morning/Turning circles round each dwelling.' The camel moans while continuing its inexhaustible motion around the camp, looking for its calf. This movement encapsulates the speaker's pangs of agony and her efforts to speak forth her loss. It also suggests that the woman and the animal are undergoing circular movements to recuperate the dead, and the figure of allegory enhances this circularity.

It is expected that the elegy can be the vessel through which the poet voices her agony and describes death, but it is essential to articulate an additional rhetorical strategy. Instead of explaining this grief and conveying her sorrow, the poet's use of allegory makes her lament even more inconceivable and obliterates any attempts at intelligibility. It is, of course, a compelling allegory in which the speaker attempts not only to lament her deceased son and mask his death or seek solace, but also to express the intensity of her grief by relating it to an animal's reaction to loss. The attempt to explain loss through the allegorical is thus not a mere choice undertaken to create a comparison between a woman's sorrow and an animal's, but an admission that the only language left for the poet to express what appears to be inexpressible is figurative. Hence, this allegorical articulation shrouds the speaker with supplementary grief and creates a doubling of the experience of death and mourning. There is a plentitude or excess in allegory, and using this figure is the only way the poet can portray her loss.

The nature of this excessive language emerges when the inadequate human response to death often fails to represent what the mourner is trying to convey. 'The only pleasure the melancholic permits himself, and it is a powerful one, is allegory,' writes Benjamin.[43] Thus, it is the allegorical structure as defined by Benjamin – more precisely, its negotiation of loss – that relies on fragmentation, incompleteness, allusion and its struggle to signify loss.[44] To be sure, allegory's central characteristics can be compared with death; it is the trope of death, as Benjamin observes, even though it tries to represent another story of loss coming from another source. Here, the source is the animal's reaction to loss, but this is not the origin of the female speaker's grief. In this context, animals and their response to loss turn allegory into a narrative of hollowness and mediation, since we have no way of measuring what it conveys with regard to the suffering of desert animals in the wake of death. The sole evidence that allegory provides is that it cannot represent loss, since it maintains a similar structure.

In another articulation, while the allegorical structure hinges on loss, it comments on its representation of death by showing that it cannot signify loss and by narrating another story of loss. But this fragmentary and imperfect language that attempts to represent suffering in the wake of death is another way of guarding loss and of preserving its affects. The effort of naming may temporarily lull the mourner's sorrow but it fails to overcome mourning itself. After all, it testifies to the fact that the melancholic response to loss remains indescribable. As a result of this figural logic, I argue that Bedouin women poets employ, in their elegies, an intricate allegorical orchestration of a similar experience of loss to convey mourning, but eventually they are unable to mourn. This allegorical expression in effect maintains the impossibility of mourning, and the poem ends without it actually being accomplished. Moreover, the speaker's figurative language shows that the melancholic is deprived of speech and therefore cannot describe loss.

In the poem about the she camel, it is notable that after the allegorical articulation, the text suddenly shifts to recounting the attributes of the dead. At first glance, this shift is rhetorically unmotivated and seems almost discrepant and perplexing, since the subject matter changes swiftly from grief to praise of the dead as a living and generous host.

In the second part of the poem, death becomes life and the dead beloved is animated in the memory of the speaker through the description 'His house is still ready/For a throng of visitors.' For the speaker, death has turned the son into an idealization of generosity and hospitality, which are highly regarded attributes in Bedouin culture. Butler thinks that the melancholic cannot break her attachment with the love object: 'For the melancholic, breaking the attachment constitutes a second loss of the object.'[45] Thus, cultivating this attachment and clinging to the lost object justifies this abrupt shift in the poem in which we see the speaker's rhetorical refusal to dwell on the imagery of grief and instead her insistence on celebrating her son's life.

The following elegy exemplifies a similar rhetorical mode. The poet, Ḥarbīyah al-Ghuwayrī, dramatically and lavishly expresses her sorrow and deep woe in an allegory in which a bewildered she falcon gazes at its broken eggs:[46]

My heart:
A she falcon
With broken eggs
Whose yolk has vanished:
Nothing left but the shell.
O my companion!
Hunter of the fleet gazelle
With long eyelashes,

This passion of his
Brought on each night.

By God! Were not the desert path
So rugged and impassable
I'd jump like a heedless one
Startled by a slithering snake
Dreading its sharp-toothed sting.[47]

A falcon, a broken egg, a loss, a bewildered gaze, an intensity of feelings at a fleeting instant, bear great resemblance to a woman's grief, although the woman can neither comprehend death nor describe her experience. Forced to confront the departure of her beloved, the poet engages the mourning process of a bird and compares it allegorically with her own grief. This initiates a scene of extravagance, grandeur and devastating impoverishment at the same time. The too fragile heart of a grieving woman is displaced by the image of a bewildered she falcon. She joins her heart with a powerful bird that is motionless in front of an irreparable loss. What is left is the void emanating from broken shells.

Once more, we notice the temporality of mourning that is captured in the recurrence of loss: the eggs were broken before hatching, their yolk vanished and the shells scattered. This image is haunting because loss is depicted by the most insignificant, trivial and abandoned entity – eggshells. We have a poem about dearth ensnared in impoverished imagery, yet the poem is extravagantly rich. It is death both in its exuberance and its dearth. What the poem grasps is the horror of loss, the ultimate image of death met with maternal sorrow and intense grief.

However, what is the significance of a she falcon in the nomadic context? Women poets allude to birds and associate them with freedom and the ability to migrate to the land of a beloved, as in: 'O bird, going whichever way you desire/Crossing barren plains by wing/Search for my beloved/I wish you would find him.'[48] Also, this poetry almost fully catalogues birds, including the nightingale, sparrow, raven, partridge, dove, duck, eagle and owl.[49] But the falcon has another significance: it can fly far to catch its prey, has piercing eyesight and is often associated with nobility and grace. It is one of the most venerated birds in the desert. Another woman poet describes the gallantry of her beloved by declaring that 'His falcons proudly show themselves and strike their prey.'[50] Because of its powerful penetrating gaze and hunting instincts, the falcon helps Bedouin in their hunting trips to supplement their meagre diet. Bedouin lyrics refer to this noble bird, which has been elegized in a few poems especially by male poets.[51]

Beyond this poem's impoverished and insignificant opening image, a rich allegory emerges. The speaker tries to capture the essence of death in extended metaphorical language that links her heart with a she falcon stricken in front of its broken eggs, vanished yolk and desiccated shells. The poet's choice of bird enhances this sense of loss in that the creation of the most honoured bird, the falcon, has been violently ravaged. By deploying this poignant reflection, the speaker attempts to create an image and empty it of its essence. The opening metaphor connects the woman speaker with the she falcon and invites a unique relation with it, demonstrating the capacity of this bird to suffer, experience loss and undergo pain and sorrow. Also, this preliminary relation stages a sense in which the she falcon can respond and is able to comprehend loss in the same way as the woman poet. A parallel might be drawn between the way the speaker perceives the she falcon's anguish and Derrida's extended reflection on the question of animal suffering. He points out that there is already a 'self-contradiction' in the question 'Can they suffer?' because it implies a sort of inability to respond or a deprivation of power.[52]

> 'Can they suffer?' amounts to asking 'can they *not be able*?' And what of this inability [*impouvoir*]? What of the vulnerability felt on the basis of this inability? What is this nonpower at the heart of power? What is its quality or modality? How should one account

> for it? What right should be accorded it? To what extent does it concern us? Being able to suffer is no longer a power, it is a possibility without power, a possibility of the impossible. Mortality resides there, as the most radical means of thinking the finitude that we share with animals, the mortality that belongs to the very finitude of life, to the experience of compassion, to the possibility of sharing the possibility of this nonpower … the anguish of this vulnerability and the vulnerability of this anguish.[53]

In these observations we can see that the affect of the she falcon's suffering allows the woman speaker to experience her own human vulnerability. The questions of 'nonpower', vulnerability, helplessness and subjection converge in the moment of finitude experienced by both human and animal. At this moment of convergence, Derrida highlights that 'mortality resides there, as the most radical means of thinking the finitude that we share with animals'. According to the poem, the she falcon must have reacted to its loss prior to the speaker, who immediately associates her heart with the bewildered bird at the moment of loss, which sets up a topography of apriority. If the woman speaker gestures toward the animal's loss to describe her own, then she figuratively establishes a primal scene of her loss. Moreover, a woman in mourning embodies the sensibility of the animal and 'the anguish of this vulnerability'. The transferential relation bridges the distance between animal and human.

The most remarkable aspect of this scene is that it is filled with silence – no cries, no wailing, only a rustling voice in its effort to assemble coherent descriptions. It is evident that the speaker cannot face loss except by turning to metaphorical language to recover glimpses of what it signifies; she does this by associating her loss with an animal's, which becomes an imitation of experiencing death and displaying her devastation. She attempts to recapture a non-human perception of life and death to understand the human conceptualization of passing.

There are many folds in this anguished reflection that seeks to grasp the meaning of death. The speaker fails to understand this loss, and the allegorical description demonstrates her failure. Furthermore, this figurative articulation bears witness to holding onto loss through the selection of incomplete images and signs that may express one's grief, but fail to recognize the passing.[54] This aesthetic mode of articulating loss through the construction of allegory is thus a pathway to melancholy. Benjamin writes: 'If the object becomes allegorical under the gaze of melancholy, if melancholy causes life to flow out of it and it remains behind dead, but eternally secure, then it is exposed to the allegorist, it is unconditionally in his power.'[55] The melancholic cannot see the object except as allegorical, as something other than itself, which is brought to a life that is eternally haunted by death. After the initial allegorical expression in the poem, the speaker unexpectedly shifts to the loved object, in a manner similar to that seen in the previous poem. The poet continues:

> O my companion!
> Hunter of the fleet gazelle
> With long eyelashes,
> This passion of his
> Brought on each night.
>
> By God! Were not the desert path
> So rugged and impassable
> I'd jump like a heedless one
> Startled by a slithering snake
> Dreading its sharp-toothed sting.

Instead of reckoning with death, instead of realizing that she lost her husband, the female speaker resurrects the dead and elevates her attachment with the loved object to the extent of incorporating it into her ego. The elegy perpetuates its resistance to death and no longer expresses any solace in its tunes. It assumes the pushing of death beyond its limits and refuses the rhetoric of normative mourning.

These images of animals and birds are not only associations that provoke other memories but are also poetic attempts to capture the response to loss as a pre-linguistic experience. Most significantly, these allegorical depictions of desert animals align the melancholic with these pre-linguistic moments or with aphasia, since, as we have seen, the melancholic loses the ability to speak her loss. In previous elegies, the woman poet is not trying to gratify her poetic imagination by employing images of animals and birds. Rather, there is a keen and profound relation with nature as meditation on poetry and language. Male poets describe their horse or camel in a manner that reflects their valour and gallantry, in a narcissistic tribute to themselves and by extension to their tribe.[56] They tend to boast about their conquering audacity, mastery of desert routes and knowledge of the stars.

Women poets present a different and unique perspective, as we have seen. Because the allegorical representation of animals invokes ethical and metaphysical implications, reading their poems cannot be confined to anthropological or empirical dimensions. The relationship of women poets to the desert and its wildlife is not an attempt to conquer, to appropriate or to master; rather, it is persistently receptive, for it is intended to establish reverence and generosity toward otherness in nature.

These poems put forward a set of allegorical and ethical questions with regard to identifying with and relating to animals, as well as towards sympathy, pain, or awareness of animals and the depiction of a unique attachment. The fellowship of animals and women extends the domestic boundary in a rather contemplative way, attesting to a benevolent affinity with the absolute other – the animal. Evidently, these poems assert the compatibility between humans and animals especially in the event of loss, which is the most evocative, poignant and sorrowful experience. These poems suggest that loss and its affects are by no means limited to humans. More importantly, isolating the animal as a site of identification indicates that there is a reversed configuration of power between human and animal. It is, in fact, bringing to light the inability, vulnerability and powerlessness of both human and animal in the face of death.

Effectively, moving from questions of gender and sexuality to the non-human suggests another insight into the relation of a woman with the elegiac genre and the way in which these elegies turn our attention from affirming the tribal legacy to a topos that is no longer human. The poet therefore refashions this longstanding construct in conventional Arabic elegy by redirecting its concern to the animal, which is recalled as a site of identification of a woman in mourning; the poem, then, stages a critique of the question of genre and gender in connection with the tribe. If al-Khansāʾ, for example, is driven by desperate duty to glorify the tribe in the midst of her distress and mourning, then her elegies will be an extension of discursive and linguistic formations of patriarchy. Her sons and brothers die, but their memory survives in the tribe's grandeur, a tribe that is perpetually alive.

The Bedouin elegy contributes to an understanding of melancholy, one that cannot stage mourning in a discourse about death and loss, demonstrating the difficulty of achieving a 'normative' mourning in the Freudian sense. Ultimately, the elegy's registers of loss show rhetoric of denial, deferral and ambivalence towards the mourned. Each elegy is dependent on an allegorical mode in which the poet turns away from death. It is precisely this figurative turn that portrays a refusal to mourn loss and initiates an internalization of the object's image into the ego. These rhetorical strategies – the stress on reanimating the dead, the disavowal of death, and the deployment of allegory – together demonstrate that the speaker is in a melancholic bind.

A Desert Lost

O East Wind of the highlands,
When did you stir from Najd?
You journey through the night
And passion upon passion add!

Majnūn Laylā[57]

> The mind is a desert mirroring the empty stretches of Arabia.
>
> Etel Adnan[58]

The desert generates the metaphysics of loss *par excellence*. Bedouin women poets express their loss in relation to leaving the desert in several poems. The desert is usually held to be boundless, untainted and stimulating and to provide an unending freedom. Perceived in this way, its qualities offer a limitless dwelling place far from the city's confining walls. The Bedouin can predict seasonal changes by following the direction of stars in the night sky and the movement of the wind. Jaroslav Stetkevych describes the spatial and temporal 'outpourings of Arabic poetic nostalgia over Najd' (a central region of Arabia), emphasizing that the nomadic poet knew and remembered these places and yearned to return.[59] 'Within that region he knew every stretch of desert, every abandoned and possible campground, every marking of the trail.'[60] The vastness of the desert does not inhibit a Bedouin who knows its routes, can track the desert caravan and find travel posts with remarkable precision.

Yet the desert is more complicated than these idyllic and idealized inscriptions. It continues to conjure up the phantasm, generating a sentimentalized affinity with departure and travel.[61] Departure embodies both the desire and the dread that have provoked poetic expressions in Arabia since ancient times. Rather than controlling this departure, the Bedouin remain controlled by it, and it inspires songs of longing and waiting. This condition affects women poets when they are forced to leave the desert and live in an urban environment or become settled villagers, a move that causes insurmountable sorrow. They are compelled to confront finitude, as the walls of city buildings seem to distress and restrain them. This may indicate that women poets refuse the domesticating effects of living in circumscribed spaces. Unlike the city, the desert offers women autonomy, more choices and, most importantly, an endless home. When living with the al-Murrah tribe, Donald Cole observed that 'They reject the city as physically and socially polluted and prefer the desert where they can live what they habitually describe as a pure and clean life.'[62] The idea that the city is confining and the desert liberating signifies a great loss, similar to death. Moreover, the open desert is more hospitable and inviting than the city, and has no negativity associated with it. In this sense, the desert is another name for love, freedom and communal life.

In some ways the desert is the abstraction of an ideal. Hence, it is not surprising to observe that it has remained the object of Bedouin love and allure. It has never been given up without great difficulty and anguish, and when it is relinquished, a melancholic voyage begins. The inability to sever the attachment to the object of desire – the desert – shows that these women poets are performing melancholia in its most heightened state. Furthermore, these poems display an alienated female speaker who cannot contend with living in the city or bear its foreignness. Yet, it would be erroneous to suggest that these poetic moments exemplify a rejection of modern life or a resistance to modernity. There are irrefutable examples where women embrace what can be characterized as modern, in the form of instrumental technology (see Chapter 5). The following poem by Bakhūt al-Marīyah illustrates that technology, in the form of a motorcar, is in harmony with the desert:

> My longing for a tent
> After an adobe house.
> My longing to see
> Scattered herds of white camels.
> My longing to accompany
> A just-departed motor.
> My longing to gaze
> On the plain behind the mountain.
> When Bedouin nomads
> Disperse to desert camps,
> The absent beloved
> Will not be remembered.[63]

The characteristics of the poems on desert loss at the poetic and figurative level can be summed up as follows: they contain amorous diction about longing, waiting, night vigils and pain. The desert is viewed as the unsurpassed object of desire. Leaving the desert for the oasis town or city dwelling resembles falling into prison and confinement. Most significantly, these poems exemplify how the spatial change evokes a manifestation of grief in which the social space is intertwined with the psychic one. Evidently, the social world as recognized in the desert and the city is enmeshed within the psychic world, signifying a melancholic bind. The female speaker in these poems cannot reattach to new affections, cannot relate to new domestic domains and continues to preserve a phantasmic characterization of the desert. It appears that the abundant and majestic poetic splendour of the desert cannot be transferred to the oasis because it lacks serenity and tranquillity. The following poem by ʿAlyāʾ from the tribe of ʿUtaybah sets up a contrast between oasis life and the desert:

> Last night I stayed up till the moon fell down
> My eyes held vigil while the tribes were sleeping
> I heard the sound of the water wheel before sunrise:
> The rising voice of water gushing over wood.
>
> To the desert! Away from this oasis town!
> I long to embark, to make camp among my ancestors
> Whose herds, when lightning flashes, rush
> Toward the highland well like parched wild beasts!
>
> In the evening they call on fat sheep with sharp blades
> Inviting each to dangle from a tent's centrepost
> Then fire up the lamps, blazing paths between tents
> As sharp-ringing pestles increase in their clamour.
>
> The crowd of visitors swells as night waxes,
> Yet they always find space for a late-arriving guest.

I remember them on the first day of summer's going,
At the highland well encircled by thirsty throngs.
If we don't return to them, and rain falls,
Bury me beside the desert of Nafūd.

O eyes, shed your tears, let them flow
After Abū Maẓīr, and forget the others.
He welcomes whole crowds, offers wise counsel,
Never wishes harm on a companion
Or skimps with his fistful of coffee beans.

For guests he offers the best of his herd.[64]

The poem begins with the anxiety of living in an oasis where water wheels deprive the woman speaker of her sleep. The cacophony of the water wheel, its gushing noises that persist through the night, jogs the speaker's memory. In fleeting visual scenes she recognizes what the city cannot offer, and utters her command in the second stanza: 'To the desert! Away from this oasis town!'

In her nocturnal remembrance, the speaker inscribes her exuberant longing for the nomad camp and nostalgically recalls how night waxes and wanes in the desert. This convivial night scene overflows with hospitality and vitality, with guests coming and going. The ritual of making coffee is staged in the poem, signifying an important tradition in Bedouin social texture and symptomatic of a nomad camp in which people are welcoming and generous.[65] In the fifth stanza, the poet portrays an essential scene around the spring where the Bedouin water their herds.

These depictions are by no means exceptional. Like the other poems discussed, this one describes the landscape and Bedouin mores in an inconsolable tone. Indeed, it expresses a desire for an idealized and lost desert. But unlike the previous poems, this speaker signals to death: 'If we don't return to them, and rain falls/Bury me beside the desert of Nafūd.' The rhetoric of death characterizes the poems on desert loss, and the gestures used reveal this heightened state of melancholy. The poet al-Jāzī al-Subayʿīyah describes similar sentiments:

I find comfort in taking poison,
Better than the distress of a husband's presence.
My desire is a man from Subayʿī, who tracks
His dispersed camels.
He is better than Ibn ʿAskar's castle and its building.
When I die, bury me in the centre of this
Dry and endless space,
My grave in the path of departing camels,
That they may step there.[66]

Woes are often uttered in the opening of these poems. Grief and anger are not the only sentiments depicted; sometimes the speaker declares a desire for death if she does not return to the desert. If the inability to mourn the desert generates the death wish, then we are at a different stage in the process of melancholy. There is no consolation after leaving the desert, no desire in oasis life: the pain with which these speakers try to describe their confinement in the city is the only way to address a loss so devastating and disquieting: 'But the heart was cracked by blades/From the city mud, surrounding it';[67] 'I find comfort in taking poison';[68] and 'I fell into confinement/As if imprisoned high up in stone walls.'[69]

Yet these poetic lines cannot articulate this loss; nothing can describe what was lost within the desert. Butler emphasizes the enigmatic nature of this loss and shows how it obliterates something else:

> So when one loses, one is faced with something enigmatic: something is hiding in the loss, something is lost within the recesses of loss. If mourning involves knowing what one has lost (and melancholia originally meant, to a certain extent, not knowing), then mourning would be maintained by its enigmatic

> dimension, by the experience of not knowing incited by losing what [one] cannot fully fathom.[70]

Although the lost object is named, and is sometimes attached to the rendering of the desert as the ultimate ideal with its nomadic ethos, all these figurative descriptions fail to articulate this loss adequately. In brief, the loss of the desert is a loss of an ideal, yet this ideal is unspeakable. Butler emphasizes that 'melancholia is precisely the effect of unavowable loss. A loss prior to speech declaration, it is the limiting condition of its possibility: a withdrawal or retraction from speech that makes speech possible.'[71] If this loss can describe and name what was lost in the abandoned object, then it will be unproblematic to mourn it, but in this case there is something unspeakable about the loss, as Butler has demonstrated. This is the melancholic response, which is deprived of speech.

Furthermore, in these poems about loss of the desert, we can see expressions of grief and self-reproach and sometimes anger. Equally important, yet more problematic, is the rhetoric of cruelty and aggression experienced in the restricted dwellings and uttered in these poetic lines. The tone is frequently melancholic, and these aggressive tendencies are redirected toward the self. Freud comments:

> If one listens patiently to a melancholic's many and various self-accusations, one cannot in the end avoid the impression that often the most violent of them are hardly at all applicable to the patient himself, but that with insignificant modifications they do fit someone else, someone whom the patient loved or has loved or should love.[72]

The ambivalence towards the love object, in this case the desert, turns inward to the ego, as when the rhetoric of cruelty is redirected to the self. The ego drags the forsaken object inside itself, creating its semblance in a fictional manner. In this process, the ego drags ambivalence with it as well. Freud explains: 'If the love for the object –

a love which cannot be given up though the object itself is given up – takes refuge in narcissistic identification, then the hate comes into operation on this substitutive object, abusing it, debasing it, making it suffer.'[73] Hence, since the ego has failed to be a substitute for the loved object, it identifies with the object, which ultimately gives rise to this cruel and abusing voice that haunts the ego. Butler explains that the impoverishment of the ego apparently results from the relentless self-judgement and debasement that was misdirected towards the ego.[74]

Thus, the ego attempts to inflict its own annihilation by producing aggressive thoughts against itself, demonstrating that this hostility is, in fact, a misdirected ambivalence toward the lost object. These poetic examples display a death wish if the female speaker does not return to the desert: 'If we don't return to them, and rain falls/Bury me beside the desert of Nafūd;'[75] 'When I die, bury me in the centre of this/Dry and endless space/My grave in the path of departing camels/That they may step there';[76] and 'I find comfort in taking poison.'[77] As Freud observes:

> The analysis of melancholia now shows that the ego can kill itself only if, owing to the return of the object-cathexis, it can treat itself as an object – if it is able to direct against itself the hostility which relates to an object and which represents the ego's original reaction to objects in the external world.[78]

At this point, the ego can neither articulate nor speak this aggression that was once associated with loss. As observed in these poems, there is both a departure from the desert and a refusal of this departure. Through this twofold turn, the abandonment has ultimately been incorporated into the ego. 'In this sense, to refuse a loss is to become it,' as Butler has indicated.[79] I argue that this inability to articulate what was lost within the forlorn object is the predicament and the demise of the melancholic. Butler sums up this relation to speech: 'the prohibition on grief registers as a loss of speech for its addressee.'[80]

Obviously, the melancholic talks a great deal and complains, but it is a misdirected speech, since it is addressed to the ego instead of to the absent other. Consequently, the speech of the melancholic becomes unceasingly withdrawn to the extent that she is deprived of it. Butler motivates the analysis of speech in relation to melancholia: 'If melancholia designates a sphere of attachment that is not explicitly produced as an object of discourse, then it erodes the operation of language that not only posits objects, but regulates and normalizes objects through that positing.'[81] This melancholic response to death, then, is a response to the other, which is figured in its judging and sometimes cruel voice that is misaddressed to the ego. This is clarified by Butler:

> The melancholic would have said something, if he or she could, but did not, and now believes in the sustaining power of the voice. Vainly, the melancholic now says what he or she would have said, addressed only to himself, as one who is already split off himself, but whose power of self-address depends upon this self-forfeiture.[82]

Because the melancholic is shrouded with loss of speech, she cannot explicitly communicate her own predicament. Through a circular path, she speaks to the other that she has internalized and whom she could not mourn. Viewed in the context of the preceding discussion, melancholia works at an ironic level where the subject clings to the mourned object and appropriates it in a narcissistic way, to the extent that there is no interest in giving it up. Unlike mourning, melancholia is not a passing moment of sorrow where the subject recovers from her grief; it is instead a continuing voyage of holding onto the object of loss and generating a formation of fictional desire. Through a complex trajectory of internalization and incorporation, the melancholic develops an external voice that once meant to utter its aggression to the lost object, but instead turns this hostility towards the ego. The cruel voice bruises the ego until it becomes impoverished and loses its desire to live, as exemplified in the poems of desert loss.[83]

In this and the previous chapter I have explored melancholic desire and the malady of grief as they intertwine with Bedouin women's poetry on loss. Even though the readings of Freud's 'Mourning and Melancholy' have influenced many disciplines in the humanities and informed literary analysis, to date there is no single study of Arabic poetry and melancholy. This theoretical eclipse has motivated my examination of Bedouin women's poetry in the context of feminist philosophy and psychoanalysis. I have argued that Bedouin women poets offer different inscriptions of melancholic motifs to signify several topoi – desire, malady of grief and desert loss – while they focus even more precisely on the articulation of melancholy and images associated with death.

Chapter 4

Masquerading Tropes: The Fiction of Face and Voice

It may appear somewhat paradoxical, given the cultural and historical context of Bedouin poetry, to wonder whether it displays parallel rhetorical tropes and similar figurations of address to those of European poetry. Although de Man, Chase, Culler and other literary theorists indicate that prosopopoeia, for example, pertains to lyrics, they devote their discussions exclusively to eighteenth-century European Romantic texts. Prosopopoeia as a mode of address is undoubtedly a pervasive feature of Romantic lyrical poetry, but we also find it carefully stated in Bedouin women's poems,[1] where meditations on loss exemplify diverse gestures of address. In these poems prosopopoeia is aligned with melancholic motifs (see Chapter 2). I shall now explore loss again, but this time as expressed in the configuration of prosopopoeia.

While evoking a comparative reading, I shall show how Bedouin women's poetry employs similar modes of address and registers of speech and voice to those in canonical European poetry. More specifically, Bedouin women poets often gesture to silent or dead entities, and their poems and elegies embody a fundamental figure that fits de Man's description of prosopopoeia in his influential essays, 'Autobiography as De-Facement' and 'Hypogram and Inscription'.[2] De Man explores this trope and its performative force in producing voice and face, and explains how it has been misread and collapsed with apostrophe and personification. In the Bedouin elegy discussed in this chapter the staging of prosopopoeia emerges twice, first in the poem's rhetorical positing of voice and face and subsequently in its self-reflexive relationship to language and death. Voice as a figure is fictionalized and, more significantly, is generated through prosopopoeia.

As a figure of speech, prosopopoeia appears as a central poetic moment in a number of well-known European poems, such as Keats's 'Ode to Psyche' and 'Ode on a Grecian Urn' and Shelley's 'Ode to the West Wind'. It is exemplified in opening lines: 'O wild west wind'; 'Thou still unravish'd bride of quietness'; and 'O Goddess! Hear these tuneless numbers, wrung.' Yet, literary critics of lyrical poetry often collapse personification with prosopopoeia.[3] Although it resembles personification in some ways, prosopopoeia is significantly more precise. It does not simply ascribe full human attributes to inanimate objects or description. Rather, it produces specific illusions of voice and face, assimilating language as a speaking subject. Moreover, prosopopoeia suggests face and voice making, since its Greek root is derived from *prosopon*, 'face or person' and *poiein*, 'to make'. It is this distinction – the giving of face and voice – that de Man seeks to assert. As he later demonstrates, prosopopoeia is the fiction of an apostrophe, and its most distinctive aspect is that it suggests voice as a disembodiment rather than as attached to an empirical body. That is to say, the figure of prosopopoeia proposes voice and face making as figures detached from a body or a locus of a coherent subject in the empirical world. Prosopopoeia is, indeed, the disfiguration of figures and this performative feature is germane to the present discussion.

Personification describes objects by giving them familiar body-like human attributes, unlike prosopopoeia, which resides in a moment of disembodiment of voice and conjures up a disfigured face. As such, it dislocates voice and blurs its origin. Thus, voice is neither subjective nor a fixed presence of a human or authorial voice. Indeed, that this trope fails to name voice in its etymology but rather insinuates it through a figuration of face accentuates the figurality of voice and amplifies its staging. A reading of prosopopoeia is therefore crucial to any examination of questions about voice and its fictionality. According to de Man, such fictionality is precisely what prosopopoeia generates. In this regard, Cynthia Chase's analysis of de Man's 'Autobiography as De-facement' is very informative, because it questions face and voice making in the lyric and proposes a theoretical reading of prosopopoeia and its configuration of address.

There is a tendency in recent literary theory towards overlapping the tropes of prosopopoeia and personification, apostrophe and address regardless of their differential effects. Some critics overlook the distinction implied in the complexity of prosopopoeia and in how it hinges on its assumption of face and of fictionalizing voice and speech. For example, Chase suggests that 'the ode's distinctive trait is a special kind of prosopopoeia, or personification, the gesture of address.'[4] In this statement she nearly collapses the two figures into one and the difference between prosopopoeia and personification seems to pass unnoticed; rather, they are assembled together as equivalent tropes. De Man shows how Michael Riffaterre also confuses prosopopoeia with personification: 'He calls it personification and dismisses it from his commentary by stressing the banality' of apostrophizing.[5] But such conflation is far from rare. In fact, this convergence characterizes recent critical studies and has suppressed the reading of prosopopoeia and its significance or difference from other tropes. Perhaps part of the overlapping is that all these rhetorical figures seemingly stage voice – although prosopopoeia conjures face as well as voice, thus presuming vocalization in a distinct way.

A number of literary critics have examined the dismissal of prosopopoeia. More particularly, Chase, in a de Manian analysis, describes the dismissal of the apostrophic gesture in prosopopoeia by George Shuster and Riffaterre as 'insignificant because it is simply conventional'.[6] De Man and Chase suggest that to reduce the address in this figure to a mere source of embarrassment would discard its rhetorical and specular force. Jonathan Culler, on the other hand, comments on the avoidance by critics of any theoretical discussion of apostrophe, since they treat this trope as inconsequential. He descibes the sense of embarrassment that apostrophizing, in the form of 'O mountain', 'O bird', has introduced to this form of address:

> One can argue that this embarrassment is linked to the obviousness that apostrophe is a figure, an empty O, for which one can scarcely make cognitive or transcendental claims of the sort that are routinely made for metaphor: it is embarrassing for the high callings of lyric to depend on, or even be linked closely with, this sort of figure.[7]

Almost all theoretical discussion of this rhetorical trope has been confined to the Western poetic discourse, implicitly dismissing the possibility of exploring prosopopoeia in other poetic traditions. Ironically, however, as we shall see, all texts depend on it regardless of their cultural context.

De Man's discussion of prosopopoeia begins with an analysis of Wordsworth's autobiographical *Essays Upon Epitaph*, in which he shows that 'prosopopoeia is the trope of autobiography'. He continues:

> It is the figure of prosopopoeia, *the fiction of an apostrophe* to an absent, deceased, or voiceless entity, which posits the possibility of the latter's reply and confers upon it the power of speech. Voice assumes mouth, eye, and finally face, a chain that is manifest in the etymology of the trope's name, *prosopon poien*, to confer a mask or a face (*prosopon*) [my italics].[8]

Here prosopopoeia is, in effect, the staging of 'the fiction of an apostrophe' by addressing a mute entity. There is a continual interplay of address and addressee in the analysis of this silent trope and the way in which it fictionalizes face and voice. To elucidate de Man I draw my examples from the entirely different context of

Bedouin women's poetry, and examine the emergence of face and voice in prosopopoeia – or, as Culler puts it, 'the giving of face and voice to and thus the animation of what would not otherwise be a living interlocutor'.[9]

First, it is crucial to illustrate how this rhetorical trope has characterized the opening lines of pre-Islamic odes. These poems depend precisely on their imperative opening, such as: 'Halt, friends, let's weep,' a rhetorical motif that figures in classic English epitaphs and assumes a sentient being who will eventually respond to this summons.[10] The pre-Islamic poet Imru' Al-Qays deploys this mode of address: 'Halt, friends both! Let us weep, recalling a love and a longing by the rim of the twisted sand,'[11] and ʿAntarah begins his *muʿallaqah* or ode with a similar invocation: 'Have the poets left anywhere/In need of patching? Or did you/After imaginings/Recognize her abode?/O abode of ʿAbla in al-Jiwáʾi/Speak! Morning greetings/Abode of ʿAbla/Peace!'[12] These two openings capture the scene of absence and abandonment in which the pre-Islamic poet begins his poem after recalling his beloved's departure. He apostrophizes as he gazes at *al-aṭlāl*, the ruins, and the residual marks on the sand after his beloved has deserted the camp site with her tribe. The poet thus addresses a silent and voiceless abstraction of separation, and this poignant moment inspires his poem.

In Bedouin women's poetry there are many attempts to inscribe an address by means of inanimate addressees – a bird, the desert, a highland, lightning, a mountain, a deceased or absent subject, and other abstract concepts such as separation and death. 'How happy you seem with blissful music, O dove!/O you in the greenery of palm branches singing';[13] 'O wolf on the summit of Madabī mountain';[14] 'O highland of the valley';[15] 'O generous lightening, glimmering';[16] 'O Lookout Mountain';[17] 'O rider of the swift-legged GMC!'[18] 'O black-camel rider traversing pale mirage';[19] 'O bird, going whichever way you desire;'[20] 'O bird, great the travellers,'[21] and 'O beloved'[22] among many others. These poetic openings not only raise the provocative question of address, but they also mediate the relationship between voice and address that rests on the figure of prosopopoeia. This figure presupposes a voice that may belong to the deceased, or to a silent entity such as the mountain, highland or animal with which the speaker has identified in relation to loss (see Chapter 3).

It is important, however, not to reduce this to a narrowly defined concept of personification, and to highlight that in Bedouin poetry this mode of address is a recurring trope and is always a fiction of apostrophe in the form of prosopopoeia. We have seen (in Chapter 1) how these poets are fascinated with the topoi of voice and speech and that the voice is always related to an absent addressee. There are lyrical dialogues between a woman and a man, a woman and her mother, or a woman and her beloved, which are usually broken into fragments.[23] In one poem an anonymous poetic dialogue takes place between two poets, female and male, in which he seeks her love and she rejects him. The man apostrophizes five times while addressing the woman as a mountain covered with lush meadows, but she sneers at him in her reply. He says:

O mountain,
O you who are covered in verdure,
I admire the blossoming flowers in you,
And they have converted me by force
To their faith.
O mountain, lovely mountain.

I want to graze in you,
I have only eight goats.
They won't overrun the town
Or disobey its laws!

She responds:

Watch your goats, Ibn Ḥusayn,
They're headed straight for a chasm,

Headed for a hard fall – the end of your precious goats!
They might all tumble in, or maybe just the first four,
And regret would seize shepherds who'd hide the affair.

He replies:

I graze it so guiltily, I have no rights. It's a habit.
And the one with habits steals kohl from her eyes.
I graze it all night, though dawn's the time of prayer …
Whether or not you've accepted it yet.

She replies:

O scurrilous coward!
Your hand guides your tongue
Towards the abyss of fallen women.
Your hands show the proof!
There's no doubt your right hand
And left hand are sisters,
O son of Ḥusayn!
Your right hand's the hand
Of an ungainly woman.
Hers and yours are the same.[24]

Bedouin women's poetry offers several examples of this sort of interplay between a speaker and addressee. The addressees are extensions of a desire to establish a relationship with the other, who not only cannot be faced, but can only be spoken to through the figuration of such an address.[25] In these declamations the speaker presumes that the addressee is capable of a linguistic exchange. Some hint of her insistence on this is exemplified in the openings to a bird, the desert and death. Another example, in which the poet Kannah al-Shammarīyah asks the mountain about her dead beloved, stages 'the fiction of an apostrophe':

O Lookout Mountain, have you seen Abdullah?
Has he not climbed into you by the twilight hour?
O Lookout Mountain
I ask you
By God
Which is hope
Which despair?
I have sworn not to marry any of God's creation,
For I still hope to see him on Judgment Day.[26]

One could say that the act of speaking forth this address to an apparently familiar and identifiable object restages the act of addressing an interlocutor who is capable of responding. Thus, addressing a poem or an elegy to a voiceless addressee is inseparable from the question of the interlocutionary realm. Equally important is the assumption of the addressee's ability to speak, which reinforces a fictive reciprocity between the speaker and what has been addressed. Since these are non-human entities or abstract concepts, it manifests a desire to bestow voice onto a silent and unresponsive world.

With the address as an embodiment of the site of addressing or speaking forth, the poem emerges as the site of assuming an interlocution. The postulation that the addressee is capable of speech expresses the speaker's desire to have linguistic access to the unknown through the form of known entities – bird, desert and highland. Everything the poet attempts to unmask and make familiar is in fact a masked unfamiliarity. For instance, even if she addresses the desert highland as the most familiar and closest landscape, she unmasks the unfamiliarity of the addressee by appropriating the object as a cognitive subject.

As the openings of these poems reveal, the address presupposes an ability to hear, which again suggests access to expression and vocalization. Chase suggests that by creating an I–you relation the speaker seeks to confer an empirical status on the world. Through this apostrophic address, she attempts to change the world of objects and abstractions into subjects, which in turn will create a cognitive relation between addressor and addressee. The addressee is thus perceived, projected and imagined as an interlocutor or a listener.

Speaking to 'Abandonment of Death'

Although there are a number of poems with apostrophic openings, to give a close reading I have limited myself to one particular elegy. In fact, any elegy or poem with an apostrophic address could be included here (see Chapters 2 and 3). The following elegy stages a prosopopoeia through addressing the 'abandonment of death'. The projection of voice can be read in relation to death in the poem's fundamental question, 'where is my love?' The woman poet here assumes death's ability to speak,[27] and declares:

I jumped to the highland;
Gesturing, with five fingers,
I said:
O abandonment of death,
Where is my love?
Into a knot
Twice over
He tied me
Without a touch,
And I tied him
Into one knot
That cannot be undone.
If yesterday is as today
And if tomorrow is the same
My sorrow will grow.[28]

The poem begins with two movements: climbing the high plateau and pointing five fingers, which are spread out in a preparatory gesture to face death before the moment of addressing loss, the assumed listener. This act of gesturing, of pointing to the time of death, to an absence and separation, refers to pre-signification. Perhaps it implies the speaker wrestling with her desire to communicate with loss, since what occurs is a gesture instead of words – and her hand is caught in a web of threads and knots. From the outset, the poem's dominant mode is interrogation. We are prompted to ask who or what is the addressee? The speaker is anxious to ask death about her beloved, and addresses the 'abandonment of death'. The trace of separation is undiminished. The hand gesture appears in a gap or void between life and death. It precedes speech, but carries an interrogation: 'where is my love?' Death swiftly seized the beloved from the midst of the living, and is hence being summoned.

The elegy repeatedly bestows speech on the silent world because, as we have seen (in Chapters 2 and 3), it cannot acknowledge death and passing. The speaker seems to be suggesting that loss does not deaden as much as it dislocates, and places a demand on us in ways that evoke keen interrogations about its meaning. Perhaps the speaker deliberately throws open her fingers questioningly in contrast to a silent, motionless world, to reveal just how baffling this condition of death is. The words she uses describe the sudden intrusion of loss: 'Oh abandonment of death/where is my love?' The greatest threat of 'abandonment' is the anguish it sheds on the lives of those attempting to understand why death steals and deprives. But the boundaries between what speaks and understands, and what lies on the highland infinitely mute and inanimate, have become hard to distinguish, let alone rely on. That is why they are perpetually overlapping and creating this false identification.

In these lines we can recognize the poem's main figure as prosopopoeia, an embodiment of face and voice. The speaker in this elegy initially recognizes the absence of her beloved, but refuses to lament and instead searches for him. She attempts to substitute death for life and imagines the dead beloved as speaking. In a sense, she is drawn into what cannot speak, and bestows speech on it by addressing and gesturing towards it with her fingers.

At issue here is the linguistic relationship between address and reply. The movement of prosopopoeia, however, allows the initial address to be both stated and undermined, because of the irreducible effects of another interplay between address and language. Pointing towards what cannot speak, then, presents a moment in which the speaker assimilates language as a speaking force. Furthermore, pointing the hand with fanned fingers causes us to wonder whether it is accusatory. If so, then the speaker is accusing death of taking her beloved away. But if this pointed hand is a gesture during speech to a listener, then we have a moment in which death is treated as a listening subject. The speaker therefore climbs up to the lookout in the desert and begins by speaking to death. The poem indicates that her gesture precedes her words. The gesture is complicated, in so far as the speaker describes the staging of this address and how it was initiated in the moment of gesturing. But the poem reverses this a priori structuring because the gesture is articulated in language; it is a linguistic signifier, even though the speaker attempts to posit its priority to the moment of addressing death. The poem has come to depend on its address and the question it poses. It bypasses the other senses and continues to be obsessed with speech, which it bestows onto inanimate and dead entities – death, the deceased and so on. The interaction between the responsive and non-responsive worlds culminates in an extraordinary exchange between the speaker and the deceased.

The staging of this address is dramatized in the poet's preparatory movement of jumping onto the lookout, the high plateau in the desert from which nomads can spot newcomers. *Al-rajm* could be a heap of stones stacked up to create an observation post. Nomads often stand on such a high place to gaze out and await the arrival of absent ones. It can also be a guard post, overlooking an entire camp site and its surroundings. Several Bedouin women poets describe this moment of climbing as *al-rajm* and say: 'Last night I climbed a mountain';[29] 'I climb to the peak of Mount Jawa at dawn';[30] 'Yesterday I scaled the lofty summit at forenoon';[31] or 'I climbed the lofty place and stayed waiting.'[32] In the present poem, however, *al-rajm* dramatizes the scene of loss. The elegy emerges when the poet is on the high place in the open desert from which poets recalled their beloved, as other poems show. Standing there, the speaker observes loss and interrogates it, at the same time searching unceasingly for her beloved to the extent of turning objects into sentient subjects in her apostrophic address.

If the signification of prosopopoeia is complicated in the articulation of an address to loss – 'O abandonment of death' – the site of this radical positing of face and voice is similarly multilayered. It is not only a phrase or a proper name, but a pre-linguistic 'O'. In the moment of utterance the speaker invokes an empirical voice, but it is an empty voice or cry because it is embedded in the opening sound, 'O'.[33] This sound is a moment in which the speaker is interconnected with language and its ability to name. Yet, the address does not embody a localized addressee whom we can identify as the poem's recipient. It carries the speaker's insistent demand to be listened to by 'abandonment of death', which makes it even more intricate.

The figure of address has been investigated by Derrida, who says:

> If I may now make use of the apostrophe, let me tell you this much at once: *I do not know* to whom I am speaking. Whom is this discourse or lecture addressing here and now? I am delivering it to you, of course, but that doesn't change the situation much. You will understand why I say this. And once you find this intelligible, it becomes at least possible to demonstrate that, beginning with the first sentence, my lecture has not simply and purely missed its destination [my emphasis].[34]

The Derridian questioning of address is a continual investigation not only of this kind of lyrical address, but also of the function of address in texts. When delivering a public lecture Derrida stages another form of apostrophe as he addresses his audience, thus highlighting the relationship between address and addressees (*destinaires*). He reflects on the moment of address and subverts it by recognizing apostrophe, yet questions the chances of arriving at a destination. Derrida marks the unknowability of his words arriving at specific addressees and calls attention to the fact that destination is always exposed to deferrals, divergences and holdups.

Still, Derrida's emphasis on the deviations and delays of the dispatch leads us to recognize the indetermination of the topos of address. He problematizes the question of address in so far as it combines the unknowability of both trajectories – to whom one speaks and who is listening to one's speech. He writes: 'Regarding those to whom I now speak, I do not know them, so to speak. Nor do I know you who hear me.'[35] Because, as the addressor, Derrida neither knows for sure who his addressees are nor who will hear his delivery, he advances his questions regarding the trajectories of both speaking and hearing in the formation of address. It is in the context of this subversive critique of apostrophe that he dismantles the speaker's determination of a designated addressee.

Thus, Derrida's explication of the knowability of addressees helps us to continue reading the poem, while keeping in mind that the poem's addressee is never determinate in and of itself. Following Derrida, we can see how address in texts presupposes an arrival at a destined receiver, but its trajectory reveals a contradiction of what it rhetorically displays. Even after a poem projects knowability of its addressee, it is paradoxically entangled in the uncertainty of whom or what it is addressing.

To what extent does the working of address, in general, deploy systematic illusions of listening and speaking? It presupposes an immediate perception of exterior perspectives that is located somewhere else, and by so doing it inscribes an alignment between itself and what it structurally fictionalizes. The assumed voice of the dead, otherwise silent, is imagined as hearing the speaker's address; the deceased will speak and, more significantly, will enter the world of the living. This is clear in other openings in which the speaker addresses a wolf, bird, dove or lookout mountain and dramatically aligns the poem with loss. She inscribes her address to a dead, silent concept and presupposes its ability to respond. The silent world of death has been transformed into a world in which the dead can hear and speak by means of the apostrophic address and its staging of prosopopoeia.

Culler views the lyric as 'a poetic naming that performatively creates what it names'.[36] In this sense, it is death that the poem rhetorically creates. If a poem invokes death, it often rhetorically generates its own theme, which is already inscribed in its address. As a result of this self-referentiality, the poem rhetorically and thematically serves as a poem about death. More problematic is that the language names death and speaks loss. As a concept, 'abandonment of death' is given life in the form of address and the poem aligns it with cognitive power. The speaker thus initiates a condition that if death as an event is cognitive, then finitude can be understood. She summons death and asks: 'Where is my love?' This question sets forth the knowledge that she claims to have. Later, she presupposes knowing what death is, since she asks it about the dead. Thus, the poem displays the figuration of voice in relation to understanding the mystery and predicament of death. If death has a responsive power, then the speaker would comprehend finitude.

By assimilating death, a non-cognitive abstraction, into a cognitive subject, the poem implies an understanding of the metaphysical world. The speaker's desire to comprehend persists, in that she perceives a non-cognitive concept as cognitive and creates a possibility that death might involve a verbal exchange. Furthermore, if the speaker claims an understanding of finitude then she presumes knowledge of life – and of death.

Examining the word 'abandonment' in the poem helps to clarify this. The Arabic *hajr* has a connotation of separation from a beloved, of leaving, forsaking and abandonment. If death implies infinite separation, then it is identified with what it generates. In this case, one can suggest that the speaker not only addresses death as a cognitive subject but at the same time cancels this assumption, since she associates death with something identical to itself. According to the poem, death resembles itself, which negates the speaker's presumed understanding of what death designates. Yet, despite the poet's claim of understanding, the poem encompasses a tropological system that not only disrupts any presumed knowledge of finitude, but also denounces the language of trope. For de Man, 'the language so violently denounced is in fact the language of metaphor, of prosopopoeia and of tropes, the solar language of cognition that makes the unknown accessible to the mind and to the senses.'[37]

De Man's theoretical elaboration has a bearing on how figurative language attempts to explain and reveal the unknown, assuming knowledge and understanding. Having inscribed figurative language in relation to a cognitive process, he seeks to demonstrate how the language of prosopopoeia is precisely 'the language of cognition' that attempts to make language meaningful. It is a language that ceaselessly assimilates the unknown by inferring a possibility of knowledge and perception, which prompts him to dismantle the primacy of figurative language and its promise of a cognitive manifestation. Paradoxically, understanding as part of the process of reading depends on this trope. In another context, de Man deconstructs the generic name of the lyric and explains how such a name is related to a 'defensive motion of understanding'.[38]

In the present poem, the dividing line between what is inanimate and what is living is repeatedly blurred and diminished. The implication is that if the speaker treats objects as subjects, then she herself also mirrors such a process, for she turns out to be mute like the addressee. De Man refers to this as the 'threat that inhabits prosopopoeia, namely that by making death speak, the symmetrical structure of the trope implies, by the same token, that the living are struck dumb, frozen in their own death'.[39] The poem exhibits this danger because it identifies death with intelligibility. To perceive death as a responsive being implies another assumption – that death can address us in return. Moreover, this threat, as de Man demonstrates, extends to implicating us in the symmetrical structure of prosopopoeia. For him, this symmetrical structure of the trope is ultimately applicable to us as readers. In other words, if we perceive text as having voice, then by the same token we 'are struck dumb' in this process.

One can read de Man's assertion by focusing on the I–you relation created in the fiction of address. In this sense, an abstract concept is called on by a you that is listening to my lament. Following de Man, if this I–you pattern is already inaugurated between the speaker and the concept then one might also be able to demonstrate how the speaker will be objectified through the same process. The proposition of a commutable exchange cannot, therefore, overcome the I–you configuration.

In the poem, the 'abandonment of death' is addressed and summoned to respond through the fictive trope of prosopopoeia. As noted, summoning a concept to listen proposes that the speaker expects to hear a voice in return. The figure of address as a topos of voice bears its own fictionality; that voice is only a fiction of a voiceless entity. Hence, the address that permits the voiceless, the mute, to speak is confined in what it cannot confer. What the address confers audibly is only presented through it and proves that voice is not its own. This, of course, implies that the figure that allows the voiceless to speak is embedded in its own illusion. The fictionality of this trope creates an assumption that linguistic signs are given voice, since they are perceived as a medium or mediation of this voice. By addressing what cannot speak, the female speaker in the elegy is, in fact, entangled in linguistic signs that are incapable of achieving responsiveness. Language is here treated as having voice and perception. Chase explains: 'How the *figure* of voice is, precisely, voiceless. The intelligibility of language depends on a figure itself mute, unable to make itself intelligible.'[40]

Once that assumption is made, of course, the addressee's ability to speak sheds more light on its fictionality. 'At stake is the possibility of hearing writing – of hearing a voice in, and putting a face or a name to, linguistic signs.'[41] Chase illustrates how prosopopoeia ascribes audible and cognitive aspects to linguistic signs. Conceived as such, prosopopoeia as a linguistic sign appears speechless and stages what it does not have. It bears its own inability to speak but continues to project its voicelessness. Linguistic signs cannot offer this presupposed exchange and reflect only their own specular movement. As the address suggests an intersubjective relationship, it never overcomes its inability to fulfill such a fictive exchange. In a sense, the speaker faces a perpetual loss and attempts to name it as 'abandonment of death', which arouses once more a desire to unravel this loss. The speaker summons the addressee to speak, and attempts to bridge a loss that is brought about by death. The poem shows that loss cannot be traversed or overcome, and its language continues to produce another loss, which is discussed below.

Unravelling Loss

In the remainder of the poem there is a suggestive configuration of a knot. But if the addressee is death, what does the speaker seek to establish between the elegy and what it elegizes? Is loss elegized by suggesting a possibility of lacing the knots? The knot functions not only as a link between the speaker and the deceased; it also reproduces a linguistic figuration of a wish to unravel this loss.[42] We have a web of threads in the poem that needs to be deciphered. The speaker moves her hand in this web, fastening knots and producing a chain of signification in the poem. Time repeats itself, turns back on itself. The function of the 'knot' multiplies and does not allow for easy disclosure. It serves as a centre through which the man and woman are contracting with each other. In Arabic, the word *'uqda* captures many significations – knot, problem, a puzzle, and in popular culture it refers to magic. However, the root *'aqada* has several meanings, some of which are 'to fasten with a knot, join, to contract a marriage', and one can read it as 'pact' of love in the poem. But what is the signification of a knot, a contract or a promise in the face of death? And how can one generate a reading of a contract with the other after death?

In the poem, the question persistently arises of what can counterbalance this bereavement in the face of death? Can intimacy be re-established and inaugurated as the speaker weaves it, proliferating knots in the face of absence? From what does the speaker weave these unlikely knots? Does she interlace knots of intimacy and love out of absence and deprivation, or plait reunion from imagined memories while she attempts to overcome loss and perhaps refuses mourning? In an astonishingly minimalist manner and with fewer verbs than the listener expects, the woman speaker condenses this love pact: 'Into a knot/Twice over/He tied me/Without a touch/And I tied him/Into one knot/That cannot be undone.'

Who can comprehend such a relationship? Who can articulate it more vigorously than in the sign 'knot'? Only an inert language can enunciate it, and no trope is more forceful to carry it forward than prosopopoeia, which has been inaugurated once again. This poem displays the force of language and death; it inscribes the lovers' bodies, attaching them, interlacing them, snaring them and curling them up inside a web of knots. These movements are intertwined without a touch, as the speaker's emphatic assertion indicates. In the prevailing loss and its melancholic setting, we see the poet's consciousness struggling to knit itself together as she tries to merge with the deceased in the process of interchanging knots. It seems that she wishes to reach what lies beyond death, beyond face and voice, and to convey it through a pact with the other, inscribing a promise of an endless relationship that cannot be undone. Yet, when and if the speaker does unite with her beloved through the tied knots, the question becomes: can she maintain a joined relationship rather than become forever untied, rushing into the death from which abandonment emerged?

It should be emphasized that this second prosopopoeia is initiated in the contractual movement between the speaker and the deceased. In other words, the poem restages another exchange between the living and the dead through the making of the knot. In so doing, it collapses the living with the dead or with the I–he distinction. The 'I' takes the position of the 'he', since both are knotted in a contract of being one. Consequently, the distinction between the addressor and addressee is no longer obvious. Because the speaker refuses to mourn the deceased, the apostrophic figure that assumes the vocalization of the silent world again expresses her desire to bridge the chasm between herself and the dead beloved. After this boundary has been blurred, the fundamental gap between them becomes interchangeable. It ignores apostrophic limits and repositions the site of speech into death, linking silence and absence with voice and presence, a discourse that bestows on language an ability to resuscitate the dead from the grave.

If Bedouin women's elegies are compelled to deny loss (as shown in Chapters 2 and 3), so does this poem. Attaching oneself to the dead is evidently a defiant act of denying death and clinging to the love object. The speaker ties herself to the deceased, who can be neither mourned nor relinquished. Perhaps she entangles herself with the lost object to continue her refusal of loss. In fact, this poem performs the melancholic bond in a remarkable way, for the speaker insists on being attached, tied to and bonded with the forsaken object. In its iterability, the 'knot' performs rhetorically how the speaker refuses mourning yet is bound to the melancholic province.

In its final lines, the poem raises another question: what is time? The relation with death is kept in constant motion, starting with the question, forming myriad knots and finally returning to specular time. Time that obliterates its trajectory annihilates itself by repeating itself. There is an absent time, the moment of death. This repetitive time in front of the 'abandonment of death' is complicated in the closing lines. The differences between present, past and future are repetitions of ceaseless and identical temporal motion. The poem suggests that the days are equivalent, but more importantly it is this 'knotted' time that is uttered and repeated. It is this moment – a knot between past and future – that is produced in speech. Futurity is 'knotted' in front of death, a knot that generates the anxiety of acknowledging death along with the speaker's unwillingness to accept mourning. Three knots, like the three days, 'yesterday, today and tomorrow', are revolving around themselves. There is a suspension of time in front of an eternal separation. The text refers to the distance, or rather addresses the rift, between life and death, by signing the contract with the other. Indeed, what the poem conveys is this contract with the other. The hand appears at the beginning and ultimately disappears in death's mystery.

As we have seen, the 'knot' generates many interpretations, each of which reflects indeterminate meaning. The poem stages the unreadability of the knot and continues to resist deciphering. What it says is exposed to this trope, this silent knot.

The question of the suppression of prosopopoeia in literary studies becomes one of what we suppress when we dismiss reading this trope. For de Man, as for Chase, to avoid theorizing prosopopoeia is to dismiss its discursive effects in all texts. Chase observes that critics tend to dismiss this trope, but that all discourse depends on it:

> What we suppress when we ignore apostrophe is the dependence of all discourse, including what we call perception, on the figure of address. *For what the address does is to claim the existence of an addressee capable of hearing it: capable of giving ear, of giving voice, to a text*; passing from a sign to a sound and a sense; passing between cognition and perception [my emphasis].[43]

Precisely by virtue of that exclusion, we can recognize that 'discourse and perception' depend on this trope's irreducible effects. Let us now consider prosopopoeia's reflexive aspect. In the act of reading we produce a configuration of this trope because we assimilate linguistic signs as having voice and perception. For Chase, this trope's transferability displays its effects to include also the process of reading. Thus, while the contract with the dead or inert object emerges as prosopopoeia in the poem, this positing of voice initiates another relationship between the reader and the poem that suggests that the poem has been animated – like death – and therefore might speak to the reader. This relationship with reading arises because of the specular movement inherent in the language of tropes. It creates a sort of vertigo to follow the trope's mirror-like effects, its layering and reflecting in a process of *mise-en-abyme*, in which the figure signals towards the scene of reading.

In 'Autobiography as De-Facement', de Man discusses the self-referentiality of this voiceless trope. This self-reflexive movement is specular, but not intersubjective, cognitive or imperative.[44] Address in prosopopoeia, then, must itself be related to a tropological movement that both reduces it to a sign and draws it into a specular realm. The notion of specularity to which de Man refers is grounded in the topos of a mirror. To consider this trope specular posits the existence of mirror images of itself, of sending its effects somewhere else. De Man calls this 'the doubleness of specularity', implying that prosopopoeia induces a symmetrical movement between itself and what it attempts to reanimate.[45] As a figure of speech, it projects life when it reanimates the 'abandonment of death'.

This movement is analogous to another device by which the figure infuses death and muteness into what it tries to reanimate. In both movements there is symmetrical specularity, which allows the figure to attribute animation and to take it away. The figure of prosopopoeia generates life through its illusionary effects of face and voice, yet, paradoxically, it offers muteness as well. The specular functioning reveals that this trope embodies animation and death at the same time. But de Man stresses that it perpetuates a contradiction. The self-reflexive 'Oh, abandonment of death', embodies this contradiction of prosopopoeia's specular movement, in which the speaker gives voice and face to the faceless but also takes it away. At the point of assuming face, de-facement begins, since the speaker bestows a hypothetical face on death. De Man focuses on reading prosopopoeia as giving a face, which becomes a 'de-facement'.[46] In fact, by giving face, the poem disfigures or de-faces the very face it creates, displaying the contradictory mechanism of this rhetorical trope.[47]

Indeed, can there be a reading without prosopopoeia? Chase says that 'reading – our conception of reading on the model of a perceptual process, like hearing or seeing – depends on this prosopopoeia; signs must be actualized by an act of perception in a responsive subject.'[48] If there is 'no lyrical poetry without apostrophe', then de Man's deconstructive reflections assert that there can be 'no reading without prosopopoeia'. The self-reflexive prosopopoeia presents a mirroring of its own; a silent trope that is already proposing what it cannot communicate. Through its self-projection it denounces its own illusions of animation and voice, which it attempts to construct in the form of its address. Yet, the exchange between poem and reader in the fiction of address refers to another proposed exchange: between reader and reading. The poem is about its address, 'abandonment of death'. It reflects on itself, and the movement of the apostrophic gesture from poem to addressee corresponds to that of reader and reading. If 'abandonment of death' is the object of the poem's address, then the poem produces its own object of reading. The self-reflexivity of this figure passes to the linguistic signs, and through this double movement the address aims towards reading. For de Man, the banality or embarrassment of apostrophe does not remove it from its own continual revolving mode, or what he calls 'the tropological spectrum'.[49] The relationship between the poem and its reading can never overcome the specular movement inherent in the first trope. Accordingly, through the figuration of its address the poem restages guidelines for its reading. Here, reading is by turn both a reproduction of the figure it analyses and a staging of this figure's 'revolving' effects, since the figural operation resides in a revolving moment. Tropes, for de Man, do not produce an either/or polarity but cause the effects of a revolving door – a metaphor that Genette once used.[50]

What is crucial about prosopopoeia is not only its difference from personification but also that it propels itself to the plateau of reading. Within prosopopoeia's specularity, the fiction of address goes beyond a mere subject/object relation to involve both text and reader. The scene of reading arises from within the specular effects of this trope because reading reproduces it in so far as we conceive of text as a speaking entity. If we claim that the text has a voice and speaks to us, the scene of reading then becomes a staging of this trope we are addressing. The movement of conferring cognitive power on mute objects is inextricably related to our reading. To this extent, readers of prosopopoeia are implicated in their critique. De Man recapitulates:

> And to read is to understand, to question, to know, to forget, to

> erase, to deface, to repeat – that is to say, the endless prosopopoeia by which the dead are made to have a face and a voice which tells the allegory of their demise and allows us to apostrophize them in our turn.[51]

If readers bestow life on texts, they consequently generate the same trope, prosopopoeia, creating another exchange – of death for life. In this case, the question of this trope's self-reflexivity is a question about how reading is always a reading of the language of tropes. As de Man puts it: 'Since it can be and has been argued that no theory of reading can avoid being a theory of tropes'.[52]

Thus, when the speaker in Bedouin women's poetry addresses 'abandonment of death', 'the desert' or 'the mountain', she tries to give consciousness to these inanimate objects. By enduing them with life, she creates a possibility of voice and expressive power. In this respect the addressee cannot be understood empirically as the receiver of the poem. In turn, the responsive aspect in such an address is re-enacted in prosopopoeia. However, neither 'abandonment of death' nor the language that tries to describe it has life.[53] The double movement is that the 'abandonment of death' not only fails to exist, but also that neither does its referentiality.[54] As a speechless concept that can be addressed, 'abandonment of death' prefigures absence and deficiency in language.

Language, on the other hand, is an embodiment of this loss in so far as it tries to name and identify, but it lags behind, implying that this address appropriates the inability of language to say what it is. Thus, 'abandonment of death' does not signify the concept of death itself so much as a condition allowing speech and perception. However, it should be emphasized that in the act of reading we infer understanding, which implies perceiving linguistic signs as having voice. What is at stake is that language has no voice or perception of its own that could be addressed as a cognitive subject. Rather, it is a figure that perpetuates its muteness, as de Man affirms: 'To the extent that language is a figure (or a metaphor, or prosopopoeia) it is indeed not the thing itself but the representation, the picture of the thing and, as such, it is silent, mute as pictures are mute. Language, as trope, is always privative.'[55]

De Man emphasizes that language is a metaphor, a figure. He makes explicit the problematic nature of language in relation to a perpetual lack by proposing that it is a representation of the thing and not the thing itself. As such, it appears as mute as a picture. He asserts unequivocally that language as a figure is privative. Moreover, we have seen how he relates the language of tropes to understanding. If this is the case, does it entail understanding, and how can understanding become privative? According to de Man, understanding is connected to the process of reading, which is already a process of apostrophizing, as discussed above.

Prosopopoeia has been dismissed, viewed as insignificant or inaccurately collapsed with personification. But we have seen that it is a distinctive poetic device that pervades language.[56] The poem is concerned with the trope of voice, since it attempts, through language, to bestow cognition and expression on mute abstraction. In confronting death, its address evades loss and by so doing presumes to restore life. The speaker presupposes an interlocutor, and attributes voice and face to voiceless and faceless linguistic signs. The figure in the poem ends up producing a mirror reflection of its own, so that its tropological movement extends the conception of voice and its fictional manifestation to include our relation to the poem as readers. However, the figure's self-referentiality operates at many levels, to the extent that the mirror-making played in prosopopoeia ends with a provisional tempo – but nothing as inexplicable or unpredictable as the death that the speaker attempts to address.

Chapter 5

Technology and Postcoloniality: Algeria and Arabia

The early decades of the twentieth century were a turning point in the history of Arabia and the Middle East and in the proliferation of new technologies. Yet, literary critics of Arabic writing have neither addressed nor researched the implications of technology in Arabic literature; neither have they examined its impact on non-Western cultures. It could be argued that this lack of reflection is a result of the gap between disciplines in the humanities and social sciences. Indeed, recent philosophical studies investigating the representation of technology in Western texts have, with a few exceptions, shown such dissociation.[1]

It is nevertheless important to highlight the role of the humanities, for this allows us to reflect on texts that incorporate significant material that crosses over to other disciplines, such as technology. But there is a tendency to confine the definition of technology to the instrumental instead of exploring its relation to poetics. In *Rethinking Technologies*, Verena Andermatt Conley writes:

> In the research in the humanities and social science over the past two decades, technology has been initially defined as *instrumental*. It pertains to human creations that alter or manage what is constructed to be the natural environment. Seen in this light, it is thought, in the wake of Martin Heidegger's

> speculations on science and poetry, to be a means of *execution*, ranging from an 'application' to a generalized technics, that is, to something that is 'always already' there and that could be said to circulate ineffably. Following Heidegger, we are compelled to ask not only what our positions are in relation to technology, but also, how and where do we locate the latter? Everything is somehow technical, and technics appear to be a defining trait of all investigation and knowledge. Technics must be distinguished from instrumental technology that amounts to one of its particular uses and that consequently has been tied to specific ideologies.[2]

As Conley observes, technology has been defined quite restrictively. Heidegger's 1953 essay, 'The Question Concerning Technology', remains one of the most influential discussions on this topic and helps to locate technology in the area of poetics and the arts. It allows us to reconsider the etymological poetic mark that does not limit technology to empirical tools associated with political ideologies.[3] Furthermore, according to Frantz Fanon, Abdelrahman Munif and Bedouin women poets, the interplay between the different approaches to technology not only highlights the diverse non-Western responses to technology but also shows their proximity to similar perspectives in Western discourse. Conley notes that in humanistic commentaries on technology in the West, 'elegies on the death of nature and the dangers of automation and dehumanization counter the expression of praise.'[4] This binarism has a counterpart in non-Western texts and needs to be kept in mind when unfolding the question of technology.

Fanon's essay, 'Ici la Voix de l'Algérie', and Munif's five-volume *Cities of Salt*, are exemplary for examining the notion of technology in non-Western locales and are strikingly analogous in approach.[5] These texts may help us to reconfigure an analysis of the relation between technology and non-Western contexts and, by juxtaposing their assumptions with Bedouin women's poetry, a theoretical reading of technology can become very evocative. It is imperative to examine technology within a theoretical framework that goes beyond the empirical approach that is of genuine concern to Fanon and Munif. Their approach is to analyse technology within the confines of instruments and instrumentality and to show how both colonizer and colonized have utilized, appropriated and expropriated it. Munif does not deploy these postcolonial categorizations in his novel, but uses as surrogates the people of the oasis and the Americans. Interestingly, in his essays and interviews he talks about the effects of colonialism on Arabic culture. Perhaps he conceives his role as offering a critique of oil imperialism, which has become the paradigm of American expansion in the Middle East.

I propose to take a theoretical feminist approach to technology, related to these compelling texts but drawn from the counter image that Bedouin women poets present. Women have no role in either Fanon's or Munif's exploration of instrumental technology. Likewise, both writers have overlooked the etymological implications of the word 'technology', which I argue are performed and inferred by Bedouin women poets who present a strikingly different narrative about instrumental technology in relation to poetics. I have selected a few poems in which these poets speak of motorcars, trains and aeroplanes when expressing their longing to travel in the desert. It is essential to ask what the function of the motorcar is in these poems. What does a technological topos reveal, designate or even bear in the vastness of the desert during the third decade of the twentieth century? Which approach to technology is more revealing about non-Western perspectives? And what do we make of the discrepancies between male and female technological narratives?

Before addressing these questions I shall examine Fanon and Munif's core thesis, namely that technology is both Western and political, which redefines the relation to technology as one marked by the colonial enterprise. In fact, both writers echo some of the early European and American approaches to materiality in African cultures.[6] More specifically, postcolonial thinking about technology leads to assumptions about what is called the Third World and its relation to

Western technological topoi. I argue that the postcolonial critique tends to inscribe totalizing claims of disseminated technological tropes – in Fanon's case the radio – by assimilating them to cultural and political modalities. Certain postcolonial interpretations often appropriate non-Western settings to illustrate how resistance to and ambivalence towards technology originate in the very structures of non-Western cultures.

Needless to say, if these contestations circulate unaddressed – if technology in non-Western domains is invoked to insinuate a binary opposition between different cultures – then one is confined to linking technology to a totalizing effect that eventually leads to viewing it in terms of enframing and instrumentality. This tendency to subsume all the reactions to technology into one coherent experience without heterogeneity has characterized certain postcolonial studies. Although there is a long theoretical investigation of the question of technology in the American and European tradition, no substantial work examines it in a non-Western context.[7] However, in a number of postcolonial essays, critics have treated technology in developing countries, for example in Egypt, Algeria and Arabia, as places where the West encounters the East and new conflictual relations arise.[8]

In their analyses, technology is attached to the Western imperial and colonizing power and aligned with the concept of the foreign. If an examination of technology rests on these fundamental hypotheses, then other presuppositions of ambivalence and/or resistance arise. I suggest that any ambivalence to technology cannot be reduced to a reaction of the East to the West, or of developing countries to the industrialized world, but needs to be addressed beyond these hierarchies. Also, this psychological ambivalence cannot be limited to non-Western cultures while its occurrence in American and European cultures is ignored.[9] Otherwise, such interpretations construct a non-Western setting, for example in Algeria or Arabia, as one in which technology is interpreted as an opposition to the indigenous culture and/or a threat to moral and social principles.

Ambivalence and the Radiophonic Voice

In 'Ici la Voix de l'Algérie', Fanon examines the notion of the Third World's relationship with technology. He asserts that in the conventional Algerian milieu the radio conveys a challenging immoral message. Is the perception of technology always symptomatic of such cultural and political formations? This notion of a systematic cultural rejection of technology can be dismantled by showing a poetic production – Bedouin women's poetry – in which there are no signs of a coherent refusal of technology.

The voice of Algeria transmitting itself through '*un instrument technique précis: le poste de radio*'[10] was well known. In his essay, Fanon describes the Algerians' new 'attitudes' to the radio and notes 'some' resistance to technology. During colonization Algerians were undoubtedly ambivalent about the radio. There was a discomfort, uncertainty and a sort of declared resistance to this 'alien' instrument. According to Fanon, the radio became, among other things, a colonial apparatus, echoing Frenchness and encountering an unspoken refusal in the Algerian psyche: '*Il n'y a pas de résistance organisée à cette technique. On ne met pas en évidence, même après enquête, de véritables lignes de contre-acculturation, telles qu'on en trouve décrites dans certaines monographies consacrées à des régions sous-développées.*'[11]

Fanon seeks to situate the radio in a sociopolitical and cultural context and to show the reaction to it. There is a class affiliation, because the privileged Algerian families resisted buying radios.[12] Fanon attributes this to a sociocultural construction peculiar to Algerian society, an anxiety provoked by this high-frequency instrument. Yet, this resistance is not an 'organized' rejection and produces no political protest: '*Voici donc, à un certain niveau explicatif, l'appréhension d'un fait: les postes récepteurs s'imposent difficilement à la société algérienne. Dans l'ensemble, elle refuse cette technique qui met en cause sa stabilité et les types traditionnels de sociabilité.*'[13]

Fanon creates a polemical presupposition. He assumes that Algerians view this instrument as a cause of instability. A radio, while not a 'threat', is still a colonial presence. Elites in Algeria often listen to it. In other words, it is accessible only to a minority and continues its figuration in Fanon's language as a sign of colonialism: '*Le poste de TSF, comme symbole de la présence française, comme système matériel inclus dans la configuration coloniale, est affecté d'une valence négative extrêmement importante*.'[14] He argues that the radio is aligned with colonial and political stratagems that influence how both Algerians and European settlers perceive it.

Fanon is convinced that technology, as represented in the radio, creates a gap between national struggle and the modern Western world. This unspoken chasm carries psychological and pathological symptoms engendered by colonial violence. The radio slips away in his account, although he tries to capture its presence during the revolution. In 1947–48, according to Fanon, to circulate this foreign body the colonizer had to cover it up, mask it by using a native dealer. The Algerians' ambivalence to technology – an ambivalence in which Fanon himself engages – is problematic. It is a semantic ambivalence that displays itself in the text even though Fanon attempts to limit this technological trope by a specific construction. But in his discussion the radio is there as a non-presence, a presence that is rejected. Even his argument is structured in terms of ambivalence, as it fluctuates between negating and affirming his relationship to the radio.

Fanon lapses into uncertainty about technology, which suggests that we must become aware of its complex layers. He tries to record a noticeable change towards technology in the Algerian psyche: '*Avant 1954, la radio est, dans le domaine psychopathologique, un mauvais objet, anxiogène et maudit*.'[15] He thus distinguishes between two historical phases in the perception of technology – before the revolution and during the resistance. He presupposes that the embracing of this 'Western' technique marks a national shift in Algerian society from a period of subjection to one of finding its identity and, as a result, it appropriates Western colonial imports. For Fanon, the radio during the war of liberation became a national voice and a sign of political struggle, whereas before the 1956 revolution it had haunted the native psyche not only as the enemy's voice but also as the enemy broadcasting its abusive French voices into the ears of troubled paranoid and schizophrenic patients. He observes how the radio delivered aggressive and insulting messages, which became friendly after the revolution. But how can we conceive of the voices in hallucinatory psychoses as being 'protective and friendly'? This is not to deny the complicated discursive formation of the radio in the colonial context, but to call attention to its emergence as a perplexing trope, both because of its relatedness to 'the voice of Algeria' and its elusive movement in relation to war, paranoia and colonial conflict. In Fanon's thematization, the topos of voice multiplies in this cultural and political scene.

The voice penetrates Algeria, which is systematically feminized in Fanon's discussion.[16] He identifies this voice as that of France: '*Radio-Alger, la voix de la France* en *Algérie, constitue le seul centre de référence au niveau de l'information.*'[17] But it has a different meaning for the European settlers, to whom its message becomes '*une invitation à ne pas se métisser, à ne pas oublier le bon droit de sa culture*'.[18] In this articulation, the settlers are connected to their own culture and the absence of the radio carries a threat of becoming Arabized. For Fanon, the radio implies an identificatory moment between the settlers and their culture, which confirms a civilized Western origin. He compares the way in which these two communities come to think about the radio. Indeed, it emerges *in between* communities as it dispatches its messages in different languages. Moreover, a binary structuring arises in the figuration of this instrument between what Fanon depicts as the uncivilized Algerian community and the civilized European one. The European community embraces the radio rapidly, just as it incorporates all technological changes. It owns the motorcar, the telephone and the refrigerator. This conspicuous adaptation of different technological topoi by the European settlers implies a desire to be civilized. In Fanon's formulation, civilization becomes technologized.

Nevertheless, Fanon's attempts to assign the radio a fixed Western origin cannot overcome the elusiveness and fragmentary nature of this technological trope. The radio resists a fixed and unified cultural presencing that is surrounded by political upheaval. Rather, it appears as an elusive trope that cannot conform to oppositional structuring or fixed conceptual moment. It not only renders all the important bearings that Fanon follows carefully, but affirms its resistance to representing specific modes of cultural interpretation.

Following Fanon's construction of the radiophonic voice, one is obliged to ask what and where is the location of this voice. Fanon presents it as marked by political conflict, and later tends to locate a national identity in its fuzzy broadcast. For him, the voice has an identificatory association with Algeria and during the revolution it encompassed a specific Algerian referent. When its soundwaves were lost during the war of liberation, this loss inaugurated a determination to interpret the voiceless moment as a definite voice (or voices) of the battle.

The rhetorical configuration of Fanon's compelling interpretation of the radio as a voice that can be appropriated and reappropriated following political upheaval imposes an empirical analysis that excludes discussion of the radio as instrumental or as a mechanical topos. Correspondingly, the radio is marked with instabilities in its encounter with the French and Algerian sites and is doubly transformed during the national struggle into a useful tool for the resistance. In Fanon's text, it is arguable that the locus of the radio's voice emerges as a loss of its source. In other words, the radio's voice is in fact a loss of its identifiable locus in the radiophonic transmission. This loss displays itself in an exemplary moment in the text:

> *En fin de soirée, n'entendant pas* la Voix, *il arrive à l'auditeur d'abandonner l'aiguille sur une bande de brouillage ou de simples parasites, et de décréter que là se trouve la voix des combattants. Pendant une heure, la salle s'emlit du bruit lancinant et pénible du brouillage. L'Algérien, derrière chaque modulation, chaque grésillement actif, devine non seulement des paroles, mais des batailles concrètes. La guerre des ondes, dans le* gourbi, *réédite à l'intention du citoyen, la confrontation armée de son peuple et du colonialisme.*[19]

In this passage, incorporating the radio indicates confusion about its function, so that it overlaps with the realm of imagination. When the Algerian resistance began, the appeal of this broadcast voice reached the realm of illusion and fantasy. Reading Fanon's vivid description, we can easily imagine a community of listeners surrounding a disconnected radio set. Out of the fuzzy sound, they assemble a fictive noise. The scene is amplified when Fanon adds the sounds of battle to the lost airwaves. By conjuring up imaginary voices, his text negates his attempts to locate a specific radio voice, as he describes how voice loses its presumed origin. He employs '*la Voix*' as a detached signifier that does not identify any referent. We can follow how the listener reacts when he does not hear this *voice*. He listens to 'jammed waves' and produces a radio announcement indicating that what he hears is the sound of the battle.

Fanon has already mentioned another conflict between the French and Algerians over the radio. It is a battle of soundwaves as the French authorities repeatedly attempt to jam 'Ici la Voix de l'Algérie'. The listener hears an endless noise, detached from any voice. In moments of linguistic absence, he imagines the combatants. The noise of the jammed waves produces an absurd staging of the war. Voice, as an imagined construction, is situated in the war zone. Ironically, the passage dislocates this voice as it disappears in the endless soundwaves. This is why, in its most defined status – that of the jammed broadcast – the radio reveals an uncertainty of voice rather than originating a definition of its source.

In Derrida's discussion of voice, one can see how it 'detaches itself, that is its way of "attaching itself"'.[20] Derrida demonstrates how voice does not refer to a given locus where its source can be located. He dislocates voice in telephony, where we can listen to it as it detaches itself and dispatches its messages. Despite Fanon's efforts to inscribe stability to the radio in the colonial context, the radio contests this by putting on the air multilingual programmes punctuated by interruptive and discontinuous static. This instrument, in Fanon's configuration, thus crosses the road from '*une radio d'infidèles*'[21] to a friendly voice that inhabits the troubled psyche. It was once identified as an '*objet de l'ennemi*',[22] but lost this identity because of the radio's slow acceptance among Algerians.

To interpret the radio on different cultural, political and psycho-pathological levels is indeed to propose its negation as a singular category; furthermore, interpreting it as a coherent French presence stages a desire for assigning to technological tropes a determinate cultural and political origin. In Fanon's portrayal we have seen how the radio operates on many distinct levels. It cannot be culturally specific in Algeria because it operates in different dimensions and its function is unstable. Here again, the radio does not connote a stable referent. It crosses national and political configurations into more discursive and semantic fields. In Algeria, the radio cannot be limited to a designated locus and we cannot infer that it signifies a paradigm of Frenchness or foreignness. Fanon, in his ambivalence, reminds us that this instrument has failed to bring satisfaction: '*Dans la situation coloniale, le poste ne répond à aucun besoin du peuple algérien.*'[23]

Instrumental Technology: Fantasy and Conflict

In Abdelrahman Munif's *Cities of Salt* (*Mudun al-Milḥ*), the reactions to technology are less subtle and far more controversial. Munif's narrative uncovers the seeds of the alliance in Arabia between the American arrivals and the ruling class with its supportive elites. I am not attempting either to equate Algeria with Arabia or to make general observations about Arabic literature and its approach to technology. Instead, I offer a comparative framework of the reactions towards technology in Arabia as dramatized in the first volume of Munif's quintet.

Unlike French imperialism in Algeria, the American oil enterprise in Arabia was perceived not as a civilizing mission involving progress and education, but as a model of a new oil economy to be instituted, regulated and administered. Munif thus scrutinizes modernity in relation to a technological project that is devoid of any cultural or aesthetic dimension. Despite the extensive interest in oil, the world's fascination with it and the oil panics especially in times of conflict, one crucial aspect of its history – the traumatic cultural encounter between the Arabian people and American oil technology – has remained unacknowledged.

The symbolic power of oil carries a wide range of political, economic and scientific significations and continues to influence the global economy, but perhaps we should conceptually reconsider its first discovery. How did the search for oil influence, transform and radically distort Arabic culture, especially in the regions where drilling operations were conducted? *Cities of Salt* invites technology theorists to examine this long-forgotten moment in the history of American–Arab contact and the prolonged, ironic staging of the Western obsession with oil.

While Arab and Western scholars have disregarded this crucial era, Munif's momentous quintet, written in 1983–88, covers the human encounter with the machine, capturing the story of people who once lived quietly in their oases. In its epic quality, *Cities of Salt* relates a suppressed history of these anonymous inhabitants and unearths a crucial epoch in the history of oil discovery. This period has been almost eclipsed in the official history of Arabia and has been similarly ignored by American writers. Munif's narrative confronts this historical amnesia with candour and carefulness. He charts a politics of memory, which Derrida calls for in affirming the need of individuals and researchers to have access to the past. However, Derrida and Stiegler warn about inattentiveness: 'We must awaken to critical vigilance with regard to the politics of memory: we must practice a politics of memory and, simultaneously, in the same movement, a critique of the politics of memory.'[24]

Munif reveals the tragedy of the oil industry's impact on the people of the oasis, and that its development was embedded in violence against both humans and nature. He exposes the ruthlessness of the search for oil, in an attempt to provoke his readers to re-examine the previous articulation of technology and of the American oil enterprise in Arabia. For Munif, any reading of the history of oil and modernity in Arabia has to confront and negotiate with the brutality of its emergence. Indeed, tracing the history of what preceded oil becomes integral to understanding technical and urban modernity.

Many critics have highlighted the significance of *Cities of Salt* not only as a landmark in the development of Arabic fiction but also as a novelistic space that offers a different historiography of the immeasurable transformation of Arabia from a tribal and nomadic culture to the age of the oil boom, with all its economic and political ramifications. In this narrative, we can see how rapidly oil technology altered the fabric of Bedouin society and prompted a radically different structure to emerge. What happened was not a typical transformation, but a singular rupture that altered the very existence of the desert community and later made an impact on the entire Arabian Peninsula. Munif displays a historian's and an economist's knowledge of the language of oil, reflecting his training in oil economics.[25] As Edward Said remarked, it is 'the only serious work of fiction that tries to show the effect on a Gulf country of oil, Americans and local oligarchy'.[26]

Cities of Salt portrays a fictional oasis town named Wādī al-ʻUyūn, 'valley of springs', a name connoting a source. It is the site of the beginning, of things to come, but ironically this beginning is represented by its fleetingness. Although Munif does not refer to specific dates, the historical events and political references suggest that the location is Arabia and that the beginning of the nineteenth to the early twentieth century is the era, which he investigates in non-linear fashion. I have assumed that the first volume, *Al-Tīh*, meaning 'desert' or 'wilderness', is set in the 1930s and that the third volume, *The Variations of Night and Day*, is set in the 1920s.[27] Oil was first found in Arabia in 1938 and its discovery coincided with the acceleration of American scientific and technological dominance after the Second World War.[28]

In an interview, Munif highlighted the implications of his book in relation to colonization and oil:

> *Cities of Salt* deals with the question of the relationship with the

> 'other' that developed between the West and ourselves as Arabs from the beginning of the twentieth century. Western imperialism had always tried to obtain raw materials, extending its hegemony over markets and exploiting people in one way or another. But until the discovery of oil, most of our countries, especially the coastal states, were merely passageways for the colonizing power. Portuguese colonialism, then British colonialism, established a number of installations on the coastlines, the functions of which were to safeguard and facilitate their transport routes to India. Apart from this, the coastal states did not have any particular significance, except that the typical [colonial] relationship between ruler and colonizer was created. However, after the discovery of oil this region was transformed into a [commercial and political] target and a vital territory. In terms of colonization, this probably became more important than [relations with] the ruler. Thus, we can call this century the century of oil. In effect, the first oil concession Britain obtained was in Iran in 1901, and other concessions followed to include Bahrain, Kuwait and Saudi Arabia.[29]

The present reading is limited to a few passages from the first volume of the quintet, *Al-Tīh*. It focuses on the period after the First World War and describes the arrival of technology in Arabia with a team of American oil engineers, geologists and surveyors who came to Wādī al-ʿUyūn. The sudden appearance of American oilmen and their exploration machinery baffled the Bedouin dwellers in this oasis settlement. Munif depicts modern oil exploration in a series of scenes of cultural discord and confusion between drilling crews and tribes. This extends to the latter's conflict-ridden relationship with technology as a Western influence on Arab culture, with negative social and political consequences.

Most importantly, Munif links the arrival of oil technology to destruction and shows how this unexpected mechanical onslaught shocked and scarred the human psyche. He perceives technology as a complex field of reflection signifying, above all, modernity as a swift and unforeseen transition. He represents the search for oil primarily as a violent event that caused the demolition of the oasis, followed by several distressing episodes in the life of the people. Technology is perceived as both instrumental and material. What is at issue is the historically important transition of a tranquil desert oasis in the early twentieth century through a chain of events that unleashed turmoil and destruction. Munif dramatizes the swift change in nomadic life, and his opening lines anchor what would have been the past life of the Wādī al-ʿUyūn oasis by staging it in a romantic, nostalgic and almost poetic description:

> Wadi al-Uyun: an outpouring of green amid the harsh desert, as if it had burst from within the earth or fallen from the sky. It was nothing like its surroundings, or rather had no connection with them, dazzling you with curiosity and wonder: how had water and greenery burst out into a place like this? … For caravans, Wadi al-Uyun was a phenomenon, something of a miracle, unbelievable to those who saw it for the first time and unforgettable forever after.[30]

The oasis was a place of wonder where springs of water flowed and green trees grew in the midst of a desolate desert. But this pivotal description of Wadi al-Uyun empirically and figuratively almost vanishes from the novel's language. It seems that Munif has in mind the oasis as a paradigm of a premodern condition, portrayed as an earthly paradise: 'Where are you, Wādī al-ʿUyūn, earthly paradise?'[31] The opening scene captures an ubiquitous elegiac mode because this earthly paradise is annihilated by an urban apocalypse and lost forever. The metamorphosis of the desert from a peaceful oasis into a graveyard suddenly flattened by tractors invokes an immense sense of alienation and foreignness. Eventually, the narrative articulates the varied reactions to technology in multilayered accounts. The first is deeply rooted in a state of anxiety and fear, which I argue is correlated with a traumatic experience; the second is associated with the ambivalence and wonder that systematically accompany inscriptions of the West and/or the foreign in postcolonial novels,[32] and is also comparable with Fanon's analysis of technology. This critical discrepancy dominates the novelistic account of technology.

More importantly, the arrival of the foreigners or of the West appears sudden and mythical. Munif describes the initial explosions as the geologists conducted their survey:

> As soon as the camp was erected, the men paced off the area, put up wire fencing and short white pickets, scattered some strange substance around the tents and sprayed the earth with water that had a penetrating smell. Then they opened up their crates and unloaded large pieces of black iron, and before long a sound like rolling thunder surged out of this machine, frightening men, animals and birds. After several minutes of the rumbling, one of the Americans raised his hand and signalled to another, who extinguished the sound, but it was a long time before it stopped ringing in the ears.[33]

The people of the wadi witnessed the machine's appearance in terrifyingly aggressive, thundering explosions. The reverberating sound and 'blinding light' generate terror and sheer silence.[34] The text refers to a 'marvellous incident, so crystal and yet impossible to believe', which emphasizes its Gothic and supernatural quality. The novel draws attention to the effect of the oil exploration on wildlife and includes figurative descriptions of the reactions of plants, trees, birds and animals: 'The animals who drew near retreated in fright; the camels fled, and the sheep stirred uneasily.'[35] Munif continues:

> With the first light of dawn, a huge iron machine began to move. Their deafening noise filled the whole wadi. So gigantic and strange were these iron machines that no one had ever imagined such things even existed; the lights that shone from

> them were like shooting stars. They moved on the same open track the caravan used, and within a short time the noise grew louder, and the machines arrived in the wadi.[36]

This passage stages the arrival of the machine at dawn, a temporal moment with implications of a cherished time in the Bedouin setting and its associations with suddenness and surprise. The reaction is dread and awe of the machine because of its violent features. The machine is 'gigantic and strange', indicating both its foreignness and power. It is so alien that language cannot describe it, pointing up the sublimity of this terrifying moment. 'No one could describe the moment in which the machines moved into the wadi or know the feelings that gripped the people as they watched the huge yellow hulks move along and roar, then stop at the border of the camp.'[37] Munif seems to suggest that there is no reconciliation between a modernity conducted by mechanical degeneration and a nomadic life nestled in an oasis landscape. If this reconciliation cannot take place, what, then, is the future of this mechanized modernity?

The second reaction to technology is the account of different inventions, culminating in the fictional emir's fascination and wonder with the telescope, the telephone, the radio and the motorcar.[38] Munif's candid critique of the emir's relationship to instrumental technology during that period is replete with the latter's conceptually absurd responses. The emir discovers new gadgets and becomes enamoured of them. His absorption is depicted as a parody of his idolatry of things American.[39] This political satire also illustrates how these instruments are related to a new social order. Elite status is created in relation to the possession of technology among the ruling class, which is linked to access to power and control. These new technologies create a separation between the elite, power and the ruling class, and the workers, powerlessness and the poor, installing new patterns of hierarchy.

In his important study of the oil industry and race, Robert Vitalis uncovers racial discrimination by the Arabian American Oil Company

(Aramco) and draws attention to the transfer of discriminatory practices and 'the setting up of the Jim Crow systems' in the eastern shores of Arabia 'in the 1930s and 1940s',[40] where drilling crews and geologists began to establish their camp according to race and class divisions. He quotes from a letter: 'A few mud huts and dirty natives mark the metropolis of Khobar. One of our Ford cars with large tires conveyed us some six kilometers inland to a temporary camp consisting of tents for the white men and straw-huts for the natives.'[41] This image of modern Americans traversing the desert in a powerful Ford motorcar and gazing at the 'dirty natives' reveals a colonial perspective imbued with a sense of superiority. This phantasmic superiority is expressed in the setting up of a segregated camp where the 'dirty natives' return to their 'mud huts'. The logic of exclusion likewise dominates the representation of new technologies in Munif's narrative. The instruments start to enhance and affirm the political power of the ruling class and its fascination with technological surveillance.

Interestingly, Munif also focuses on the emir's relationship with another new device, the radio, and his illustration of different responses to the radio bares a certain resemblance to Fanon's argument. The radio is a 'gleaming box' that Rezaie offers to the emir.[42] Everyone reacts with fear and curiosity, while Rezaie says: 'This is a gift I have brought you from far away, Your Highness, and it will bring the whole world to you and bring you to the farthest point of the world, as you sit there.'[43] While the emir and his men are experiencing 'fear and alarm', they are startled by the sudden 'sharp voices' that start bursting 'from no one knew where'.[44] Rezaie patiently instructs the emir on how to operate the receiving set and explains about broadcasting, its precision and ability to relay numerous stations. 'With pleasure mixed with terror the men listened to the music in silence.'[45] The narrator ridicules the emir's infantile and irrational remarks about 'the new wonder', which are similar to his reactions to the telescope and the motorcar.[46] 'They look uncomprehendingly at one another: How could this box speak and make music? Who was playing the instruments? Where did he sit? How could he eat up and sleep, and how did that tiny space hold him?'[47]

Like Fanon, who suggests that the radio induces paranoia and the illusion of hearing voices, Munif emphasizes how the people at the coffee house start hearing distant voices over the air at night: 'They had heard unusual noises coming from the north hill; the noises, they said, could be heard, though indistinctly, when the night fell and the sea waves calmed.'[48] The townspeople are haunted and 'gripped' by this instrument, because they want to identify it. The presence of the radio brings a compelling desire to understand it. Thus, these imagined voices and the indistinct clamour illustrate the desire to know.

Cities of Salt casts considerable doubt on technological modernity, which the author stages throughout *Al-Tīh*, starting with the rush for oil and then the American hegemonic expansion. He dramatizes his perspective of modernity by situating it within the ruling class, which he displays in an unreflective and almost comical relation to the proliferation of instrumental techniques. Through the emir's reactions Munif depicts a cynical, unsettling and perhaps menacing outcome for the future of modernity, for the emir and his associates are incapable of lucid questioning about the consequences of the new technologies or the values being imposed on them. For Munif, this modernity is mechanical and devoid of any coherent and rational reflection. The ruling class sought the machine to search for oil without consideration of what would follow. Culture and history were eclipsed and devalued because of this unreflective relationship with modernity and lack of rational judgement about it.

Munif assumes that a mechanical modernity cannot offer any formula of recognition or identification. This modernity was at first inhuman and startling, bringing destruction, madness and exilic characteristics. Later, with each technical object that the elites cherished and feared, it became a process of fragmentation. Munif charts this dichotomized response in a setting where there is only a spectator and a victim, suggesting that such a division cannot offer hope for a future with modernity. In his bleak vision, modernization is consumed only by the elites, who have failed to appreciate its aesthetic or moral value.

Obviously, Munif limited his exploration of technology to American oilmen and the ruling class in Arabia, along with a few responses of a religious character, and in general he overlooks the reactions of ordinary people. In *Al-Tīh*, the women who comprise half the population are largely absent, and their relationship to technology and modernity is nonexistent throughout this dominant male account. The masculinization of instrumental technology in the novel creates a gender imbalance in the portrayal of its arrival. Is it possible to recover another narrative that focuses on women's responses to technology? In fact, Munif's novel helps us to clarify the wider context in which we can make a distinction between Bedouin women's relationships with technology and aesthetics. In stark contrast with both Fanon and Munif, there is no ambivalence about the way in which Bedouin women relate to instrumental technology and modernity; their poems illustrate a feminine desire for the machine. The perspectives of the two male writers need to be scrutinized alongside the feminine approach to poetics and to *techné* – craftsmanship and the arts of the mind.

The poems I have chosen both prefigure and problematize the limitations of anti-technology sentiments in Fanon and Munif. I am not, however, trying either to simplify their critique or, given the historical contexts in which they wrote about Algerian and Arabian societies, to overlook its political urgency. Nonetheless, in postcolonial studies the relationship between developing regions and technology remains undifferentiated. There is a tendency in the 'Third World' context to equate alienation and foreignness with instrumental technology. Also, any account of the reactions to technology in non-Western literature needs to explore critically the differentiated articulations around this topic and to include women's responses.[49] At stake is perhaps another level of intimacy, a level in which Bedouin women poets navigate between the desert and modern technologies such as the motorcar and aeroplane. In contrast to the almost 'silent' resistance that Fanon tends to endorse, or the dichotomized reactions in Munif's novel, these oral poems reveal a dynamic and positive relationship between women and technology. But how can we analyse the encounter between technology and gender in a nomadic space in the desert? What motivates the conceptual and speculative approaches of Bedouin women's poetry compared with Fanon and Munif's complex approaches?

It should be emphasized that these poems invite a theoretical rather than empirical reading of poetics and technology; otherwise the mechanical inscriptions could simply be taken as corresponding to empiricism and cultural essentialism. I also distinguish Bedouin women's poetry from Fanon and Munif's interpretations on the basis that technology is not assimilated to a cultural or political materiality from which any binary opposition arises. These poems cannot be read as postcolonial or presumed to be representative of such a discourse, since they do not exhibit the dialectics of negotiation with the colonizer or the matrix of conflict and ambivalence that profoundly characterize postcolonial writing. Rather, this poetry demonstrates that Bedouin women are not technophobes in their approach and that technology is not confined to instrumentality.[50] Their poems show no signs of refusal; the machine does not belong to a national or cultural struggle and the technological topoi are not aligned with national or colonial schemas. I also wish to resituate that suspended political event, the automobile protest,[51] in women's poetry and women's relationship to motorcars.

Dying to Travel in a Motorcar

By about the third decade of the twentieth century – long before the Gulf War of 1990 – Bedouin women in the desert had expressed in oral songs their desire in relation to instrumental technology. More specifically, they desired the motorcar, which arrived in Arabia in 1925.[52] In a series of 15 oral poems there is a repository of many technological figures – including binoculars, motorcars, water carrying trucks, aeroplanes and railways.[53] What stands out is that some of these instruments are inscribed in English: Ford, Dodge, GMC, a Mack truck and a black-wheeled Mack, raising questions of translatability (see Chapter 6). In general, these are love lyrics in which images of parting, crossing the desert, voyage and movement are systematically articulated. References to technological devices often emerge as poetic tropes. The relationship with the machine is personal, connecting the woman with the other in the vastness of the wilderness. Yet, the desire for the machine is aligned with characteristics of the desert; the vastness and infinity can only be crossed, or imagined as crossed, by the ability of the machine to traverse this challenging space at significant speed. The motorcar, train and aeroplane are represented as innovative transport, promising rapid arrival at the destination and sharing an ability to overcome the desert expanse.[54] In some respects, then, they are part of an evolutionary process.

Indeed, these poems indicate that Bedouin women welcomed the evolutionary process by embracing the motorcar's ability to overcome desert travel and the distances between camp sites, or between the desert and the city. Their references are almost always manifested in the configuration of *raḥīl*, 'journey'. Departure, distance, waiting and long voyage can be better endured by the accelerated speed of a modern form of transportation. The motorcar signals a dream of departure, a departure that has a long literary history since it was constituted in pre-Islamic poetry. The departure as an event is always evocative and marks the moment of speech. The motorcar in these poems is invariably travelling in the direction of the invisible, carrying a promise of the future, of reaching its destined end. This is articulated in language. A continual movement of travel, trace, trail, voice and motorcars is set in motion in the poems. The technological figures in this vernacular genre wind towards the unconscious. Recollection and memory are essential in preserving and transmitting the oral composition. Thus, one can read here the auto-mobility of oral poetry and its ability to travel and to be transferred.

Moreover, the machine is aptly incorporated within the poetic genre. One could argue that Bedouin women poets neither stray from the old generic form nor lose or eschew their intimacy with nature after mechanized transport arrives in the desert. Clearly, there are no inscriptions of loss with regard to the desert or nature. This identification with the world of things does not indicate mere replication or mimesis, but another understanding of what lies beyond the self, the distant other. In fact, unless nature is threatened by irreversible destruction and extinction, the world of things that encompasses both the machine and the desert is in synchronization.

Cole distinguishes between the romantic Western perspective, which conceives of a threat contained within decadent modernity and laments the loss of the old nomadic ways of life, and the nomads' own attitudes towards urbanization. He stresses that the Bedouin perceive no dichotomy between modern and premodern eras. 'Furthermore, they do not agree with either the Westerners or the governmental officials that nomadic pastoralism is doomed in the modern world.'[55] He shows that the members of the al-Murrah tribe retained their nomadic traditions despite their settlement in 'the most remote and isolated desert region of Arabia, the al-Rubʿ al-Khālī or 'their love for the fine herds of purebred camels which they cannot imagine abandoning'.[56]

Likewise, Bedouin women poets do not perceive technology as a destructive force that destabilizes their nomadic culture, yet their viewpoint is not an unreflective embracing of new devices. There are no efforts to assimilate technology into the nomadic space and these poems express no need to adapt to it. One notices immediately an amusing spontaneity in responding to the machine and wanting it closer: 'Salamah, rise and/ bring me the binoculars',[57] and 'My desire's the motorcar of Dāmir/set in motion for my sake.'[58] Ḥiṣah al-ʿAnayzīyah sarcastically mocks her sons whose frequent travel in the Ford has been fruitless:

O sons, how extended is your absence!
Why not just stay away for the rest of the month?

Your travel! Such a waste!
Following the Ford's driver down every tortuous desert trail,
You finally returned when least expected.
She hoped you would come back with the goods,
But your earnings barely cover your fare.
All that's left:
A cheap trinket
For the wife.[59]

As indicated, there are no signs of psychological resistance or ambivalence. The machine is not an alien entity that engenders disquiet and it does not constitute a threat. Instead, it allows the woman poet to make a momentous leap from traditional camel to modern motorcar. Speed is the only comparison made between them, though red is the preferred colour for the vehicle.[60]

It is significant to ask about the relationship between technology and poetry in Bedouin poems. According to Heidegger, technology is not analogous to the essence of technology and this essence is not itself technological. The standard definitions of technology are that it is a means to an end or to a human activity, but these limit technology to the instrumental, which correlates with its Latin meaning, *instrumentum*. For Heidegger, the two possible meanings of technology can be called instrumental and anthropological and, as we have seen, they are accepted by Fanon and Munif. However, although accurate, these definitions cannot explain the essence of technology as Heidegger noted it.[61] If we trace technology carefully we find that its meaning is related to the concept of revealing, and Heidegger articulates 'revealing', *aletheia*, with regard to the essence of technology. He also identifies the proximity between technology in its etymological Greek origin and a poetic trace:

> *Technikon* means that which belongs to *techné*. We must observe two things with respect to the meaning of this word. One is that *techné* is the name not only for the activities and skills of the

> craftsman, but also for the arts of the mind and the fine arts. *Techné* belongs to bringing-forth, to *poiesis*, it is something poetic.[62]

This conceptualization illuminates the encounter between technology and poetics in Bedouin women's poetry and is precisely what Fanon and Munif overlooked. Even so, one has to take into account that the machine is integrated as a poetic metaphor with multi-referential implications: 'The longing of my heart is the hum of a black wheeled Mack';[63] 'the moan of a heart/Pierced by iron nails whose dark metal/Pins it to its own aching veins/A sound like the clattering wheels of a train';[64] and 'O hum of my heart/A Mack truck groaning'.[65]

The following poem by Bakhūt al-Marīyah demonstrates *techné* and *poiesis* and a desire both for the motorcar and the desert:

> The longing of my heart is the hum of a black-wheeled Mack
> The driver shifts gears and leaves a trail,
> Climbing the grade, he double-shifts,
> Descending, he lets it rest until the end.
> My desire is neither a driver nor a boss,
> But rather the one who sees lightning
> And sets out to graze.
> A boy's family settled at the banks of a stream
> Lined with athel trees,
> Its water good for camels, but not for the one who tended them.
> My moan is that of a she camel whose calf
> Has been slaughtered.
> She ascends to the lookout, reunited with the herd,
> Then returns to search for her lost calf.[66]

This is clearly a love lyric in which the woman expresses her sentiments toward her beloved, who dwells in the desert. A melancholic and plaintive tone enfolds her desire. She begins with an extraordinary metaphor in which she aligns her heartache and yearning with the sound of a motorcar's engine, suggesting a familiarity with and responsiveness to non-human objects. T. S. Eliot in the *The Waste Land* drew a similar image: 'When the human engine waits/Like a taxi throbbing waiting'.[67] Clearly, the speaker apostrophizes by way of comparing her heart's longing with 'the hum of a black-wheeled Mack', which is animated through this figurative turn. The dead entity is brought to life in this trope. To convey an image that appears imprecise at first, this powerfully subversive metaphor extends to the movement of the motorcar and the driving mechanism. Does the speaker want to elaborate her longing by orchestrating it with how the motorcar manoeuvres in rugged terrain? Or does she become involved with the mechanization of driving, after recalling the first image comparing her heart's moaning with the humming of the truck?

The question that arises is what motivates this amplification on the technicality of driving? The woman speaker seemingly creates a poetic image of her longing for her beloved based on an attentive listening to the motorcar's reverberations and sounds. She is not simply a spectator gazing at this apparatus, and in turn, the motorcar is neither objectifying nor subjecting. But it has multifaceted poetic insinuations. The trace of the motorcar, 'The driver shifts gears and leaves a trail,' leads to memory, since her beloved is absent and what remains are shards of recollections. The poem depends on the speaker's memory of her beloved, but why do we have the juxtaposition between her nostalgia and this extended metaphor of a driven motorcar, especially when we encounter a sudden rift in the second stanza? As discussed in Chapter 1, poetic and thematic rifts of this kind mark these oral poems. However, this particular poem intensifies this seemingly staged rift or break, because the speaker, after the figurative turn, declares her desire unambiguously:

> My desire is neither a driver nor a boss,
> But rather the one who sees lightning
> And sets out to graze.
> A boy's family settled at the banks of a stream
> Lined with athel trees,
> Its water good for camels, but not for the one who tended them.

In a remarkable way the speaker sketches the traits of her beloved. He is neither a driver nor someone who oversees a farm in the oasis, but a Bedouin who lives in the desert and leaves to graze his herd after he sees lightning. He is an integral part of the desert landscape: lightning, water spring, camels, athel trees and grazing land. This portrayal affirms the speaker's desire to be part of the desert and negates any wish to live in an oasis. What is essential is that the motorcar and the desert are in accord with each other, while an affirmative relationship with the past is vividly articulated. The speaker depicts her longing as a hum of a motorcar, yet rejects the oasis and longs for the desert. The poem elaborates on these affinities in the last stanza. These sentiments about wanting to be in the desert may shed light on Bedouin women's relationship with modernity and technology. However, an equivalent depiction of this mechanized metaphor is found in another poem:

O hum of my heart
A Mack truck groaning
Up a grade,
Double-downshifts through the gears
A heavy-bodied truck
Straining beneath its load
Working the pedals
It's never enough.[68]

In both poems the speakers' attentive listening generates a poetic resonance and displays their skill in composing the mechanics of driving into a rhythmical oral poem. The motorcar remains a register of poetry. But the first poem (see also Chapter 3) concludes with the compelling melancholic image of a grieving camel:

My moan is that of a she camel whose calf
Has been slaughtered.
She ascends to the lookout, reunited with the herd,

Then returns to search for her lost calf.

In a self-reflexive manner, the speaker draws a comparison between her grief and that of a she camel whose calf has been killed. What she and the animal have in common is loss. The camel roams around in utter devastation, climbing to the highland where the herd grazes, then descending to search for her lost calf. By capturing this image of restlessness and continual movement, the poet attempts to represent her own loss. The same melancholic desire characterizes her relationship with her beloved. More significantly, after invoking the hum of a truck, she concludes with a sound that captures the traditional Bedouin ethos – the bereaved she camel. Both metaphors inscribe the poet's affinity with non-human entities and convey her longing. Thus the motorcar, the metaphor of the modern, does not clash with the conventional image, the bereaved camel. In another example of combining traditional and modern, 'O rider of the swift-legged GMC!/Your destination: an encampment',[69] the GMC motorcar is depicted as a fast camel travelling to the desert camp site. The affirmative relation between the modern motorcar and the traditional encampment and camel is clear.

In the next poem the speaker addresses a male poet and we find a sketch of another technological topos – the aeroplane. Emerging as a lyrical address to an absent interlocutor, the poem begins with an apostrophic gesture requesting permission to speak. In so doing the woman undermines her role as speaker and comments ironically on the triviality of feminine speech:

Permit me to say six words, Muḥammad:
It is useless banter and I am ashamed to prolong it.

Oh, Muḥammad, females are not worthy of good treatment;
  their speech is
Not strong and needs no response.

The passenger of that which is in heavenly space walks by the movement of
Its sound, because of its speed, throwing it behind.

It leaves the airport in the forenoon
Passing the camels' herdsman, who has not left his home.

It crosses the passengers of the Dodge before Dumwāt, cutting across the
Red Ṣulba and the encampment below.

A trained pilot does not fear death,
Five minutes pass and its destination is reached.[70]

The speaker goes further in this ironic opening, indicating that her request requires no response. After asking permission to utter 'six words', her focus shifts to another nameless object. In this poetic rift, we finally realize that she is describing an aeroplane traversing the desert and passing the herdsman and the Dodge at riveting speed. But what is she addressing when she depicts her words as inconsequential and meaningless? If we read the aeroplane as a comment on new socio-historical circumstances, we would dispense with the striking analogy between the aircraft and the poem.[71] The sudden shift exemplifies the movement from a moment of passivity to a description of a nameless flying object.

At first it is uncertain what the poem's thematic concern is, but we eventually realize that it characterizes an aeroplane and its speed across long distances. In fact, it is a praise poem of an aeroplane that supports what was indicated above about sustaining the genre, even though the poem incorporates references to new machines in an innovative language that has not been previously deployed in Bedouin poetry. But this language represented in the Dodge, the aeroplane and the airport creates no estrangement between the speaker and her nomadic composition. The pilot and the aeroplane are not named as such, and the airport is referred to literally in Arabic as 'the place of aeroplanes'. If the poem depicts and praises an aeroplane, what does the woman reveal to the absent interlocutor? In fact, this poem reverses the conventionality of thematic or topical poetry.

If we ask what it is about, we will find there is no other theme or topic except the poem itself. The aeroplane is only comprehensible as an allegory of the poem. Thus, the permission to say 'six words' refers to the poem *per se*, which interestingly consists of six lines in Arabic; when the aeroplane 'walks by the movement of its sound/Because of its speed, throwing it behind', it portrays the poem's movement and rhythm. The poem inscribes the traversal as language.

All these poems illustrate that the encounter with the machine can be seen as an attraction at first sight, revealing a fascinating openness to new technologies. The machine is not idealized, romanticized or projected as something other than itself, and it is not a mechanical marvel generating fear or wonder. Rather, it is connected to a spatio-temporal trace in which the machine's characterization resides in its speed and remarkable ability to traverse the endless desert, and the choice of the aeroplane over the motorcar obviously confirms this. These technological topoi reflect the influence of urbanization on nomadic society. Cole spent the years 1968–70 with the al-Murrah tribe in al-Rubʿ al-Khālī (the empty quarter) and recounts that 'Trucks, motorcars, and airplanes have replaced camels, which had been the only means of transportation within the lifetime of people no older than thirty.'[72]

Feminine Desire and Technology

If we trace the articulation of the machine as a technological site in these poems, we will see that it marks a woman's desire: 'My desire's the motorcar of Dāmir/Set in motion for my sake.'[73] Another poet utters, 'I wish riding the water truck/When it sets off, it traverse the vast desert.'[74] A woman in love speaks of her desire in relation to a travelling motorcar.[75] A motorcar leads the way to her imaginary reunion with her beloved. It is as if the desert, in these poems, turns auto-friendly. Driving in the desert, then, neither creates a dichotomy between public and private spaces nor generates a traffic jam. Unlike urban space, the desert is traffic free, yet it evokes the desire for faster transit and mobility. Knowing the nomadic itineraries, always moving towards rain and pasture land, constructs a continuous separation between the woman and her love. Love in the nomadic discourse is inevitably related to separation, and anticipation is linked to a figuration of absence. Her beloved is never there; he is crossing the desert towards rain, or he is on a raid or wandering in the desert. The separation is enigmatic and encounter seems impossible. The motorcar therefore often serves as a figure of *raḥīl*, and is equated with desire. The eye is always on the road, a road to the unconscious, and the attention of the speaker is on the trail of a fast vehicle: through speech, it can connect the woman with her desire.

However, in the poems that I believe were composed before the discovery of oil we notice a different tone describing separation. A dramatic scene of waiting frequently accompanies it. The distinction lies in this waiting scene, which seems to be concealed or delayed in the poems about instrumental technology. In examining a couple of the earlier poems, the distinct articulation of absence and separation in the waiting scene is evident. The speaker expresses the moment of waiting for her beloved in vivid imagery and the entire poem focuses on this anticipation. Is her beloved going to arrive? Is he coming home from his travels? The poet peers into the distance, waiting until the end of the day:

> I climbed the lofty place and stayed waiting;
> When I descended, sunset bent down in me.
> O I wish I were riding a fast camel,
> Noble, which would carry its rider across the mirage's heart
> To follow a beloved who would capture me
> While the rest of the tribe had no effect upon my mind.[76]

For the speaker, waiting is a spontaneous act that sounds like a daily practice – climbing up, sitting on the high place and gazing towards the sun. In her heart is a burning desire to unite with her beloved, but the day ends without his arrival. The image of the 'sunset bent down in me' intensifies the melancholic tone, as if the day collapses in vain. The sun's descent within the speaker is highly evocative, carrying a notion of finality in the desert. A temporal moment is followed by a desire to be with her beloved, in an attempt to overcome this loss. This endless horizon, containing only a mirage, brings the poem to its thematic and anguished end.

In contrast, another poem illustrates a similar tone of waiting, but offers a different description:

> I shiver from the transparent north wind;
> It marks me every morning and afternoon,
> Because I always cast a glance at the travellers
> While I wait for his exhausted, old, fatted camel.[77]

The speaker exposes herself to the cold wind, which leaves its chilly marks. She repeats the act of waiting twice a day, with no result. In this poem the gust of wind embodies temporal movement, contrasted with the waiting that alludes to frozen time, or withholds its motion since time repeats itself without any consequences. Unlike waiting, the cold wind reminds the speaker of the passing of time and of seasonal change while her beloved remains absent. Effectively, the waiting scene mixes the language of love in the desert with philosophical speculation about presence and absence. It attentively re-enacts the classic theme of *raḥīl* and the absent love. This scene of waiting is essential in oral Arabic poetry, for it is intertwined with an existentialist moment that plays off this endless waiting. The description of this scene echoes other poems, yet this unintended echoing does not sound repetitive. Often a poem ends with no fulfilment of the waiting. The desert has to have this plenitude of absence, as if that were one of its unpredictable realities.

In contrast to these two poems composed before the discovery of oil, the other poems about motorcars, trains and aeroplanes do not stage the scene of waiting in this way. There is still waiting, but it may be deferred or momentarily detached from the poem's thematic concerns, as if these rapid machines alleviated its distressing presence. ʿAmshah from ʿUtaybah captures the speed of the train and the motorcar while maintaining the pathos of separation:

I ride the train and my heart is tight with worry,
Tears of my eyes shedding all their water.
Departing early from al-ʿĀriḍ with a menacing crowd,
In the afternoon the train arrives in al-Dammām.
Get up, Saʿad, and gently write my greetings,
One overflowing like the rain and its pebbles,
Overflowing like the desert's sand and those who walk,
Overflowing like rainfalls from its sky.
Write it in a letter and send it off safe
In a new make of car, expensive, difficult to buy.
Send greetings to my people until they hear
And mention that my soul is revealing what was concealed.
The sons of Mināʿīr are a fearless battalion,
Their tents pitched up high to greet their guests.[78]

A consideration of poems about the absent desert demonstrates the powerful relationship between these Bedouin women and their desert environment. The intensified melancholic bond was explored earlier (Chapter 3), but there is another aspect of Bedouin mores and the desert. The poet Bakhūt al-Marīyah unambiguously conveys her longing for the desert as well as her wish to travel in a motorcar:

My longing for a tent
After an adobe house.
My longing to see
Scattered herds of white camels.
My longing to accompany

A just-departed motor.
My longing to gaze
On the plain behind the mountain.
When Bedouin nomads
Disperse to desert camps,
The absent beloved
Will not be remembered.[79]

The speaker affirms her yearning by portraying the desert expanse as a highly picturesque setting, where 'Scattered herds of white camels' graze and the 'Bedouin nomads/Disperse to desert camps'. She dismisses living in the adobe house and reiterates her desire to be in the desert three times, one of which is related to the motorcar, 'My longing to accompany/A just-departed motor.' As discussed earlier, the motorcar is compatible with the desert and not in conflict with it, as is an urban house or oasis dwelling. Describing the animated nomadic scene introduces a moment of elation because, after a long journey, the Bedouin have reached their grazing land, far from the disconnected and monotonous life in the oasis. The speaker is passionately immersed in tribal life and could almost forget her beloved. What has been conveyed so far is related to seeing, since the speaker, in her melancholic mode, yearns to see the desert. But, because the desert is obstructed by mountains, her longing gaze cannot see: 'My longing to gaze/On the plain behind the mountain.'

This rejection of urban or oasis life has been articulated in a number of poems, such as: 'But the heart was cracked by blades/From the city mud, surrounding it',[80] and 'Tell the mountain that after openness/I fell into confinement/As if imprisoned high up in stone walls.'[81] Obviously, living in an urban building evokes despair, confinement and everything that is contrary to the openness of the desert. The following poem by al-Jāzī al-Subayʻīyah (see also Chapter 3) is relevant because it elaborates on this strong attachment to the desert:

I find comfort in taking poison,

Better than the distress of a husband's presence.
My desire is a man from Subayʿī, who tracks
His dispersed camels.
He is better than Ibn ʿAskar's castle and its building.
When I die, bury me in the centre of this
Dry and endless space,
My grave in the path of departing camels,
That they may step there.[82]

The speaker intensely rejects her husband. However, her longing for the desert is doubly amplified because it is both a gesture towards freedom from an undesirable marriage and a return to her past.

These poetic samplings demonstrate Bedouin women poets' attachment to the desert. But the question becomes: What does the desert stand for, especially when juxtaposed with technology and urban life? Why do these poets fervently reject urbanity and its buildings while they embrace the motorcar? Their poems categorically differentiate between technology and urbanity, and it appears that urbanity strips the speaker of her desire to live: it cannot measure up to what the desert offers. Thus, I argue that the desert is the vessel in which the Bedouin ethos is preserved. Unlike urban space, it does not separate the poet from her nomadic culture, and the motorcar as a technological topos makes the desert even more attainable.

In these poems, the various makes of motorcar are not merely signs of a foreign presence. Clearly, the motorcar does not generate an anxiety of the foreign or a conflictual relation with technology. Both the motorcar and the aeroplane become poetic figures. These technological instruments are incorporated into the language of poetry, while the generic texture is not disrupted. If it is a love or a praise poem, the inclusion of these mechanical inscriptions does not change the configuration of the genre. Bedouin women poets seem to hold onto past forms, preserving conventional poetic qualities and their attachment to the desert. At the same time this inviolable clinging to the past can be read as an innovative gesture that connects the modern, the motorcar, with the oral genre and with traditional forms of nomadic culture.

Thus, one can argue that Bedouin women's poetry stages a fundamental link between the conventional and the modern without any visible linguistic distancing or disavowal. The approach to modernity is grounded not in alienation and destruction but is an exemplary reading of the past in relation to modern life. Neither parameter – the traditional or the modern – threatens or cancels out the other. This is in striking contrast to Munif's novel, where we saw a linguistic estrangement between the premodern and the modern, in which the latter is always attached to anxiety about creating a rupture with the past.

It is noteworthy that Bedouin women poets' articulation of instrumental technology conveys no sense of overcoming or conquering the desert. The motorcar does not mark the limits of these voyages: it is unmarked, like the desert. The correlation between technology and the desert does not carry a hierarchical relation. It is as if the machine blends with the desert in the Bedouin setting. Once the motorcar, as a better practical choice, has won out over the slow camel, it is aligned with desire because it travels faster – as fast as a woman's pulse. The camel and the motorcar, this alternating pair, function as a motif of the nomadic desire of dispersing and moving on in an open space. The motorcar has affinities with the desert, especially in its speed, and there is a desire to utilize it in order to be with one's beloved:

Last night I slept, O son of Thāmir,
Among my people, and today
I cannot trust the shrunken camel
As endless mountains block my way
My desire's the car of Dāmir
Set in motion for my sake,
And when its wheel begins to jammer
The distant place draws near to take.[83]

The speaker expresses her longing for her tribe, but suffers from distance and separation because 'endless mountains block [her] way'. Her view is obstructed and she cannot see the tribe's land. She states emphatically that she relies on the faster motorcar rather than the 'shrunken' camel, and there is an affirmation of speed and desire in relation to the motorcar. The mechanism of desire is clearly inscribed in this poem and is essential to its reading. But desire, in so far as it relates to a technological object and never achieves the satisfaction it seeks, is complicated. This movement creates its double in the poem – the movement of speech. Desire transmits and transfers itself in language. This 'automotive' desire should be read with a Lacanian insight. Desire designates itself to another: 'desire desires the desire of another. Desire has a movement, an energy that is always trans-personal, directed to another.'[84] This desire for 'the car of Dāmir' is in motion, on the road as transpersonal. Desire is always linked to something not there: 'Desire is a fundamental lack, a hole in being that can be satisfied only by one "thing" – another's desire.'[85] Desire exists beyond 'conscious articulation' and in this sense it is like language:

> Like both need and demand, desire exhibits the structure of the wish; it is based on the absence or privation of its object. Like demand, it preserves an absolute or unconditional element and an orientation towards the other. In opposition to demand (and in accordance with need), desire is beyond conscious articulation, for it is barred or repressed from articulation. It is structured like a language, but is never spoken as such by the subject.[86]

What has been engaged earlier will lead to another domain, 'the domain of the drive'. Both Lacan and Freud articulate the drive, and Lacan explains what inhabits its domain by referring to Freud: 'Freud says that it is important to distinguish four terms in the drive: *drang*, thrust; *quelle*, the source; *objekt*, the object; *ziel*, the aim.'[87] The drive cannot be 'regulated with a movement'[88] and always returns in a circular course. At issue is the satisfaction of the drive:

> The satisfaction functions only in the category of the impossible, which is defined by the field of the Other. The drive is indifferent to its object: it is not an object that satisfies it, for this object reveals only another want, another satisfaction for which it yearns.[89]

We have to remember that we are in the realm of speech. The woman inscribes her desire in poetry; there is no satisfaction attained in the poem unless it is said to be in the act of creativity. The poems are produced by the mouth, which is an erogenous zone, and they are designated to another rim – the ear.[90] The echo of this 'oral' poetry can be heard. In its circularity, nomadic poetry travels from one border to another, carrying its trace from a woman's mouth to my and your ear. It seems that the mouth is speaking to itself in the domain of language, which suggests a Freudian model. Elizabeth Grosz writes: 'Lacan asserts that the drives' source is always defined by the erotogenic rim, the orifice, or a cut on the body's surface that marks a threshold between its interior and its exterior, and thus also a site of exchange between the subject and the world.'[91] In the movement of this exchange, in the speaking forth of the poem, which travels from mouth to ear in a repetitive manner, a certain satisfaction coincides with speech. From this circular motion of this drive, from a woman's mouth creating speech, we have another figure of this reading of desire – the motorcar. To what does the motorcar refer in this oral poetry? The woman realizes its presence and her awareness is not devoid of suggestive interpretations.

Heidegger's thinking is appropriate here because he assures us that technology is embedded in poetry. In 'The Question Concerning Technology' he reiterates:

> Because the essence of technology is nothing technological, essential reflection upon technology and decisive confrontation

> with it must happen in a realm that is, on one hand, akin to the essence of technology, and, on the other hand, fundamentally different from it. … Such a realm is art. But certainly only if reflection upon art for its part, does not shut its eyes to the constellation of truth concerning which we are questioning.[92]

As we have seen, these poems present women's unique relation to technological topoi. The speaker apostrophizes the motorcar, and the machine is animated by her feelings. The noise of the motorcar is a heart pulse. This quasi-human quality sheds more familiarity on a woman's relationship with a motorcar. The speaker invokes life into this silent object by animating the motorcar through the configuration of prosopopoeia.

What has been transferred in these poems? Is the signifier, as the name of a motorcar, able to transfer itself from one language to another without diminution? How can one read the English utterance in a nomadic dialect? To speak of transferring is to raise a question of translation, which sheds light on our understanding of the multiple significations of Bedouin ethos in women's poetry and its translatability into English, issues that are discussed in the following chapter.

Chapter 6

The Translatability of the Nomadic

> Translation is the most intimate act of reading. I surrender to the text when I translate.
>
> C. Spivak[1]

The notion of origin and the original has been much debated, especially in the two separate but related domains of translation and oral composition. Their systematic interplays are not, however, incompatible. In oral poetry, searching for the original is impossible, since it does not exist as such (see Chapter 1). Instead, a critique of its representation must replace the quest for an authentic, accurate and uncontaminated poem, because the original cannot be derived from its various recitations and transmissions.

If we are reading a nomadic poetry that continues to perform translative configurations, and if translation is characterized by loss, interpretation, homelessness, borrowing and alteration, and infinitely performs and sets off these modes, then it is important to recognize that this unique oral poetry retains what seem to be the effects of translation. In fact, Bedouin women's poetry incorporates a number of aspects associated with translation. Translation is also prefigured in its context and should not be confined to questions of fidelity.

Translation Theory and Bedouin Women's Poetry

There is a need first of all to ask how Ibn Rāddas's role prefigures and problematizes translation. How can we reconcile the role he played, since he is the one who collected these oral poems from diverse transmitters unknown to his readers? As a transmitter, inscriber and commentator, Ibn Rāddas continually enacted the translation process. How much did he capture and what did he relinquish in these different acts of translation? He neither explains the scene (or scenes) of performance where he listened to the different poems nor discusses the difficulties of transcribing them. However, gathering these oral poems and subsequently transcribing them embodies a forceful suggestive movement of 'translating' orality into writing. In Ibn Rāddas's collection, all these processes already mark what remains for the reader, bringing the realization that translation is another matrix of loss. In many instances Ibn Rāddas presents inaccurate meanings of certain vocabulary, either because he misread some poetic lines, dismissed the rhetorical, presumed the poet's intention, or sometimes attempted to withhold or conceal women's erotic imagery (see Chapter 2).

What happens in translation to the marginal subject and the minor language, dialect or dialects? Gayatri Spivak asks the question of how a translator should attend to the specificity of the language.[2] Is it possible to translate inscriptions of gender and how can they be understood in translation? In Spivak's view, 'the translator from a Third World language should be sufficiently in touch with what is going on in literary production in that language to be capable of distinguishing between good and bad writing by women, resistant and conformist writing by women.'[3] But Bedouin women's poetry has been silenced and suppressed, as it were, not because it is 'bad' composition, inferior to 'good' poetry, but because no one surrendered to it or read it on its own terms within its gendered context. There is a double exclusion, first, because no commentator attempted to examine Bedouin women's poetry in order to classify it; and second, because this dismissal is embedded in a long Arabic tradition that can be traced from Ibn Khaldūn to the present day.

Spivak cautions about certain cultural politics that emerge in translating the writing of Third World women: 'There is an ethno-cultural agenda, an obliteration of Third World specificity as well as a denial of cultural citizenship.'[4] This is generated by the progressive realism that proliferates in the West, which attempts to render otherness in material registers – what Spivak calls 'metropolitan materialism'.[5] Similarly, one cannot appropriate Arab women's texts, in this case Bedouin women's oral poetry, as a homogeneous cultural commodity. Spivak emphasizes that the selected text or texts for translation should be those that undo and dismantle these presuppositions assigned to non-Western women's texts and their mirroring of the cultural majority. She adds:

> I remain convinced that the interesting literary text might be precisely the text where you do not learn what the majority view of majority cultural representation or self-representation of a nation state might be. The translator has to make herself, in the case of Third World women writing, almost better equipped than the translator who is dealing with the western European languages, because of the fact that there is so much of the old colonial attitude, slightly displaced, at work in the translation racket.[6]

In this context, Bedouin women's poetry cannot escape the question of translation as modern literary theorists have examined it. Two seminal essays, Walter Benjamin's 'The Task of the Translator' and Paul de Man's 'Walter Benjamin's "Task of the Translator"' are relevant because they present and problematize the question of translation in relation to a preoccupation with language, while staging translation as a theoretical performance of reading.[7] In 'The Politics of Translation' Spivak argues persuasively that the notion of translation resembles reading, and her vision of cultural translation underlines the specificity and singularity of translating non-Western women's poetry into English.[8] These three writers are not only significant for translation theory, but they also lead to certain observations about translation and oral poetry that echo compatible modes in the process of reading,

Benjamin's essay was written in 1923 as an introduction to his translation of Baudelaire's *Tableaux Parisiens*. It is noteworthy that de Man insisted on keeping Benjamin's title in his own essay title. The interpretive suggestion of this repetition reflects ironically on translation and its relation to the original, as well as on reading and citationality. From the outset de Man evokes the compatibility between translation and reading, and performs his interpretive shift by moving back and forth between the French translation by Maurice de Gandillac and the English one by Harry Zohn, alongside the original German text.

Remarkably, then, de Man promises to stay close to the text, staging simultaneously the movement of translation and reading as he interweaves his remarks. He observes that readers of Benjamin are always entangled in 'what happens to the original' but that this cannot be the focus, since many readers of orality have already subverted the notion of the original.[9] An understanding of Arabic poetic history shows that the idea of the original in oral poetry has been challenged and debated since pre-Islamic times, as well as in the context of more modern oral forms.[10] In fact, an oral poem will always be detached from the original in the process of its transmission. I cannot therefore argue for an original text except in a provisional sense.[11]

Both the reader and translator of orality know very well that they face disparities, lapses, appropriations, alterations and so on. The proposition of an original poem can only be a fantasy, since there is no evidence, contestation or confirmation of its existence in one form or another. Certainly, one can attempt to compare several versions of the same poem, if found, but no single version of the original will be more persuasive or authentic than any other. Every poem has already gone through literary exploitations and has been exposed to exilic forces. It will always be appropriable and its origin is irretrievable. The poem resides in its nomadic ability to stay always in motion, which suggests that it is in perpetual translation. Indeed, it is a translation of what has been retained in memory and through many recitations. Reciters who intervene in modifying a score of lines, who embellish a few utterances, alter or amplify the rhythmical patterns, contribute to this unending process. What is presented is the translation of translation. Even the idea of continuity of oral poetry can only be read as a discontinuity in the sense that the linear historical progression of transmission cannot be confirmed. In this way, it is like a translation that is manifested in the discontinuity between the original and what has become the translated text.

Benjamin suggests that we consider translatability as an essential moment of translation:

> Translation is a mode. To comprehend it as mode one must go back to the original, for that contains the law governing the translation: its *translatability*. The question of whether a work is translatable has a dual meaning. Either: Will an adequate translation ever be found among the totality of its readers? Or, more pertinently: Does its nature lend itself to translation and, therefore, in view of the significance of the mode, call for it? [My emphasis][12]

According to this analysis, translation emerges from the original work, and its translatability is contained in 'the law governing the translation'. Benjamin stages two meanings for translatability, although conveyed in rhetorical questions – a strategy that disarticulates the attempt to establish what translatability truly signifies. Meanwhile, he initiates the relationship between translation, understood as a mode, and translatability, which depends on the former and if contained in the work will call for translation. Thus, the work states a demand in an apostrophic gesture, in a summoning call for translation.

Subsequently, Benjamin tries to highlight the notion of translatability: 'if translation is a mode, translatability must be an essential feature of certain works.'[13] How can we read translatability as a feature emerging within the work considered for translation? And how can one assume its occurrence? Translatability cannot be addressed in terms of success or failure, difficulty or effortlessness, ambiguity or clarity. However, this feature, according to Benjamin, does not mean that the work should be translated, but rather that 'a specific significance inherent in the original manifests itself in its translatability'.[14]

Another significant point is his assertion that translation contributes or 'serves the purpose' of displaying an interrelation, 'a reciprocal relationship between languages', a sort of kinship that shows itself in the moment of convergence between languages during the process of translation.[15] This convergence cannot be read as historical. A theological or a dialectical motif resonates in Benjamin's theorization of language and in the concept of kinship, but it is not relevant to the present discussion. The kinship, however, does not imply or necessitate a likeness between the original and the translation.[16] De Man says of Benjamin's concept of kinship:

> The translation does not resemble the original [in] the way the child resembles the parent, nor is it an imitation, a copy, or a paraphrase of the original. In that sense, since they are not resemblances, since they are not imitations, one would be tempted to say they are not metaphors.[17]

De Man reads this commonality as something different from mere semblance, duplication or mimesis, and he negates any attempt to collapse the interrelatedness between languages into conventional theories of representation. He underlines the proximity of translation to other activities such as philosophy, criticism and literary theory: 'Translation is also, says Benjamin, more like criticism or like the theory of literature than like poetry itself.'[18] All these activities, though, are dependent on the original, just like translation: 'they are therefore singularly inconclusive, are failed, are aborted in a sense from the start because they are derived and secondary.'[19]

In his discussion of Benjamin, de Man brings translation into the scene of reading. Translation would be impossible if one were confined to capturing a likeness of the original in the adaptation.[20] However, this semblance amounts to mere intention: 'kinship of languages rests in [the] intention underlying each language as a whole – an intention, however, which no single language can attain by itself but which is realized only by the totality of their intentions supplementing each other: pure language.'[21]

Following Benjamin, consider the word 'rain' in English and *maṭar* in Arabic. The object of their intention is the same, but the 'modes of their intention' are incompatible. Rain may evoke different things to an American from what *maṭar* does to an Arab. In fact, Benjamin goes further, to indicate a rather conflictual relation in the modes of intention between languages.[22] He does not perceive foreignness in the interrelationship between languages, since they share a semblance in the way they express things, but he notes that a trace of foreignness is revealed in the movement of translation. 'This, to be sure, is to admit that all translation is only a somewhat provisional way of coming to terms with the foreignness of languages.'[23] More specifically, the interrelatedness and kinship between languages does not suggest an exclusion or obliteration of the foreign, which inhabits language. But can one articulate this foreign and can the target language contain it as such or would it lose its foreignness?

Perhaps a distinction should be made between Benjamin's and de Man's articulations of the foreign. De Man writes:

> We think we are at ease in our own language, we feel a coziness, a familiarity, a shelter in the language we call our own, in which we think that we are not alienated. What the translation reveals is that this alienation is at its strongest in our relation to our own original language, that the original language within which we are engaged is disarticulated in a way which imposes upon us a particular alienation, a particular suffering.[24]

What is striking is the repetition and echoing of 'our own language' and 'our own' at least three times, ironically reinforcing that language is ultimately not our own and is something we can never claim to own. One tends to assume effortlessness in one's own language, but de Man implies that the notion of original language is already displaced, since it carries a sense of uneasiness and a certain lack of familiarity. By negating homliness and cosiness, is he destabilizing the notion of an original language? Unless one is at home in the original language, then the notion of origin cannot be located or assumed. De Man demystifies this presupposed familiarity and homliness in relation to one's own language. It is perhaps for this reason that translation becomes a factor in revealing the foreignness inherent in one's own tongue, indicating a negation of the original language.

While de Man postpones the notion of a mother tongue and shows its destined displacement from a home it never owned, the same could be said of Bedouin women's poetry, with its impressive capacity to assimilate a number of leftovers and remnants of genres and histories, deferring the notion of the mother tongue. Indeed, one notices a trace of the foreign in oral poetry that resists translation. This foreign is the echoing of difference, the transparency that allows the reader of translation to see a different landscape from her own. Bedouin women's poetry protects what seem to be foreign traces: it reappropriates dialects, pre-Islamic poetic vestiges, inscriptions of historical events and runaway English words, all seeking refuge and all being incorporated and embraced. The notion of foreignness is already exemplified in these fleeting traces: echoing myriad motifs is Bedouin poetry's enchanting difference.

Nothing could be more allegorical than a discussion of translation. I am not suggesting that translation is a metaphor – which Benjamin categorically negates – but that it has to be metaphorical and allegorical, since the translator is striving to communicate a process that resides within the interlinguistic realm.

Obviously, Benjamin's essay cannot escape the language of tropes, from which he presumes to turn away. De Man underlines Benjamin's gesture: 'Benjamin, who is talking about the inability of trope to be adequate to meaning, constantly uses the very tropes which seem to postulate the adequation between meaning and trope.'[25] It seems that an analysis of translation has to try to convey what the 'task' is by deploying associative figures. One of the fascinating tropes of translation in Benjamin's essay is that of 'the royal robe'. He writes: 'while content and language form a certain unity in the original, like a fruit and its skin, the language of the translation envelops its content like a royal robe with ample folds.'[26] This image conveys allure, exaltation, the intricate and elaborate layering and pleating of meanings. The metaphor of the fold also suggests a point at which these gather to create an assemblage. But the folds do not prevent the original from shining through the translation. Benjamin emphasizes that 'Real translation is transparent; it does not cover the original, does not block its light, but allows the pure language, as though reinforced by its own medium, to shine upon the original all the more fully.'[27]

De Man wonders why Benjamin focuses on the translator rather than on the poet as an exemplary figure. He thinks that Benjamin considers the translator, and not the poet, to be exemplary precisely because of his failure.[28] 'The translator can never do what the original text did. Any translation is always second in relation to the original, and the translator as such is lost from the very beginning.'[29] For Benjamin, the translator can never capture the original, which is inaccessible and perpetually displaced. Thus, translation resides in its impossibility.

In discussing Benjamin, de Man makes observations about the French and English translations as well as the original German, to demonstrate how the translator disarticulates some of the author's remarks. Of course, he is showing ironically how translation is necessary but impossible and, more importantly, that it is a process of reading:

> The text about translation is itself a translation, and the untranslatability which it mentions about itself inhabits its own texture and will inhabit anybody who in his turn will try to translate it, as I am now trying, and failing, to do. The text is untranslatable:

> it was untranslatable for the translators who tried to do it, it is untranslatable for the commentators who talk about it, it is an example of what it states, it is a *mise en abyme* in the technical sense, a story within the story of what is its own statement.[30]

De Man indicates, evocatively, that Benjamin's essay is self-reflexive and bears the tracks of what it tries to theorize. The essay that attempts to explicate and reflect on translation ends up, ironically, performing translation. Stemming partly from its elusiveness and paradoxical texture, Benjamin's essay enacts its own untranslatability, and de Man comments: 'The text is untranslatable: it was untranslatable for the translators who tried to do it, it is untranslatable for the commentators who talk about it.'[31] If translation generates a *mise en abyme*, then it overlaps with reading. Such an analysis of translation, of course, entails its relationship with reading: 'The translation is a way of reading the original.'[32] In Benjamin's essay one encounters the untranslatable as what will characterize every reading of it and reading in general, and it is always present in the language.

Bedouin Ethos and the Untranslatable

I have experienced relatively few problems with purely linguistic issues in translating Bedouin women's poetry, and my familiarity with Arabic dialects has allowed me to elucidate some of the dialectal aspects. However, with regard to this poetry's cultural fabric, the translation decision has to negotiate a fine line between accuracy, intelligibility and poetics. It is a process of reading at many levels. I had to examine these poems in their varied Bedouin dialects from different parts of Arabia, study the mediator's introductory remarks and explanations of unfamiliar words and then reflect on the poem itself, while approximating some of the old or obscure vernacular phrases with classical or modern standard Arabic and sometimes with my own Arabic dialect. This process of translation as reading is manifested in moving from one language to another while encountering delays until the poem's arrival – or incomplete arrival – in English. Indeed, translation becomes analogous to the nomadic. But what sort of rupture appears between the original and the translation and what transcends translation? A few examples may shed light on what is untranslatable in this poetry.

Despite Ibn Rāddas's brief comments before each poem and the clarification of some obscure vocabulary, an accurate and literal translation may not make sense to a reader who is unfamiliar with Arabian culture and the Bedouin ethos. In these instances, I have either worked the necessary information into the poem as unobtrusively as possible or added it as a footnote. Something is lost, however, because an Arabic word often has connotations that are entirely absent from the English equivalents. In such cases the semantic richness of the original Bedouin dialects cannot be matched, but one can either use more than one word to carry the multiple implications, or a richly connotative English word that does not entirely reflect the sense of the original but creates an analogous poetic effect for the Anglophone reader.

The first and most obvious translation problem with Bedouin women's poetry is its exceedingly rich vocabulary, which differs from and often far exceeds that of modern standard Arabic in several areas. For example, the *Al-Mawrid English–Arabic Dictionary* lists two words for camel, *jamal* and *ba'īr*, and one for a she camel, which is *nāqah*.[33] Bedouin women's poetry, by contrast, features in excess of one hundred words to describe the different types of camels – and in pre-Islamic poetry the range of words for camels, riding beasts and other modes of transportation exceeded one thousand.[34] Most of these are very difficult even for contemporary native speakers of Arabic to understand; scholars trained in standard Arabic find them even more opaque. Of course, this linguistic abundance stems from the reliance on animals in desert life. In Bedouin women's poetry, dialectal camel words include *khalūf* (milk-camel), *wasāgah* (a camel taken by force), *sawānī* (work camels used for irrigation), and *khalūj* (she camel whose calf has been slaughtered). One also finds a host of words for camel characteristics, such as fast, slow, patient, young, old, strong, weak, of particular lineage, or referring to a particular colour such as, black, white, pale, brown, red or blue. Cole describes the sheer variety of these animals:

> There are many types of camels. Some are specialized as beasts of burden and are strong but slow and rough in their gait. Others, mainly for riding, are fast and nimble, while still others mainly provide milk. The al-Murrah keep all three types, but their milk camels, most of which are black or dark brown in color, are their most valued possessions.[35]

In English, a white or brown camel would seem adequate, but a blue one would be regarded as strange, even humorous. In his classic study of Rwala Bedouins in the 1920s Musil gives a detailed description: 'The camels are variously colored, the Bedouins having a special name for each shade. They dislike white animals with some black hairs, *zerka*. Calves of this color are generally killed', or sold since they are undesirable. 'Pure white is the most favored of all.'[36]

To translate the word *zarqā'*, 'blue camel', I have chosen 'blue-grey', while I interpreted *ḥamrā'* as a red camel, since it captures the irony when juxtaposed with a red motorcar (see Chapter 5). However, red is metaphorical in this poem: 'O rider on the swift red camel/Blood-tinted.'[37] The poet prefers a red camel that is tinted by blood in battle, praising the rider who is a courageous warrior. Bedouin women revere and admire heroic, brave and noble men and despise those with cowardly attributes. But because an English reader would be unable to differentiate between white, red or blue camels except at the representational and visual level, and would miss the semantic and allegorical connotations, the figurative signification is lost in translation.

Allusions to water camels likewise resonate with suggestive cultural nuances. The poet says of her beloved's camels: 'O eyes, gaze at his harvest and guard it/Look at his water camels, look at his well.'[38] An English reader would be unsure what water camels represented or implied. Another motif used is the water wheel or scoop. Some alteration occurs in an English rendering: 'My eyes held vigil while the tribes were sleeping/I heard the sound of the water wheel before sunrise:/The rising voice of water gushing over wood.'[39] Choosing to translate *sānīyah* (plural *suwānī*) in the Bedouin dialect – *sānīyah* (plural *sawānin*) in classical Arabic – as water wheel transforms the image and sound into a more accessible illustration for the casual reader of English. However, this is not a precise rendition. Kurpershoek describes the classical Arabic word *sānīyah* as 'a camel upon which water is drawn from a well by a man riding or leading it away from the well, having the two extremities of a long rope tied to the saddle, and the upper end of the well-rope being tied to the middle of the former rope.'[40] Altorki and Cole describe this process:

> Water was drawn from the wells by a mechanism known as *sawānī*. This consists of up to five pulleys which were made of wood and attached to the trunks of *'athal* trees. Ropes made of palm fiber or of camel leather were used to pull leather buckets filled with water which were emptied into basins for distribution through runnels to the farm.[41]

Other distinctions can be demonstrated in the expressive and figuratively deployed words, *wāridāt* (camels converging thirstily on a well) and *maṣādīr* (camels leaving a well having drunk their fill). These expressions, which reflect the significance of water and rain in Bedouin life, are often used metaphorically to render human emotions of love, longing, mourning and distress. The process of converging on wells and drawing water, in all its concrete and laborious detail, can become a mode for expressing desire and loss: 'My heart is like a well dug ever-deeper/Towards water the herds ebb and flow';[42] and 'I am a spring whose water tastes fresh and pure/Rough-hooved camels can't reach it in the summer heat.'[43] The act of drawing water, at risk of loss, can convey the poet's longing and desire:

> The pull of my heart:
> The pull of a bucket

Drawn up from the well
By three strong young blue-grey camels.
They let it descend till the water pours in,
Then powerfully pull as it rises with the rope.
I long for the night raider who unbinds tethered camels
When sleep steals their guardians just before dawn.[44]

These lines contain three important words that frequently appear in Bedouin women's poetry: *mā'* water; *dalw*, 'leather bucket'; and *bīr* in the Bedouin dialect, *b'ir* in classical Arabic, which means both 'well' and 'water'. One of the recurrent expressions, 'the pull of my heart (*jarr galbī, wa-tall galbī*) is like the pull of the well-rope', portrays the speaker's suffering and longing for her beloved. The torment of her heart is equivalent to the strenuous effort of drawing water from a deep well with a rope pulled by three camels. The poet portrays how the leather bucket navigates this testing process and she implies its fragility. We can only imagine this heart's ordeal allegorically in this figure. Watering camels is a methodical process that remains obscure to urbanites and most Westerners. Bedouins carefully decide when and where to water their camels, for how long and which ones should drink first. It is an elaborate traditional practice with a known set of conventions. Musil describes the different stages:

> As some of the wells are as much as a hundred meters deep, the drawing of water is very fatiguing, especially on account of the bulges in the rocky sides which impede the bucket in coming up. The right hand must not only hold the rope firmly, but must shake it most of the time so as to keep it in the center.[45]

Drawing up the leather bucket is a difficult activity for men and 'often also the rope is tied to the saddle of a camel which [it] is then made to pull.'[46] Thirsty animals react in a compelling way, as is implied in these poetic passages. Musil observes that 'A thirsty she camel murmurs pitiably, *tahenn*, refuses to graze, her eyes overflow with tears.'[47] Given this background, we can begin to appreciate the intensity of the woman poet's emotional condition in the above stanzas. Obviously, water is the substance of life and signifies love, the thirst for which is equally ubiquitous and unquenchable. Although thirst is part of the rhetoric of love regardless of cultural boundaries, it has distinctive evocations in the desert. One also finds references to the mirage, that unforgettable desert image that torments thirsty travellers by the semblance of water shimmering before them under the blazing sun.

In general, poets employ 'thirst', with its myriad desert and nomadic allusions, to capture their utter yearning for their beloved. Musil writes:

> *Ẓumā'*, thirst, is a word commonly used by the Bedouins. Thirst tortures travellers. Dispersed raiders often perish of thirst; the lack of water makes both the women and children in camp lament. Often a woman with parched lips goes from tent to tent begging with dumb gestures a drink of water for her child. … A person tormented by love resembles a thirsty man.[48]

The speaker's perceptive gaze and her ability to render a common scene – watering the camels – while aligning it with her psychic state, creates a lyrical image that turns the ordinary into a subtle poetic allegory. Another poet constructs a similar analogy:

> The day it swept across sun-livened herds
> My heart ripped open like a waterskin torn
> As the water-carrier hoisted it onto its mount.[49]

An expression like *farī galbī farī dalw*, 'My heart ripped open like a waterskin torn', conveys loss by comparing a torn heart with a torn waterskin or leather bucket, a disaster that can threaten life itself if read literally. Significantly, the poet's agony allows her to envision the semblance, but the reader of the translation will not arrive at this metaphorical matrix. Consider also: 'I weep like a ruptured waterskin/ Carried till nightfall on a jittery camel.'[50] What kind of translation can simultaneously render both the empirical practice of watering animals and its poetic nuances? The incorporation of so many animal and water references in poetic figures raises the question of the untranslatable.

Another distinctive element that challenges translation is the multi-faceted signification of clouds, lightning and rain that have inspired pre-Islamic and modern poets alike. There is a plethora of poetic and cultural references to these motifs, which haunt Arabic poetry and delight readers.[51] Imru' Al-Qays, towards the end of his *mu'allaqah*, has an extraordinary image of changing weather:

> Friend, do you see yonder lightning? Look, there goes its Glitter
> Flashing like two hands now in the heaped-up crowned
> Stormcloud
> Brilliantly it shines so – flames the lamp of an anchorite
> As he slops the oil over the twisted wick.
> So with my companions I sat watching it between D'arj
> And El-Odheib, far-ranging my anxious gaze;
> Over Katan, so we guessed, hovered the right of its deluge,
> Its left dropping upon Es-Sit'ar and further Yadhbul.[52]

Without discussing the mythological pre-Islamic undertone in these lines, suffice to say that Bedouin poems are replete with similar motifs.[53] Bedouins pray for rain during seasons of drought and dearth, just as their forebears did in pre-Islamic times. A vocabulary of clouds, rain and a variety of downpours is vividly represented in their poetry. In translation, however, the variants of clouds disappear into a few English renderings and the same could be said about rain. The following lines are in the realm of desire and longing invoked by weather imagery:

> O generous lightning, glimmering
> In darkest midnight,

Swift lightning dazzling
In its clarity,
Let rain fall near
My beloved's encampment.[54]

The poet begins at the instant when lightning flashes across the sky and she apostrophizes by addressing it, while offering spectacular images of the lightning's fleeting brightness and luminosity. The speaker not only enacts these effects in her poems, which become a space for an infinite voyage of light in a desert night, but generates rhythmical sounds to accompany her imagery. Through this abundant rendering of lightning she almost shifts its effects, so to speak, to where her heart belongs – with her beloved. She wishes that it would pour on his land, offering him the ultimate gift of rain. Another poet sketches luminous images of rain clouds:

When I am herding the riding camels, I see rain clouds
Gathering above the beloved's home,
Rain clouds the size of Ḥāyil's mountains accumulating
Like the night with white tips.[55]

There are numerous instances of Bedouin women poets utilizing metaphorical references to rain and clouds in an intimate manner to portray their emotional condition. 'My tears burst from worries/Like a downpour from rainclouds';[56] 'Their faces a towering summer cloud/ Pouring forth rain as thunder rumbles';[57] 'Like scraps of rainclouds torn by northern wind';[58] and 'Get up, Saʿad, and gently write my greetings/One overflowing like the rain and its pebbles/Overflowing like the desert's sand and those who walk/Overflowing like rainfalls from its sky.'[59] For the most part the translation of these lines cannot be easily rendered in English because of the richness of the language of weather, flora and fauna. This essential feature of Bedouin poetry indicates not a poetic obsession, but rather a spontaneous grasp of the harshness of survival in Bedouin life. Any translation of such allusions will always be incomplete, leaving space for uncertainty. In a sense, the untranslatable allows us to wonder about what is translatable and to redirect the translation effort to what is attainable.

These observations underline the way in which this poetry's aesthetics are bound up with Bedouin culture and dialect, making translation into a foreign idiom – that of twenty-first-century America – especially challenging. Even when the two cultures share external similarities, for example the important cultural scenes surrounding coffee drinking, the web of meanings woven around those scenes is quite different. In the USA, coffee of different brands is aggressively advertised in a society punctuated by temporal intervals, where it is associated with waking up, going to work, or taking a social break. It is also related to extended socializing in cafés, which form a third public space set apart from home and work.

There are several references to coffee in Bedouin women's poetry, some appearing in elegiac form: 'His coffeepot always on the fire for guests';[60] 'If you're hungry he'll nourish you generously/And pour coffee if you're thirsty';[61] 'You're greeted with coffee before they ask who you are';[62] 'Who increases the cardamom in the coffeepot';[63] 'O generous greeter of guests/O gallant giver of cardamom coffee';[64] 'Alas, his coffeepots/Remain abandoned/After entertaining/Many worthy guests';[65] and 'The pot, plate and coffeepots weep.'[66] In Bedouin life, coffee culture is centred on hospitality and the coffee and its flavourings signify the host's generosity. The use of costly saffron and cardamom adds to the aura of magnanimity, so that elegiac descriptions like 'he never skimped on handfuls of cardamom' may require some clarification for the English reader.[67] In Bedouin Arabic dialect, *dallah* (plural *dilāl*) is a coffeepot with a long curved spout and a handle usually made of copper, used by nomads in Arabia, Jordan, Syria and elsewhere. When it is said that a man died and left 'coffeepots like crows', *dalāl kamā al-gharbān*, that man is being praised as an extraordinarily noble and generous figure who served so much coffee to guests that his pots were blackened by endless fires.[69] It also indicates that guests flocked to his dwelling and were welcomed day and night.

Bedouin poetry often depicts the coffee-making ritual. In a long 30-line poem, Muḥammad al-Qāḍī (who died in 1868) details the preparation of Arabian coffee, turning it into a lyrical and a musical activity while recalling his beloved:

> To shake the beans as they roast is the best method to try,
> Until they sizzle and sweat and slowly yellowish turn,
> Becoming like sapphires in sight of him who passes by.
> It creates a smell of an aroma strong, a scent most fine,
> Which when inhaled is like ambergris of fragrance profound.
> Pound it in a *jurn*, so that every yearner will for them pine,
> So each heart will hear and rejoice in its crunching sound.
> Pour it into shining copper pot close by the fire.[69]

However, in one complex reference (see also Chapter 2) an anonymous woman poet employs the coffee scene in an almost riddle-like poem with sexual overtones, challenging translation. It highlights how women poets extend and subvert this conventional metaphor:

> O my brother, springtime
> Of exhausted travellers,
> Leader of horses
> Followed only by their dust,
> I ask you about a man
> With all the tools for making coffee,
> Yet it's been eight long years
> And he hasn't ground a bean!
> He should either brew something in his pot
> Like other men,
> Or else yield the pot
> To someone
> Who cares for it.[70]

In the delicate translation process, concern about sounding vague and awkward dominated the process of transferring its ironic, shrewd and unusual rhetorical strategy into English, while leaving a space for the reader to wonder for a moment about its subject matter. The riddle-like question amplifies the ambiguity. It equates translation with reading, while compelling the reader and translator to ask what kind of interlinguistic choices would be appropriate to intimate this woman's sexual grievance? It should not be overlooked that the speaker's grievance has to go through a process of translation before it is transferred to the addressee, her brother, in an allegorical address. Similarly, this allegory disguises the grievance rhetorically and postpones its arrival in translation.

In *Siting Translation*, Niranjana emphasizes de Man's notion of the unreadability of allegory as a figure of reading and translation:

> De Man has finally presented a version of Benjamin's text that most closely resembles his own concern with the figure of allegory and the unreadability of texts it embodies. Allegory always presents an allegory of its own reading; and the allegory of reading always says that it is impossible to read.[71]

Spivak, on the other hand, indicates that 'the translator must surrender to the text. She must solicit the text to show the limits of its language, because that rhetorical aspect will point at the silence of the absolute fraying of language that the text wards off, in its special manner.'[72] For Spivak, surrendering to the text, surrendering to translation, carries erotic intimations: 'To surrender in translation is more erotic than ethical,'[73] and in a footnote she refers to Irigaray's view that the erotic is ethical.

Ibn Rāddas, in his brief introduction to this poem, writes:

> It was related that one of the poetesses of the desert married a man who was impotent. She stayed with him for eight years, during which time he treated her with kindness and respect. And no one knew [about] her condition until she approached old age

> still desperate to have children. In this poem, she addresses her brother.[74]

This turns out to be an excuse for a woman's expressiveness about a sexual matter, and the obscurity persists because of her appropriation of the coffee scene. When one considers that the poet is saying that her husband is impotent and did not have sexual relations with her for eight years, the uncommon configuration she deploys to address sexuality is surprising. Ironically, she appropriates and mimics coffee making and deserted coffeepots, which belong to a prominently masculine scene, to inscribe her grievance and send it back after she deappropriates it. More significantly, if her husband had never touched his coffee tools or prepared coffee, the poem would ultimately be suggesting that the speaker is assailing his honour and generosity: she would be doubly stripping him of his manhood. Is it possible to convey this poem's conventional scene yet maintain some of its ambiguity and rhetorical force? Is it not, then, the poem's rhetorical strategy that poses a challenge, attesting that something is lost in translation and here is lost forever?[75]

A recurrent cultural translation difficulty involves the centrality of travel in Bedouin life. For example, *malfā* means a 'person or place where you will be welcomed while travelling' and connotes 'refuge', another powerful institution in Bedouin society that has no American equivalent.[76] It also connotes 'home', itself a problematic translation, since the word in English signifies a settled abode, while similar Bedouin words, such as those related to the root *n-ẓ-l*, 'settle/descend', carry the same home-like warmth without imputing permanence. Yet, words like 'camp' do not have the amiability and romantic sentiments of home implied by the Bedouin expressions. I resorted to the rather awkward term 'encampment' or 'camp site' when translating Bedouin words for the transient 'home'. Also, *dār* and *bayt* suggest 'household'; *bayt* is used to mean 'tent'; *diyār* 'abodes' and *manāẓil* 'dwellings'; *gaṣar* literally means 'palace', but indicates 'edifice' or 'castle' as well, and suggests a building in an oasis or village in contrast to a tent.

Jaroslav Stetkevych reminds us of 'the abodes of the hearts' (*fī al-qulūbi manāzilu*)[77] uttered by al-Mutanabbī: 'O abodes, in our hearts you abide/You stand deserted/While they with you abound.'[78] He explains the multifaceted inferences of 'dwelling' and 'abode' in classical Arabic poetic discourse:

> No poetry speaks more insistently of the inner space which is all memory and yearning than does Arabic poetry. As poetic image, this space may appear under many names and manifestations, but the suggestive force of Arabic etymology makes poet and reader experience an intimation of the prevailing shape of roundness. *Dār* and *diyār* are etymologically round from (*d-w-r* = roundness), and conceptually this fundamental etymology extends by associations to all the abandoned camp sites, wasted halting places, ruins, and courtyards of the *nasīb*.[79]

Many other cultural translation issues touch on marriage customs, institutions, omens, legendary and proverbial references, and throughout this book we have seen the role of animals in Bedouin life, the patterns of travel and of *karam*, 'generosity', the coming of the motorcar and diverse expressions of mourning and desire.

Bedouin women's poetry also presents many purely linguistic difficulties to Arabic speakers unfamiliar with its dialects. Some very common words in old Arab Bedouin dialects have a completely different meaning in standard Arabic. In some dialects, for example, *lā* means 'if' rather than 'no'; *lakinna* means 'as if', not 'but'; *abā* suggests 'as if', not 'father'; *tarā* indicates an affirmation like 'you know' and is not derived from the verb 'to see'; *naḥara* means 'go towards', not 'slaughter'; *yawm* suggests in many instances 'while' or 'when', not 'day'; and *ghathā'* means 'exhaustion', not 'scum'.

Along with these cultural and semantic challenges are formal ones. Traditional Arabic poetry, with its rhyme and especially its metre, depends for its effect on sonorous regularities unavailable in English. The loss of these must be at least partially compensated in English.

While old-style conventional translators have sometimes tried to imitate both rhyme and metre, this usually cannot be done without distorting the meaning, because English, a rhyme-discrete language, is short of the suppleness afforded by Arabic's vast rhyming storehouse. I have chosen to go instead with the metre, reproducing a rhythm like the Arabic metre in the rare instances when this is practicable, and otherwise putting metre to work in a manner that recalls the Arabic, while (as far as is feasible) preserving the semantic effect of the line, the crucial verbal unit.

The result, metrically speaking, falls somewhere between the unrelenting accents of the original and the looser idiom of contemporary English free verse, with liberated line breaks affording new poetic possibilities. I tried to minimize the inevitable limits of translation and its failure as a task – as both Benjamin and de Man agreed – by using cultural sensitivity, aptly polyvalent word choices, smatterings of alliteration and assonance, as well as attempts to recreate the evocative effect of this poetry's abundant verbal images. The focus of translation, then, is not on producing an effortless and fluent line or a familiar image to the target readership, but rather on maintaining traces of the foreign that may interrupt the reading, demonstrating that translation cannot be transparent or complete, especially when thematized cultural and historical differences pervade each poem.

Translation and the Metaphor of Modernity

The question of how the rift between premodern and modern poems should be read and whether this division transfers itself to translation is problematic. Is it possible to theorize a notion of modernity based on a few technological tropes? A theory or even a speculation cannot be elaborated because of the limited number of poetic examples – only 15 poems that contain technological traces. Any proposition will therefore be hypothetical and general unless more oral poems about technology are located.

The poems discussed, which I argue were composed after the discovery of oil, bear witness to the historical transition not only as they incorporate these topoi, but also as exhibiting the time span in more readable language. The dialects in which they are composed appear easier to follow, but ironically the difficulty lies in translating the operation of these instruments, especially the motorcar and aeroplane. The language of driving, for example, becomes difficult to transmit into English because, in an amusing way, it is profoundly intertwined with the metre and rhythmical patterns. I have argued that these technological references to the motorcar, train, aeroplane and binoculars offer a metaphorical inscription of modernity in the desert. Likewise, they extend a metaphorical configuration of automobility and transfer. But what connects metaphorical language with the means of transport?

In 'The Retrait of Metaphor' Derrida tells us that the metaphor is an ancient subject, the preoccupation of rhetoricians and philosophers through the ages, and it still continues to fascinate us. He asks: 'What is happening, today, with metaphor? *Qu'est-ce qui se passe, aujourd'hui, avec la métaphore?* And without metaphor what is happening? *Et de la métaphore qu'est-ce qui se passe?*'[80] After posing his questions in two languages, Derrida proceeds to show that 'the notion of transportation' is already inscribed in the etymological Greek meaning of metaphor. After installing this transit system within the proximity of metaphor and generating a rhetorical play on the language of transport, he continues:

> *Metaphora* circulates in the city, it conveys us like its inhabitants, along all sort of passages, with intersections, red lights, one-way streets, crossroads or crossings, patrolled zones and speed limits. We are in a certain way – metaphorically of course, and as concerns the mode of habitation – the content and the tenor of *this vehicle*: passengers, comprehended and displaced by metaphor [my italics].[81]

Metaphor here belongs to the realm of circulation and movement, but all sorts of transportation markers, like an urban system, evidently punctuate this realm. Of particular interest is Derrida's emphasis on metaphor as a vehicle in motion. It transports us, displaces us and seizes us as its mode and content. It is as if we move by it and through it and it carries us from one destination to another. It inhabits speech and language. But 'it is not only metaphoric to say that we inhabit metaphor and that we circulate in it as in a sort of vehicle, an automobile.'[82] Derrida elaborates on the metaphoric effects on the speaker/writer who utilizes this figure:

> Neither metaphoric nor a-metaphoric, this 'figure' consists singularly in changing the places and the functions: it constitutes the so-called subject of statements [*sujet des énoncés*] (the speaker [*locuteur*] or the writer [*scripteur*] whom we say to be, or anyone who would believe himself to be *making use* of metaphors and speaking *more metaphorico*) into the *content* or into the (both still partial, and always, already 'embarked,' 'aboard') *tenor* of a vehicle which comprehends the subject, carries him away, displaces him at the very moment when this subject believes he is designating it, saying it, orienting it, driving it, governing it.[83]

According to Derrida, the speaker or writer who deploys metaphor, which is always in constant movement, is thus paradoxically controlled by it and under its effects. If metaphor 'comprehends the subject, carries him away, displaces him at the very moment when this subject believes he is designating it', then how can we read these effects on the speaker in Bedouin women's poems? Extending Derrida's reading to this poetry, we can contemplate the implication of the motorcar as a metaphor on the speaker, who assumes she is saying it, directing it and 'driving' it in her language. She says: 'My desire's the motorcar of Dāmir/Set in motion for my sake.'[84] How does this device/motorcar displace the woman speaker and where does it take her? Is this a temporal displacement?

Following Derrida, we can see how the technological references prompt a metaphorical movement to the extent that the motorcar or aeroplane is already transferring the speaker to a different site. In the desert, this site indicates the modern. One can argue, then, that the auto-mobility of the poem transfers itself and the speaker, metaphorically or literally, beyond a dichotomy between traditional aesthetics and modern techniques. Modernity is coming and is changing nomadic life, like the vivid displacement in the poem in which the motorcar ironically displaces the camel:

> I cannot trust the shrunken camel
> As endless mountains block my way
> My desire's the car of Dāmir
> Set in motion for my sake.[85]

In this poem, the camel is rejected on account of its slowness. From these fleeting references one can recognize that the woman is expressing her fascination with modernity and inscribing her relationship with change – a change that does not destabilize her affinity with the past (see Chapter 5).

Yet, these technological figures again transport us in their rapid transit system. The speaker is being relocated and transported to the modern through her utilization of the motorcar as a metaphor in a vernacular poem, particularly as she deploys the makes of American motorcars in English words: 'O hum of my heart/A *Mack* truck groaning';[86] 'The longing of my heart is the hum of a black wheeled *Mack*';[87] 'O rider of the swift-legged *GMC*!'[88] 'It crosses the passengers of the *Dodge* before Dumwāt';[89] 'My longing to accompany/A just-departed *motor*';[90] and 'Following the *Ford*'s driver down every tortuous desert trail' (my italics).[91]

Also, the word 'motor' referring to a motorcar is *mutar* in the Bedouin dialect, and 'train' is *rail.* These English utterances are incurporated while preserving their own tenor and suggestive relevance. More importantly, the poets composed these English words into their lyrical texture without either destabilizing the integrity of the English or disintegrating the Bedouin dialect, and amused their listener/reader at the same time. This rhetorical strategy connects the heart to the machine, so that the heart hums its longing and this hum or noise disappears in the rhythmic sounds. The rhetoric of driving becomes poetic and rhythmical in Arabic. I tried to capture parallel words in English:

> The driver shifts gears and leaves a trail;
> When he climbs the grade he double-shifts,
> And when he descends he lets it rest until the end.[92]

Without doubt, the poetic genre in Bedouin women's poetry remains intact to the extent that the inclusion of modern technological devices in English fails to change, disrupt or modify the metre. In fact, we can read how the motorcar as a poetic device regulates the rhyme and belongs to the poetic register. 'Mack', as a signifier in the poem, is transferred from English to a Bedouin dialect and returned once more to English in the translation. Has it arrived home?[93]

Following the Derridean insight I raise a different question about metaphor, that of translation. Derrida links the metaphoric transfer to another mode of transferring, 'the modes of trans-fer or of translation.'[94] Was the translation as a mode of transfer and transport able to transmit these technological signifiers abroad? Can the reader of English reach the implications of these inscribed vehicles in oral poems by Bedouin women during the early decades of the twentieth century? What has been rendered? What has been lost? Or more aptly, what is untranslatable in these poems?

To sum up, it is fitting to recall another variation of the notion of the untranslatable that has appeared persistently in Derrida's influential combined essay, 'Living on: Border Lines':

> 'translation' overcome[s], equivocally, in the course of an equivocal combat, the loss of an object. A text lives only if it lives *on* [*sur-vit*], and it lives *on* only if it is *at once* translatable and untranslatable. … Totally translatable, it disappears as a text, as writing, as a body of language [*langue*]. Totally untranslatable, even within what is believed to be one language, it dies immediately.[95]

In this passage we see how Derrida performs a mode of translation, which he perceives as an interlinguistic process. Indicatively, he associates the first phrase, 'translation', with the notion of overcoming; translation 'overcomes' 'the loss of an object' in a combat, a struggle that remains 'equivocal', ambiguous or rather ambivalent. If translation overcomes the lost object, then Derrida is alluding to mourning, and translation is able to let go of the object. The life of a text, its futurity, 'lives *on* only if it is *at once* translatable *and* untranslatable'. This is the condition of its life, survival; it is through this double bind of the translatable and untranslatable that translation is able to live on.

De Man and Benjamin understood translation in this sense by marking its double bind. But it is imperative to recognize how Derrida is spacing his lines, using italics and bracketing French words; all these textual motifs accentuate the consequences of translation. The trace of life and death is the trace of temporality that is crucial to translation, and is being enacted in this quotation. In these few lines Derrida disperses his ideas, deploys associative utterances with subtleties and stages the effects of translation. Also, in the footnotes he unfolds a parallel text or essay, 'Border Line', grasping the nuances through citing from scores of texts in order to play on one motif, a trope or a verb. Whatever was lost in translation can be brought to life through citing, recalling lines and phrases from other texts, in order to show that translation, in fact, is dispersion between languages. He maintains both translatability and untranslatability as a double movement that is undeniably working at different levels in any given text. By arresting the translatable, one will not avoid the untranslatable, because the remnant, the trace, the mark of the original will always resist translation.

Oral Bedouin poetry finds itself in a flux of dialects between ordinary language and classical Arabic language. However, being in between or on the periphery allows this poetry to flourish and reveals its gathering mode, creating a unique set of poems that are always manifested within the process of transfer and translation.

Notes

Introduction

1. Jacques Derrida, *Of Grammatology*, translated by Gayatri Chakravorty Spivak (Baltimore, VA: Johns Hopkins Press, 1974) p. 24. For a discussion of orality and pre-Islamic poetry, see James T. Monroe, 'Oral Composition in Pre-Islamic Poetry', *Journal of Arabic Literature*, vol. 3 (1972) pp. 1–53.
2. Gayatri Chakravorty Spivak, 'The Politics of Translation', in Lawrence Venuti (ed.) *The Translation Studies Reader* (London: Routledge, 2000) p. 377.
3. Ibid., p. 377.

Chapter 1: Reading the Nomadic Voices

1. The seven pre-Islamic odes, *Muʿallaqāt*, are considered the most sophisticated poetic production in the history of Arabic letters. They were embroidered in gold and suspended on the holy shrine, the *kaʿbah*, and are thus called *Muʿallaqāt* (The Suspended Odes). See A. J. Arberry, *The Seven Odes* (New York: Macmillan, 1957), and also Sells's contemporary translation of a number of pre-Islamic odes: Michael Sells, *Desert Tracings* (Middletown, OH: Wesleyan University Press, 1989).
2. ᶜAbd Allāh Ibn Rāddas's *Shāʿirāt min al-Bādīyah* was first published in 1969 with the initial volume, and the second volume followed in 1976. The two volumes were reprinted a number of times by different publishers, and I am using the seventh edition of the first volume and the fifth edition of the second one throughout this study. See ᶜAbd Allāh Ibn Rāddas, *Shāʿirāt min al-Bādīyah* (Riyadh: Dār al-Yamāmah, 1969 and Riyadh: Maṭābiᶜ al-Bādīyah, 2002).
3. In fact, Arabic literary criticism has shunned Arabian women's oral poetry, and it has been particularly neglected in studies of orality. For example, Sowayan's significant book on Nabaṭī poetry excludes women's poetry, focusing only on male poets in Arabia. See Saad Sowayan, *Nabati Poetry: The Oral Poetry of Arabia* (Berkeley: University of California Press, 1985).
4. In his illuminating study, Iḥsān ʿAbbās sketches out the history of the Nabateans and underlines that their language was referred to as Nabatiyya, which is Aramaic. It was their official language, while they used Arabic in their daily life that was similar to the Arabic language spoken in the north. See

Iḥsān ʿAbbās, *Tārīkh Dawlat al-Anbāṭ* (The History of al-Anbat) (Amman: Dār al-Shurūq lil-Nashr wa-al-Tawzīʿ, 1987) p. 24.

5. See ʿAbd Allāh Ibn Khamīs, *Al-Adab al-Shaʿbī fī Jāzīrat al-ʿArab* (Popular Literature in the Arabian Peninsula) (Riyadh: Maṭābiʿ al-Farazdaq al-Tijārīyah, 1982) p. 54.
6. Cited by Ibn Khamīs, p. 55.
7. Ibid., p. 57.
8. Al-Kamālī's insightful knowledge and extensive analysis of the poetic and cultural aspects of Bedouin poetry make his study a rare contribution to the field. Abdul-Rahman Munif wrote an introduction to this book. See Shafīq al-Kamālī, *Al-Shʿir ʿinda Al-Badū* (Poetry for the Bedouin) (Beirut: Kutub, 1964) p. 59 (my modified translation of al-Kamālī).
9. Saad Sowayan, *Al-Shiʿr Nabaṭī: Dhāʾiqat al-Shaʿab wa Sulṭat al-Naṣ* (Nabati Poetry: The Public Taste and the Power of the Text) (London: Saqi, 2000) p. 69.
10. The terms Bedouin, oral and vernacular poetry will be used interchangeably in the following chapters.
11. Sowayan mentioned that Rāshid al-Khulāwī was known for his long poems; one consists of 1500 lines. See Sowayan, *Nabati Poetry*, p. 10.
12. Sowayan discusses literacy and its relation to vernacular poetry. He writes, 'there were a few literate Nabati poets who clearly borrowed techniques and devices from written literature and employed them in their vernacular poetry.' See Sowayan, *Nabati Poetry*, p. 169.
13. Ibid., p. 172. Also, Ibn Khamīs refers to al-Faraj's anthology as the earliest. See Ibn Khamīs, *Al-Adab al-Shaʿbī fī Jazīrat al-ʿArab*, p. 13.
14. Khālid al-Faraj's *Dīwān ʿAbd Allāh al-Faraj* (Poetry Collection of ʿAbd Allāh al-Faraj) was published in Bombay in 1920. There is no reference to the publisher.
15. ʿAbd Allāh al-Ḥātim, *Khīyār mā yultiqaṭ min al-Shiʿr al-Nabaṭ* (The Best Collected Nabati Poetry) (Damascus: Al-Matbaʿah al-Umumīyah, 1952).
16. Ghasān al-Ḥasan, *Al-Shʿir al-Nabaṭī fī Minṭaqāt al-Khalīj wa-al-Jazīrah al-ʿArabīyah* (Nabati Poetry in the Gulf and the Arabian Peninsula) (Dubai: Wizārat al-Iʿlām wa-al-Thaqāfah fī Dawlat al-Imārat al-Mutaḥidah, 1998); Sowayan, *Shiʿr al-Nabaṭī*.
17. Albert Socin, *Diwan aus Centralarabien* (Diwan from Central Arabia) published by Hans Stumme (ed.) (Leipzig: Abhandlungen der philologisch-historischen classe der Koniglich sachsischen Gesellschaft der Wissenschaften, No. 19, 1901/1) 3 vols.
18. Alois Musil, *The Manners and Customs of the Rwala* (New York: American Geographical Society, 1928).
19. Although Arabian women's oral poetry would provide invaluable material for reflection in the debates around oral culture and women's poetics, to date there is not a single analysis or translation that presents these poems to readers in the

English language. The only study that has included a few references to this poetry is Kurpershoek's discussion of the poetry of Ad-Dindan, which has 11 references to Ibn Rāddas's collection. Six of these are translations of the opening verses of Bedouin women's poems, and the seventh is a translation of the longest and oldest poem in Ibn Rāddas's collection. It was recited to Kurpershoek by Ad-Dindan and appears to be 12 verses shorter than Ibn Rāddas's version. See Marcel P. Kurpershoek, *Oral Poetry and Narrative from Central Arabia* (Leiden: E. J. Brill, 1994). We find that a few Bedouin women's poems from Ibn Rāddas's collection are included in recent collections and anthologies of Nabaṭī poetry. For example al-Khālidī includes two poems from Ibn Rāddas and one from Ṭalāl al-Saʿīd. See Ibrāhīm Ḥamid al-Khālidī, *Al-Muʿallaqāt al-Nabaṭīyah* (Kuwait: Mānshīt lil-Diʿāyah wa-al-Iʿalān, 2007); and Ṭalāl al-Saʿīd, *Al-Mūswaʿa al-Nabaṭīyah al-Kāmilah* (The Complete Nabati Encyclopedia) (Kuwait: Dhāt al-Salāsil, 1987) vol. 1.

20. Ironically, Ibn Rāddas refers to this in his introduction (p. 11), where he says he has endured many inconveniences in gathering women's poetry, 'not because of a selective process, since this poetry is not the best of composition nor is it part of a fine poetry'. This unjustified judgement stems from a long patriarchal discourse that has always placed women's poetry in an aesthetically contested space.
21. See Lila Abu-Lughod, *Veiled Sentiments: Honor and Poetry in a Bedouin Society* (Berkeley: University of California Press, 1986), and Lila Abu-Lughod, *Writing Women's Worlds* (Berkeley: University of California Press, 1993). Certainly, there are numerous studies of Arabic oral poetry, and it is important to mention Bamia's insightful analysis of the cultural and political motifs of Algerian folk poetry. See Aida Adib Bamia, *The Graying of the Raven* (Cairo: The American University in Cairo Press, 2001). Also, consider Clinton Bailey, *Bedouin Poetry from Sinai and the Negev: Mirror of a Culture* (Oxford: Oxford University Press, 1991).
22. I see in other literary traditions the same denial of theoretical investigation of women's oral poetry because it has been classified as sentimental and unsophisticated. In her study of the *trobairitz* written between 1150 and 1250, Finke highlights the discrepancy in looking at troubadour poetry by male and female authors, noting that more critical investigation is devoted to the former. She writes: 'This emphasis on the emotional, subjective, and therapeutic aspects of these women's poetry miniaturizes it, perpetuating even in feminist criticism a literary double standard by which male poets' works are judged and canonized by so-called objective artistic criteria, while women's poetry is deemed emotional and personal, more like a diary than poetry.' See Laurie A. Finke, *Feminist Theory, Women's Writing* (Ithaca, NY: Cornell University Press, 1992) p. 32.
23. I am not concerned with the periodization of oral poetry because it can never be dated accurately.

24. See Ṭalāl al-Saʿīd, *Al-Mūswaʿah al-Nabaṭīyah al-Kāmilah* (The Complete Nabaṭī Encyclopedia) (Kuwait: Dhāt al-Salāsil, 1987) vol. 1.
25. Ibn Rāddas, *Shāʿirāt min al-Bādīyah*, p. 11.
26. Musil, *The Manners and Customs of the Rwala*, p. 284. Also cited in Kurpershoek, *Oral Poetry and Narrative from Central Arabia*, p. 12.
27. 'The idea of plagiarism would have as little meaning as that of copyright; both of these are fundamental to the literary institution.' Paul Zumthor, *Introduction à la poésie orale* (Paris: Éditions du Seuil, 1983) p. 254.
28. Ibid., p. 61.
29. Jaroslav Stetkevych, *The Zephyrs of Najd* (Chicago, IL: University of Chicago Press, 1993) p. 103.
30. Al-Juhany remarks the historical importance of this poem. He adds: 'Since the 10th/16th century, the Sharifs of Mecca, rulers of the Hijaz, launched sporadic expeditions against the Najd towns and nomadic tribes. The sharifs were trying to assert their political authority over Najd, but the endless disputes among the large numbers of their clans and factions over the Sharifate of Mecca rendered that objective difficult to achieve.' See Uwaidah Al-Juhany, *Najd Before the Salafi Reform Movement* (Ithaca, NY: Ithaca Press, 2002), pp. 62–3 and 18.
31. In addition to the reference cited earlier, al-Thumayrī cites 69 lines attributed to the woman of Ziʿb. See Muḥammad ibn Aḥmad al-Thumayrī, *Al-Funūn al-Shaʿabīyah fī al-Jazīrah al-ʿArabīyah* (Damascus: no publisher, 1972) pp. 178–86. Saʿad Ibn Junaydil, *ʿĀlīyat Najd* (Riyadh: Dār al-Yamāmah, 1978) refers to the places mentioned in the poem. Kurpershoek, *Oral Poetry*, pp. 19, 202, also cites the poet and translates a different version of her poem.
32. Sowayan, *Nabati Poetry*, p. 124.
33. Ibn Rāddas, *Shāʿirāt min al-Bādīyah*, p. 13.
34. Sowayan, *Nabati Poetry*, p. 147.
35. Ibid., p. 167.
36. For further discussion of this point, see Ibn Khamīs, *Al-Adab al-Shaʿabī fī Jazīrat al-ʿArab*, p. 87, who also affirms the linguistic corruption of Bedouin poetry.
37. Ṭāhā Ḥusayn, *Al-Ḥayāt al-Adabīyah fī Jazīrat al-ʿArab* (Literary Life in the Arabian Peninsula) (Beirut: Dār al-Kitāb al-Lubnānī, 1973) pp. 23–84.
38. Ibn Khaldūn marks the similarity between pre-Islamic and other popular forms of Arabic poetry. He describes the new generation of poets as non-Arabs because of their corrupted use of Arabic. Ibn Khaldūn, *Al-Muqaddimah* (Beirut: Dār al-Qalam, 1992) p. 582, my translation.
39. Ibn Khaldūn writes: 'the new generation of Arab poets compose thematic poetry like their Arab predecessors … these themes include subjects of love, panegyric, elegy and satire. … The Arab people of the East call this kind of poetry Bedouin.' My translation, see Ibid.
40. Maria Rosa Menocal, *The Arabic Role in Medieval Literary History: A Forgotten Heritage* (Philadelphia: University of Pennsylvania Press, 1987) p. 95.

41. Adūnīs, *Al-Thābit wa-al-Mutaḥawwal* (Beirut: Dār al-ʿAwdah, 1977) p. 44, my translation.
42. Ibn Manẓūr (630–711) compiled the words spoken by Arabs of the peninsula before the influence of other languages. One wonders if there is a pure voice. See Muḥammad al-Jābrī, *Bunīyat al-ʿAql al-ʿArabī* (The Structure of the Arab Mind) (Casablanca: Al-Markaz al-Thaqāfī al-ʿArabī, 1986) p. 36.
43. Adūnīs, *An Introduction to Arab Poetics*, translated by Catherine Cobham (Austin: University of Texas Press, 1990). Ibn Khaldūn states in *al-Muqaddimah*: 'In the early period singing was a part of the art of literature because it depended on poetry, being the setting of poetry to music. The literary and intellectual elite of the Abbasid State occupied themselves with it, intent on acquiring a knowledge of the styles and genres of poetry.' See ibid., p. 16. In the discussion of Arabic poetry and musicality, James T. Monroe provides a comparative discussion of the musical in Hispano-Arabic poetry and addresses strophic songs integrated within *Zajal* and *muwashshaḥah*. He demonstrates how they influence modern Andalusian music in Maghrib. See James T. Monroe and Menjamin M. Liu, *Ten Hispano-Arabic Strophic Songs in the Modern Oral Tradition* (Berkeley: University of California Press, 1989). Also, consider James T. Monroe, 'Which came first, the *Zagal* or *Muwass'a*? Some Evidence for the Oral Origin of Hispano-Arabic Strophic Poetry', *Oral Tradition*, vol. 4, nos. 1 and 2 (1989).
44. See these lyrical dialogues in Ibn Rāddas, *Shāʿirāt min al-Bādīyah*, pp. 26, 36.
45. 'There is a presumption of song in every oral poetry; indeed, every oral poetic genre is also a musical genre, even if the users fail to recognize it as such.' Zumthor, *Introduction à la Poésie orale*, p. 178.
46. Kurpershoek, in *Oral Poetry*, pp. 42–3, marks these preparatory moments in men's poetry. In fact, they deploy almost exactly the same utterances and sounds.
47. Ibn Rāddas, *Shāʿirāt min al-Bādīyah*, p. 108.
48. Ibid., p. 339.
49. Ibid., p. 345.
50. Ibid., p. 36.
51. Ibid., p. 184.
52. Ibid., vol. 2, p.2.
53. Ibid., p. 369.
54. Ibid., p. 108.
55. Ibid., p. 339.
56. Ibid., p. 369.
57. Ibid., p. 229.
58. Ibid., p. 339.
59. Ibid., p. 258.
60. Ibid., p. 198.
61. Ibid., p. 41.

62. Ibid., p. 322.
63. Ibid., p. 70.
64. Ibid., p. 97.
65. Ibid., p. 70.
66. Ibid., p. 97.
67. Albert Lord, in *The Singer of Tales* (Cambridge, MA: Harvard University Press, 1960) p. 125, focuses on the crucial distinctions between oral song and its written transcription. For him, the encounter between the singer and the scribe problematizes the scene of performance. After the scribe has arrived at the scene, the performance is no longer the same because the singer is asked to stop many times so that the words can be recorded. The interruptions and deferral affect the performance. Lord observes: 'But bards never repeat a song exactly, as we have seen. This method [written transcription], although it has been used often, never results in a text that truly represents any oral performance.' He points out that repetition of a song is never the same. I argue that indeed the performance will not be the same and the song will always be different in the course of its transmission. Lord thinks that writing is an external, inaccurate medium, since it interposes a 'fixed' text, and he insists on this distinction between written and oral text. This division governs most of the critical debates about orality. Following Derrida, reciting a song will never be the same as any other recitation, and one can only produce a simulacrum of what is called original. Derrida questions the binary opposition that manifests itself in Western metaphysics, which presupposes an immediacy of speech and the possibility of meaning. Western metaphysics always considers writing as a representation of speech and continues to exalt the spoken word over the written one. Derrida has critiqued this binary opposition, referring to it as 'Logocentrism: the metaphysics of phonetic writing.' See Derrida, *Of Grammatology*, p. 3.
68. Ibn Rāddas, *Shā'irāt min al-Bādīyah*, p. 349.
69. Al-Kamālī, *Al-Sh'ir 'inda Al-Badū*, p. 50. Cole presents another description of the role of women in a nomadic setting: 'Males and females are expected to carry out different tasks, to spend leisure time separately, and to have different outlooks on life, but females are not secluded as they are in village and urban Arabia. They move about freely in their herding and household chores and attend urban markets when in the city.' See Donald P. Cole, *The Nomads of the Nomads* (Chicago, IL: Aldine Publishing Company, 1975) p.76.
70. Ibn Rāddas, *Shā'irāt min al-Bādīyah*, p. 52.
71. See note 1 for an explanation of the *Mu'allaqāt*. What interests me here is the opening of the pre-Islamic ode, in which the poet looks at the deserted encampment of the beloved and the traces left behind. At the same time he begins reciting his poem. Thus, this opening scene in the pre-Islamic poem bears a resemblance to the scene in which the woman poet describes her waiting for the absent beloved. See Arberry, *The Seven Odes*.

72. A reading of a non-face is found in Gilles Deleuze and Félix Guattari, *A Thousand Plateaus* (Minneapolis: University of Minnesota Press, 1983) p. 170: 'The face is a surface … the face is a map.'

Chapter 2: Melancholic Desire

1. Women scholars have explored women's laments of ancient Greece and the Homeric period. Margaret Alexiou, in *The Ritual Lament in Greek Tradition* (Cambridge: Cambridge University Press, 1974), a comprehensive study of ancient Greek laments by women, highlights the link between lament and tragedy (pp. 110). Alexiou notes how Antigone, Cassandra and Medea, among others, lamented their fate. The etymological meaning of 'lament' in its Indo-European origin is represented by *thrênos* and *goós* and suggests a shrill cry. Both words are used in Greek to refer to lament and wailing over the dead. However, the specific Greek word for lament is *moirolói*, which consists of *moira*, 'fate' and *logos*, 'word, speech'. Also, Holst Warhaft examines Greek laments performed by women and points out that in ancient religious traditions in the Middle East it was usually the woman goddess who mourned the male god: 'Adūnīs is lamented by Aphrodite, the Babylonian Tammuz by Ishtar, Phrygian Attis by Cybele, Egyptian Osiris by his wife Isis.' See Gail Holst-Warhaft, *Dangerous Voices: Women's Laments and Greek Literature* (London: Routledge, 1992) p. 24. Weinbaum claims that 'lament poetry, as sung by women, who were responsible for spiritual mediation of burials and grieving, actually gave rise to the feel, structure, and texture of the poems known as the Odyssey and the Iliad.' See Batya Weinbaum, 'Lament Ritual Transformed into Literature: Positing Women's Prayer as Cornerstone in Western Classical Literature', *Journal of American Folklore*, vol. 114, no. 451 (2001) pp. 20–39, p. 22.
2. See Lila Abu-Lughod, 'Islam and Gendered Discourses of Death', *International Journal of Middle East Studies*, vol. 25, no. 2 (1993) pp. 187–205, p. 188.
3. Bloom discusses the notion of influence as both positive and destructive, and argues that modern poetry is characterized by this anxiety of influence in its relation to classical poetry. It is worth noting that Bloom added to his 1997 edition a preface with the provocative title 'The Anguish of Contamination'. See Harold Bloom, *The Anxiety of Influence: A Theory of Poetry* (London: Oxford University Press, 1997). This anxiety of influence can be traced in many polemical discussions that attempt to create a binary opposition between Western thought and Arabic literature. There is a severing between what has been classified as the East and the West in literary criticism. This rupture in the theoretical approaches to Arabic texts suggests an assumed origin that critics need to take into account when writing about Arabic literature, as if the moments of contacts and influence can be easily circumscribed and isolated, so that a pure tradition can be celebrated.
4. It is important to emphasize that Greek was widely spoken in Syria and

Palestine during the Umayyad period (661–750) and perhaps at the beginning of the Abbasid era. It was used in theology, trade, politics and education, among other fields. For a detailed examination of the role of translation in medieval Arabic culture, see Dimitri Gutas, *Greek Thought, Arabic Culture: The Graeco-Arabic Translation Movement in Baghdad and Early Abbasid Society (2nd–4th/8th–10th Centuries* (London: Routledge, 1998) p. 17.

5. Ibn Khaldūn records that 'The Greek work … which has been translated [into Arabic] is the book of Euclid. … It was the first Greek work to be translated in Islam in the days of Abu Ja'far al-Mansur.' Ibn Khaldūn, *The Muqaddimah*, translated by F. Rosenthal (Princeton, NJ: Bollingen, 1967) vol. 3, pp. 115, 130.
6. Gutas evaluates the historical accounts that refer to the role of *bayt al-ḥikmah* and tries to argue against the references to it as a centre for translation. After an extensive investigation, he concludes that *bayt al-ḥikmah* 'was a library, most likely established as a 'bureau' under al-Mansur, part of the Abbasid administration modelled on that of the Sasanians. Its primary function was to house both the activity and the results of translations from Persian into Arabic of Sasanian history and culture. As such, there were hired translators capable of performing this function as well as book binders for the preservation of books. This was its function in Sasanian times, and it retained it throughout the time of Harun al-Rashid, that is the time of the Barmakids. Under al-Ma'mun it appears to have gained an additional function related to astronomical and mathematical activities; at least this is what the names associated with the *bayt al-ḥikma* during that period would imply. He adds that 'What the *bayt al-ḥikma* did do for the Graeco-Arabic translation movement, however, is to foster a climate in which it could be both demanded and then conducted successfully.' See Gutas, *Greek Thought*, pp. 58–9. For a historical study of the Abbasid dynasty, see Hugh Kennedy, *The Early Abbasid Caliphate* (London: Croom Helm, 1981).
7. Philip K. Hitti, *History of the Arabs* (New York: Macmillan, 1951) pp. 310–11.
8. Ibid., pp. 578–9.
9. 'Just as the ancient pathology of the humours was revived in the school of Salerno under the mediating influence of Arabian science, so too did Arabia preserve the other Hellenistic science that nourished the doctrine of melancholic – astrology. The principal source of the mediaeval wisdom of the stars has been shown to be the astronomy of Abū Ma Sar, which itself is dependent on the astronomy of late antiquity. The theory of melancholy has a very close connection with the doctrine of stellar influences. And of such influences only the most baleful, that of Saturn, could rule over the melancholy disposition.' See Walter Benjamin, *The Origin of German Tragic Drama*, translated by John Osborne (London: National Library Board, 1977) p. 148. Benjamin is referring to the medieval Arab astrologer Jaʿfar Ibn Muḥammad Abū Maʿshar al-Balkhī who was known in Europe as Albumasar or

Albumazar and contributed to philosophical discussions of cosmology and astrology in medieval Europe. See Keiji Yamamoto and Charles Burnett (eds) *Abu Ma'Sar on Historical Astrology: The Book of Religions and Dynasties (On the Great Conjunctions)*, 2 vols (Leiden: Brill, 2000).

10. Jennifer Radden (ed.) *The Nature of Melancholy: From Aristotle to Kristeva*, (Oxford: Oxford University Press, 2000) p. 76.
11. Giorgio Agamben, Stanzas*: Word and Phantasm in Western Culture* (Minneapolis, MN: University of Minnesota Press, 1993) p. 13.
12. Burton asks the reader to offer her or his interpretation of melancholy: 'take Melancholy in what sense you will, properly or improperly, in disposition or habit, for pleasure or for paine, dotage, discontent, feare, sorrow, madnesse, for part, or all, truly, or metaphorically, 'tis all one.' See Robert Burton, *The Anatomy of Melancholy*, edited by Thomas C. Faulkner, Nicolas K. Kiessling and Rhonda L. Blair, 3 vols. (Oxford: Clarendon Press, 1989–1994) vol. 1, p. 25. Williams comments on Burton's gesture to his reader: 'Because melancholy, embracing everything, ranges from being a part to being a whole, the reader may define it in any way he wishes; and yet because melancholy may also be taken as a trope, it possesses no definition of its own. Everything and nothing, however you may define it, "'tis all one"; that is, it does not really matter. Or "'tis all one": melancholy is an undifferentiated, indivisible state.' See also R. Grant Williams, 'Disfiguring the Body of Knowledge: Anatomical Discourse and Robert Burton's The Anatomy of Melancholy', *English Literary History*, vol. 68, no. 3 (2001) p. 39.
13. Critics' revisions of mourning and melancholy are not limited to the psychoanalytical framework, but extend to the political and socio-historical elements of mourning. Greg Forter, 'Against Melancholia: Contemporary Mourning Theory, Fitzgerald's The Great Gatsby, and the Politics of Unfinished Grief', *Differences: A Journal of Feminist Cultural Studies*, vol. 14, no. 2 (2003) pp. 134–70, summarizes each approach. He writes: 'Jahan Ramazani thus finds in modern elegy a "melancholic mourning" that challenges Freud's "insidious distinction between 'normal' and 'abnormal' grief."… Philip Novak makes this challenge part of an antiracist politics, suggesting that melancholia may be an appropriate and necessary response for African Americans trying to hold on to a distinctive culture threatened by white racism. … Michael Moon contends that, because gay men and women are "categorically excluded" from the "normalcy" that mourning restores, "the Freudian model of mourning may look fundamentally normalizing and … privative." He therefore recommends that gay men respond to the catastrophes of Aids with what amounts to a melancholic fetishism, through which they might extend (rather than relinquish) their erotic attachments to the dead. … And José Muñoz synthesizes the kinds of arguments made by Moon and Novak, suggesting that "for blacks and queers … melancholia [is] not a pathology or a self-absorbed mood that inhibits activism, but … a mechanism that helps us

(re)construct identity and take our dead to the various battles we must wage in their names'" (pp. 140, 191, 235, 239, 355–6). For a discussion of race and melancholic affects, see Anne Cheng, *The Melancholy of Race* (Oxford: Oxford University Press, 2000). Paul Gilroy, in *After Empire: Multiculture or Postcolonial Melancholia* (London: Routledge, 2004) examines melancholy within a post-colonial framework.

14. Sigmund Freud, 'Mourning and Melancholia', in James Strachey (editor and translator) *The Standard Edition of the Complete Psychological Works of Sigmund Freud*, 24 vols (London: Hogarth Press, 1953–74) vol. 14, p. 243; Judith Butler, *The Psychic Life of Power: Theories in Subjection* (Stanford, CA: Stanford University Press, 1997).
15. The exclusion of the female melancholic marks the Greek discussion onward. Schiesari points out that melancholy has been rendered masculine in Western cultural discourse and that women were always absent. She rightly addresses 'the notable absence of women, an absence that surely points less to some lack of unhappy women than to the lack of significance traditionally given women's grief in patriarchal culture'. See Juliana Schiesari, *The Gendering of Melancholia: Feminism, Psychoanalysis, and the Symbolics of Loss in Renaissance Literature* (Ithaca, NY: Cornell University Press, 1992) p. 3.
16. Bedouin women in Arabia express their loss by weeping and sometimes by wailing and tearing the upper front of their dresses. Some may slap their faces while crying. This observation may provoke some American feminists in Middle Eastern studies who tend to make general assumptions about women in Arabia, and claim that there is a religious sanction on women's mourning rituals. But there are no scholarly studies proving such a presupposition. However, in Egypt and Algeria, to name just two, mourning rituals are quite different and involve a display of wailing and grief. Abu-Lughod, in 'Islam and Gendered Discourses', p. 190, describes the non-verbal rituals or practices of mourning among women in the Awlad 'Ali Bedouin community in Egypt. These 'practices of grief that include tearing one's clothes, throwing off all jewelry, scratching one's cheeks, and throwing dirt on one's head, all belong to the confined time and place of the funeral mourning ceremonies (*'aza*)'. Abu-Lughod explores the notion of loss in the same cultural context in another article, and in her book. See Lila Abu-Lughod, 'Honor and the Sentiments of Loss in a Bedouin Society, *American Ethnologist*, vol. 12, no. 2 (1985) pp. 245–61, and *Veiled Sentiments*, p. 197.
17. Freud, 'Mourning', p. 243.
18. Ibid., p. 245.
19. Ibid., p. 244.
20. Ibid., p. 245.
21. Ibid., p. 245.
22. Ibid., p. 247.
23. Laplanche and Pontalis suggest that incorporation includes 'three meanings: it

means to obtain pleasure by making an object penetrate oneself; it means to destroy this object; and it means, by keeping it with oneself, to appropriate the object's qualities. It is this last aspect that makes incorporation into the matrix of introjection and identification.' See J. Laplanche and J.-B. Pontalis, *The Language of Psychoanalysis* (New York: W.W. Norton, 1973) p. 212.

24. Freud, 'Mourning', p. 249.
25. Ibid.
26. Butler, *The Psychic Life of Power*, p. 134.
27. Freud, 'Mourning', p. 243.
28. Imru' al-Qays depicts one of the most erotic encounters in his ode: 'Many's the pregnant woman like you, aye, and the nursing mother/I've night-visited, and made her forget her amuleted one-year-old;/whenever he whimpered behind her, she turned to him/with half her body, her other half unshifted under me.' See Arberry, *The Seven Odes*, p. 62.
29. Cited in Muḥsin al-Musawi, *Arabic Poetry: Trajectories of Modernity and Tradition* (London: Routledge, 2006) p. 245.
30. Ibid.
31. Ibid., pp. 245–6.
32. Gilles Deleuze opens up the texture of desire to include many human activeties: sleeping, walking, listening to music, and writing. He also considers death as desire. See Gilles Deleuze, 'What is Desire?' in Constantin V. Boundas (ed.) *The Deleuze Reader* (New York: Columbia University Press, 1993) p. 137. However, desire is absent in the Freudian texts, and Samuel Weber remarks that, unlike Lacan, Freud did not employ desire 'as a central theoretical concept'. See Samuel Weber, *Return to Freud: Jacques Lacan's Dislocation of Psychoanalysis*, translated by Michael Levine (New York: Cambridge University Press, 1991) p. 120.
33. Ibn Rāddas, *Shā'irāt min al-Bādīyah*, p. 58.
34. Ibid., p. 109.
35. Ibid., p. 155
36. Ibid., p. 22.
37. Ibid., p. 23.
38. Ibid., p. 36.
39. Ibid., p. 190.
40. Ibid., p. 347.
41. Ibid., p. 67.
42. Ibid., p. 22. Unlike the poem under discussion, another poet does not withdraw her desire, explicitly inscribing it regardless of cultural prohibitions. See note 62.
43. Freud, 'Mourning', p. 247.
44. Butler, *The Psychic Life of Power*, p. 186.
45. Michel Foucault, *History of Sexuality*, vol. 1, *An Introduction* (New York: Vintage, 1980).

46. See Judith Butler, *Subjects of Desire* (New York: Columbia University Press, 1987) p. 218.
47. Ibn Rāddas, *Shāʿirāt min al-Bādīyah*, p. 46.
48. Ibid.
49. For an elaborate account of nomadic voyages, see Sowayan, *Nabaṭī Poetry*, p. 27.
50. There is a tendency among critics to spiritualize Arabic literature, and readers sometimes force Arabic texts to be understood in a religious matrix. It is imperative to emphasize that Bedouin culture is secular in nature. Even though the Bedouin believe in God, they are not dogmatic when it comes to practising Islam. See Chapter 4 in Al-Kamālī, *Al-Shʿir ʿinda Al-Badū*, p. 39.
51. See Butler, *Subjects of Desire*, p. 218.
52. Foucault, *History of Sexuality*, p. 81.
53. Butler refers to Homi Bhabha's reading of melancholia as a revolt and 'authority's ideality is incorporable elsewhere, no longer tied in any absolute sense to one figure of the law'. Butler, *The Psychic Life of Power*, p. 190. See also Homi K. Bhabha, 'Postcolonial Authority and Postmodern Guilt', in Lawrence Grossberg et al. (eds) *Cultural Studies: A Reader* (New York: Routledge, 1992) pp. 65–6
54. Butler, *The Psychic Life of Power*, p. 181.
55. Freud, 'Mourning', p. 251.
56. Butler, *The Psychic Life of Power*, p. 143.
57. Ibid., p. 167.
58. Ibid., pp. 167–8.
59. Ibid., p. 170.
60. These references will not necessarily confirm the authenticity of the poet, as I explained at the beginning of this chapter.
61. Ibn Rāddas, *Shāʿirāt min al-Bādīyah*, p. 15.
62. Ibn Rāddas, *Shāʿirāt min al-Bādīyah*, p. 67. In his collection there are a smaller number of poems in which poets describe their desire and do not negate it. In the following example (also p. 67) the poet uncompromisingly declares her desire, names her beloved and is committed to her love regardless of social restrictions: 'I am in the valley of Rass, in a house of refuge/My beloved is following deer in the highland/I wish he caught an antelope and I could carry it/I would carry for my sweetheart all the game he hunted/My desire is Surūr and I wish for no substitute/For him I lost shame, and gave up on blame/Let whoever blames me devour thin dust/Let him slam his head into a boulder.'
63. Ibn Rāddas, *Shāʿirāt min al-Bādīyah*, p. 50.
64. Foucault, *History of Sexuality*, p. 157.
65. Butler, *The Psychic Life of Power*, p. 139.
66. Freud, 'Mourning', p. 247.
67. Butler, *The Psychic Life of Power*, p. 182.
68. Ibid., p. 183.

69. According to Ibn Rāddas, *Shāʿirāt min al-Bādīyah* (p. 159), this poet left her husband because she hated him. One day she saw a man whom she loved, and composed this poem.
70. The Arabic verb *waṭiʾa*, literally 'to step on, to tread underfoot', can also mean 'to have sexual intercourse with'.
71. Ibn Rāddas, *Shāʿirāt min al-Bādīyah*, p. 159.
72. Françoise Lionnet, 'Translating Grief', *Romantic Review*, vol. 94, nos 3–4 (2003) p. 277.
73. Ibn Rāddas, *Shāʿirāt min al-Bādīyah*, p. 197.
74. Ibn Rāddas, *Shāʿirāt min al-Bādīyah*, p. 195. A poet from the Shammar tribe was married to a man called Hagāsh, who remained a long time without touching her. Finally, it became clear that he was impotent. When she saw him trying to avoid her, she composed this poem.
75. Ibn Rāddas, *Shāʿirāt min al-Bādīyah*, p. 215. I discuss this poem in Chapter 6.
76. Butler, *The Psychic Life of Power*, pp. 183–4.
77. Ibn Rāddas, *Shāʿirāt min al-Bādīyah*, pp. 190–5.
78. Butler, *The Psychic Life of Power*, p. 183.

Chapter 3: A Malady of Grief

1. I have borrowed this term from Julia Kristeva, *Black Sun* (New York: Columbia University Press, 1989) p. 219.
2. Stetkevych, *The Zephyrs of Najd*, p. 25.
3. Al-Musawi, *Arabic Poetry*, p. 243.
4. Ibid., p. 247.
5. Allen underlines the contribution of women to this genre: 'The large number of elegies composed by women that have been recorded suggest that this communal function was a particular province of women poets, the poems themselves being part of the funeral ritual. The two most celebrated names in the early history of this type of poem are Tumadir bint ᶜAmr, renowned under the name of Al-Khansāʾ (d. before 670), and Laylā al-Akhyāliyyah (d. 704).' Roger Allen, *The Arabic Literary Heritage* (Cambridge: Cambridge University Press, 1998) p. 156.
6. Al-Khansāʾ was born around the end of the sixth century and survived through the advent of Islam, when she converted. She lost her two brothers and four sons in different battles. As a result, death became a central theme in many of her poems. Her powerful elegies exhibit her outstanding command of poetic language with forceful musical patterns. In addition, her elocution sustains her sentimentalized loss and generates powerful pathos. She addressed her brother, Ṣakhr, in the following: 'O Ṣakhr! I will ne'er forget thee until in dying/I part from my soul, and earth for my tomb is cloven/The rise of the sun recalls to me Ṣakhr my brother,/And him I remember also at every sunset.' See Reynold A. Nicholson, *Eastern Poetry and Prose* (Cambridge: Cambridge University Press, 1922) p. 19. For another translation of her

poems, see Arthur Wormhoudt, *Selections from the Diwan of Al-Khansa* (Oskaloosa, IA: William Penn College, 1973).

7. In the European cultural context there has been a tendency to perceive women's laments as threatening. They generated political anxiety, which eventually led to an attempt to regulate or suppress them. I cannot apply a similar argument to Arab women's elegies. For a discussion of women's lamentations in Greece and Rome and how they triggered social and political resentment, see E. Fantham, 'The Role of Lament in the Growth and Eclipse of Roman Epic', in Margaret Beissinger, Jane Tylus and Susanne Wofford (eds) *Epic Traditions in the Contemporary World: The Poetics of Community* (Berkeley: University of California Press, 1999) pp. 221–34. Consider also Holst-Warhaft's investigation of how the state perceived an embedded threat within women's laments and tried to sanction them. She emphasizes that 'The issue of banning laments is not a minor one, involving, as it does, issues that have affected the status of women in western society ever since. If we understand some common features of the tradition we are in a better position to know not simply why laments were banned, but how they were appropriated and turned against the lamenter, and what was lost as a result.' See Holst-Warhaft, *Dangerous Voices*, p. 97.
8. In ancient Arabia, pre-Islamic tribes would avenge the unjust death of their killed men and warriors; otherwise they would suffer disgrace and dishonour among other tribes. According to many historical accounts, the pre-Islamic poet Imru' Al-Qays swore to refrain from drinking wine until he had avenged the killing of his father, the king of Banu Asad. For details, see Aḥmad al-Shanqīṭī (ed.) *Al-Muʿallaqāt al-ʿAshr* (Beirut: Dār Al-Kutub Al-ʿIlmīyah, 2002) p. 7. Some Arabic poems embody this theme and usually invoke sentiments of revenge. Bedouin women have composed similar poems – generally elegies – in which the poet calls to avenge the death of a tribal member or hero. See Ibn Rāddas, *Shāʿirāt min al-Bādīyah*, pp. 306–12, 351.
9. Classical Arabic poetry and oral poems depict strong relationships with animals and show the poets' affinity with them. For example, male poets composed many eloquent and moving laments about their horses. Cole also discusses this relationship between the Bedouin and their animals and points out its economic significance: 'The Bedouin were strongly linked to the livestock they raised and took care of and which were dependent on the Bedouin, who themselves depended on their animals for much of their own livelihood and sustenance. This inter-species co-dependency or symbiosis was a central feature of the old Bedouin economy wherein the livestock constituted a person's and a family-household's capital.' See Donald P. Cole, 'Where Have the Bedouin Gone?' *Anthropological Quarterly*, vol. 76, no. 2 (2003) pp. 235–67, p. 238. Ibn Rāddas, *Shāʿirāt min al-Bādīyah* (p. 356) included an elegy to a sheep by an anonymous Bedouin woman poet.
10. Ibn Rāddas, *Shāʿirāt min al-Bādīyah*, p. 330.

11. Peter M. Sacks, *The English Elegy* (Baltimore, MD: Johns Hopkins University Press, 1985) p. 65.
12. See Chapter 4 for further discussion of apostrophe and prosopopoeia.
13. Butler, *The Psychic Life of Power*, p. 132.
14. Ibid., p. 134.
15. Torok points out that 'Incorporation is the refusal to acknowledge the full import of the loss, a loss that, if recognized as such, would effectively transform' the melancholic relation to the absent object. See Nicolas Abraham and Maria Torok, *The Shell and the Kernel: Renewals of Psychoanalysis*, translated by Nicholas T. Rand (Chicago, IL: University of Chicago Press, 1994) p. 127.
16. See note 64, where I refer to the ritual of coffee's preparation and its symbolic value in nomadic societies.
17. Racy discusses elegy in Lebanese villages, where it is usually sung 'at funerals by male *zajal* poets. In this case it is referred to as *qaṣīdah* ("poem"), usually qualified as *qaṣīdat al-rithā'* ("poem of elegy"). In the elegiac *qaṣīdah*, although the texts centre around the deceased, they generally recreate an idealized Bedouin world. They evoke the themes of pride and honor, speak of distinguished lineage, and refer to related virtues such as bravery and generosity'. See Ali Jihad Racy, 'Heroes, Lovers and Poet-Singers: The Bedouin Ethos in the Music of the Arab Near-East', *Journal of American Folklore*, vol. 109, no. 434 (1996) 404–24, p. 414.
18. Jacques Derrida, 'The Animal That Therefore I Am (More to Follow)', translated by David Wills, *Critical Inquiry*, vol. 28, no. 2 (Winter 2002) p. 392.
19. Of course the list could be longer, but the point is that we have an extensive body of work in Arabic that deals with the question of animality, ranging from descriptive to literary and intellectual, like al-Jāḥiẓ's *Kitāb al-Ḥayawān*. For a discussion of prime sources that focus on animals, see McDonald's brief article in which he surveys animal books. He concludes that 'The information which [these books] present is general, non-technical, drawn from literary sources, folklore, anecdotes and travellers' tales, and the audience to which they are addressed is a general one.' See M. V. McDonald, 'Animal-Books as a Genre in Arabic Literature', *Bulletin: British Society for Middle Eastern Studies*, vol. 15, nos 1/2 (1988) pp. 3–10. Also, Ikhwān al-Ṣafā (*Brethren of Purity*) from the tenth century wrote a dialogue among animals, revealing their suffering at the hands of humans; it is a fable that is rendered in mystic and philosophical language about animal rights and environmental concerns. See Ikhwān al-Ṣafā, *The Animals' Lawsuit against Humanity*, translated by Rabbi Anson Laytner (Louisville, KY: Fons Vitae, 2005).
20. Arberry, *The Seven Odes*, p. 65.
21. Ibid., p. 61.
22. In his study of pre-Islamic odes, Al-Fīfī offers a careful analysis of Imru' Al-Qays's *mu'allaqah* and explains its cultural and historical implications. He provides unique insights by relating these to crucial archaeological excavations

carried out in Arabia, especially in the village of al-Fāw. In my discussion I recapitulated some of his remarks about the historical importance of the gazelle. See 'Abd Allāh al-Fīfī, *Mafātīḥ al-Qaṣīdah al-Jāhilīyah* (Jeddah: Al-Nādī al-Adabī Al-Thaqāfī, 2001) pp. 49–51. Also see Rahman Al-Ansary, *Qaryat Al-Fau* (New York: Palgrave Macmillan, 1982).

23. Ibid., pp. 88–9. In one of his poems Imru' Al-Qays relates his adventures and refers to the ruins of his beloved Salma's dwelling. See 'Abd al-Raḥman al-Muṣṭāwī (ed.) *Dīwān Imru' al-Qays* (Beirut: Dār al-Ma'rifah, 2003) p.138.
24. Sells renders a contemporary translation of 'The Arabian Ode Rhyming in "L"' and comments on its inversion of the relationship between al-Shanfarā and his tribe, along with his satirical tone of poetic motifs in the *Mu'allaqāt* (suspended odes). See Sells, *Desert Tracings*, pp. 21, 24. Also, a number of commentators debated the authenticity and the attribution of *Lāmīyat al-'Arab* to Al-Shanfarā. See Suzanne P. Stetkevych, 'Archetype and Attribution in Early Arabic Poetry: Al-Shanfarā and the Lāmīyat al-'Arab', *International Journal of Middle East Studies*, vol. 18 (1986) pp. 361–90.
25. Al-Musawi, *Arabic Poetry*, p. 246.
26. Even though Al-Sūdānī does not provide a critical analysis of the elegies of non-humans, he has commented on and compiled remarkable selections of poetry from the Abbasid era in which poets mourn and elegize animals, birds and cities, among other non-human entities. See 'Abd Allāh al-Sūdānī, *Rīthā' Ghayr al-Insān fī al-Shi'r al-'Abbāsī* (Abu-Dhabi: Al-Majma' al-Thaqāfī, 1999).
27. Ibn Rashīq writes: 'It is customary that ancient poets would epitomize: noble kings and bygone cities, unassailable goats on mountains' summit[s], lions lurking in deserts, flocks of wild ass in barren lands, eagles, and serpents in their poetry because of their might and eternalness. For indeed, much of this is present in their poetry and it is rare to find poetry without it.' Al-Jāḥiẓ cited this statement as well. See Muṣtafah al-Shurā, *Shi'r al-Rithā' fī al-'Aṣr al-Jāhilī* (Beirut: Maktabat Lubnān Nāshirūn, 1995) pp. 64–5, my translation. Al-Shurā also devotes a chapter to animals in his study of elegy.
28. By no means do I intend to imply that classical Arabic poetic discourse on animals has an immediate influence on Bedouin women's poetry; rather, it is relevant to call for a comparative reading of animality in both traditions.
29. Benjamin, *The Origin of German Tragic Drama*, p. 230. For further discussion of melancholy and Benjamin, see Max Pensky, *Melancholy Dialectics* (Amherst: University of Massachusetts Press, 1993).
30. Jacques Derrida, 'The Animal That Therefore I Am', pp. 392, 383. Derrida refers to the question of animal in a number of texts, but for more relevant discussion see his '"Eating Well", or the Calculation of the Subject: An Interview with Jacques Derrida', in Eduardo Cadavo, Peter Connor and Jean-Luc Nancy (eds) *Who Comes after the Subject?* translated by Peter Connor and Avital Ronell (New York: Routledge, 1991). For contemporary philosophical

reflections on the animal, see Giorgio Agamben, *The Open: Man and Animal*, translated by Kevin Attell (Stanford, CA: Stanford University Press, 2004); and Cary Wolfe (ed.) *Zoontologies: The Question of the Animal* (Minneapolis: University of Minnesota Press, 2003). Consider also Cary Wolfe, *Animal Rites: American Culture, the Discourse of Species, and Posthumanist Theory* (Chicago, IL: University of Chicago Press, 2003); and H. Peter Steeves and Tom Reagan (eds) *Animal Others: On Ethics, Ontology, and Animal Life* (Albany: State University of New York, 1999).

31. Derrida, 'The Animal That Therefore I Am', p. 400.
32. Ibid., p. 396.
33. Ibid.
34. The poet elegized her long-absent son, not knowing what had become of him.
35. Ibn Rāddas, *Shā'irāt min al-Bādīyah*, p. 369.
36. See Chapter 4 for a discussion of apostrophe and its embodiment of loss.
37. Ibn Rāddas, *Shā'irāt min al-Bādīyah*, vol. 2, p. 2.
38. Benjamin, *The Origin of German Tragic Drama*, p. 166.
39. Ibn Rāddas, *Shā'irāt min al-Bādīyah*, p. 369.
40. Ibid., p. 339.
41. Al-Kamālī cites a long Bedouin poem by a male poet where the speaker refers to the *khalūj* and its refusal of loss, capturing what I have indicated. See Al-Kamālī, *Al-Sh'ir 'inda Al-Badū*, p. 170.
42. Butler, *The Psychic Life of Power*, p. 142.
43. Benjamin, *The Origin of German Tragic Drama*, p. 185.
44. Stamelman discusses this point, following Benjamin: 'Allegorical discourse, moreover, is always incomplete and imperfect, because it evokes some meaning, some image, some figure beyond the horizon of its signification, some "otherness" that it can designate but not join. The allegorical sign invokes totality that can never be possessed, an origin that can never be found again, and a referent that can never be represented.' See Richard Stamelman, *Lost Beyond Telling* (Ithaca, NY: Cornell University, 1990) pp. 53–4.
45. Butler, *The Psychic Life of Power*, p. 192.
46. Although al-Ghuwayrī is considered a fine poet, reciters have transmitted only a small part of her work to us. These few lines are from a long poem. The reciters explain that the occasion for which she composed it were as follows: her husband was in the habit of making long raiding voyages with his people in search of gain. One day a great battle took place between her tribe and a neighbouring group in which her husband, Muḥammad Ibn Ṣaqr Ibn Ḥāzim, died, and she composed this poem elegizing him. We know that in 1969 she was still alive at the age of 85. See Ibn Rāddas, *Shā'irāt min al-Bādīyah*, p. 349.
47. Ibid.
48. Ibid., p. 323.
49. This recurrent theme in literature has been utilized since antiquity. Lutwack presents an interesting study that explores birds in literary texts and

comments on their significance. Leonard Lutwack, *Birds in Literature* (Gainesville: University Press of Florida, 1994).

50. Ibn Rāddas, *Shā'irāt min al-Bādīyah*, pp. 179–80.
51. Al-Kamālī cites an elegy about a falcon in *Al-Sh'ir 'inda Al-Badū*, p. 170.
52. Derrida, 'The Animal That Therefore I Am', p. 396.
53. Ibid.
54. We can see the delay of the referent in the allegorical articulation. Stamelman addresses this point, following Benjamin's insights: 'Allegory can also be perceived as a rhetorical mode of exuberant representation whose signs, because they can never reach the object they designate, move in random, arbitrary, and extravagant patterns. These signs run to excess because a coincidence with the inaccessible and anterior referent is impossible. They are signifiers cut off from the signified and free to go their own way.' See Stamelman, *Lost Beyond Telling*, pp. 63–4.
55. Benjamin, *The Origin of German Tragic Drama*, pp. 183–4.
56. See how Imru' Al-Qays describes his horse, cited earlier in this chapter.
57. Quoted by J. Stetkevych, *The Zephyrs of Najd*, p. 116, who notes that these lines were also attributed to another poet, Ibn al-Dumaynah (died 760). Stetkevych discusses the legendary Majnūn's poetry and shows how it is marked by 'reveries over' Najd, while addressing place names that are nostalgic motifs – a device that 'Udhrī poets frequently deployed during the early Islamic period (late seventh to early eight centuries); see pp. 114, 115.
58. Etel Adnan, 'At Both Ends', *First Intensity*, no. 11 (Fall 1998) p.14.
59. J. Stetkevych, *The Zephyrs of Najd*, p. 120.
60. Ibid., p. 118.
61. Munif offers a haunting description of travel and its perplexing urgency among the people of the Arabian oasis that he calls Wādī al-'Uyūn: 'Wadi al-Uyun's people, like its waters, flooded out in times of overabundance: emigration had been a necessity for a long time. ... This impulse seemed strange and mysterious, for it was not always related to the rains or the seasons as was the case elsewhere.' He continues: 'There was not a single man in the wadi who had not at some time been seduced by the urge to travel, and it was a rare old man who had not travelled to some distant place or other.' See Abdelrahman Munif, *Cities of Salt*, translated by Peter Theroux (New York: Vintage International, 1987) p. 5.
62. Cole, *The Nomads of the Nomads*, p. 16.
63. Ibn Rāddas, *Shā'irāt min al-Bādīyah*, p. 105.
64. Ibn Rāddas, *Shā'irāt min al-Bādīyah*, p. 97. The land of Najd was afflicted by a drought that lasted many years, killing much of the livestock. Since the livelihood of desert pastoralists depends entirely on their herds, the loss of livestock leads to poverty and starvation. During the worst of the drought, when the camels could no longer carry their loads, the poet's husband, Nuwār al-Nimr, was forced to go to one of the towns in Al-Qaṣīm. He left his wife

there with all their belongings, and returned to the desert with his eldest son and their camels and sheep and prayed for rain. Since ʿAlyā' the poet was familiar with desert life and loved setting off freely across its wide expanse, she hated residing near city dwellers who were not bored living in one place. In the oasis town, the sound of water wheels, used by cultivators to irrigate their fields, shatters the silence of the darkest hours of night, whereas desert nights are calm and peaceful. In this poem ʿAlyā' expresses her irritation with the noisy town nights and recalls the lost serenity of her people's desert encampments.

65. Racy provides an interesting analysis of the coffee preparation ritual and its relation to music: 'The *mihbaj* (coffee grinder), consisting of a large wooden pestle and mortar, the *mihbaj* may be considered: a household tool; a visually ornate object that has the pleasant, and perhaps symbolically significant, scent of coffee mixed with cardamom; a musical instrument; and last but not least, an emblem of generosity, honor, and social status.' See Racy, 'Heroes, Lovers and Poet-Singers', p. 408. Sowayan, *Nabati Poetry*, p. 42, also describes the setting and its significance in relation to Bedouin virtues.
66. Ibn Rāddas, *Shāʿirāt min al-Bādīyah 6*, p. 53. It is related that al-Jāzī was an orphan living with her uncle, who married her to the Amīr of Al-Majmaʿah in Najd, Ibn ʿAskar. She hated him, and it is said that she took poison and died. She composed these lines to show the extent of her contempt for castles and urban life, and her preference for travelling with her people towards freedom and wide open spaces, the delight of Bedouins.
67. Ibn Rāddas, *Shāʿirāt min al-Bādīyah*, p. 184.
68. Ibid., p. 53.
69. Ibid., p. 243.
70. Judith Butler, *Precarious Life: The Powers of Mourning and Violence* (London: Verso, 2004) pp. 21–2.
71. Butler, *The Psychic Life*, p. 170.
72. Freud, 'Mourning', p. 248.
73. Ibid., p. 45.
74. Butler, *The Psychic Life of Power*, p. 141.
75. Ibn Rāddas, *Shāʿirāt min al-Bādīyah*, p. 97.
76. Ibid., p. 53.
77. Ibid.
78. Freud, 'Mourning', p. 252.
79. Butler, *The Psychic Life of Power*, p. 187.
80. Ibid., p. 184.
81. Ibid., p. 143.
82. Ibid., p. 182.
83. Here I am paraphrasing Butler's persuasive discussion, ibid., p. 187.

Chapter 4: Masquerading Tropes: The Fiction of Face and Voice

1. Apostrophe is a frequently deployed feature in many poetic traditions and

cannot be limited to Romantic European poetry or Western canonical texts. For example, Culler observes that 'All the verse of antiquity was addressed to somebody, primarily because it was either sung or read and the traditions of song and recitation required that there be a recipient.' See Jonathan Culler, *The Pursuit of Signs* (Ithaca, NY: Cornell University Press, 1981) p. 136.

2. My focus in discussing prosopopoeia has been informed and guided by de Man's analysis, especially in these essays. See Paul de Man, 'Autobiography as De-Facement', in Paul de Man, *The Rhetoric of Romanticism* (New York: Columbia University Press, 1984) pp. 67–81; and Paul de Man, 'Hypogram and Inscription', in Paul de Man, *The Resistance to Theory* (Minneapolis: University of Minnesota Press, 1993) pp. 27–53. Among the theorists who have addressed these essays are Cynthia Chase, Jonathan Culler, Jacques Derrida, Barbara Johnson and Hillis Miller. It is important to point out that critics of the lyric refer in their analyses to the figure of apostrophe as an 'embodiment' of prosopopoeia and not the other way round. I would stress that the configuration of address is initiated in prosopopoeia.
3. Prosopopoeia is defined in the *Oxford English Dictionary* as 'a rhetorical figure by which an imaginary or absent person is represented as speaking or acting, the introduction of a pretended speaker.' See also Nicholas Royle, 'Nuclear Pieces: Memoires of Hamlet and the Time to Come,' *Diacritics*, vol. 20, no. 1 (Spring 1990) pp. 37–55. The *Oxford English Dictionary* cites personification as an equivalent synonym for prosopopoeia, and in my view this conflation, which has characterized discussion of this trope needs to be highlighted. Miller, for instance, marks the similarity between these two tropes by suggesting that prosopopoeia 'personifies what does not in fact have personality'. See Hillis Miller, 'Prosopopoeia and Praeterita', in Laurence Lockridge and John Maynard (eds) *Nineteenth-Century Lives* (Cambridge: Cambridge University Press, 1989) p. 128.
4. Cynthia Chase, *Decomposing Figures* (Baltimore, MD: Johns Hopkins University Press, 1986) p. 68.
5. De Man, *The Resistance to Theory* (Minneapolis: University of Minnesota Press, 1993) p. 47. In clarification of de Man's reading of Michael Riffaterre's work in this essay, it should be emphasized that he is not simply critiquing Riffaterre as other critics claim. Instead, he supports Riffaterre's work on prosopopoeia and at the same time shows how he misread the tropological effects of this figure.
6. Chase, *Decomposing Figures*, p. 68.
7. Jonathan Culler, 'Reading Lyric', *Yale French Studies*, vol. 69, *The Lesson of Paul de Man* (1985) pp. 98–106. Even though Culler provides a lucid investigation of apostrophe, he does not show the differential specular aspects of prosopopoeia.
8. De Man, *The Rhetoric of Romanticism*, pp. 75–6.
9. Jonathan Culler, 'Deconstruction and the Lyric', in Anselm Haverkamp (ed.)

Deconstruction is/in America: A New Sense of the Political (New York: New York University Press, 1995) p. 44.

10. Classical epitaphs incorporate this imperative moment, 'Halt, traveller', 'from which the English epitaph borrows much of its structure and many of its motifs'. See Lorna Clymer, 'Graved in Tropes: The Figural Logic of Epitaph and Elegies in Blair, Gray, Cowper, and Wordsworth', *English Literary History*, vol. 62, no. 2 (1995) pp. 347–86.
11. Arberry, *The Seven Odes*, p. 61.
12. Sells, *Desert Tracing*, p. 48.
13. Ibn Rāddas, *Shā'irāt min al-Bādīyah*, p. 198.
14. Ibid., p. 330.
15. Ibid.
16. Ibid., pp. 339–40.
17. Ibid., pp. 322–3.
18. Ibid., p. 171.
19. Ibid., pp. 179–80.
20. Ibid., p. 323.
21. Ibid., Vol. 2, p.2.
22. Ibid., p. 52.
23. See these lyrical dialogues in Ibn Rāddas, *Shā'irāt min al-Bādīyah*, pp. 26 and 36. Address appears more frequently in these poetic dialogues and I would argue that part of addressing the mountain or the wolf, for instance, is to defer the interlocutor's identity, especially if the exchange is taking place between a woman and a man. In these poetic dialogues we do not know either the speaker or the addressee. See Ibn Rāddas, *Shā'irāt min al-Bādīyah*, p. 286.
24. Ibn Rāddas, *Shā'irāt min al-Bādīyah*, pp. 282–3.
25. The configuration of this address also brings us to the other who will have spoken first. We are left with the trace of speech that is coming from the other. Derrida comments on de Man's reading: 'this sort of theorem of prosopopoeia [sic], which, figuratively addressed to us, looks at us, describes and prescribes to us, dictates to us in advance, with the voice and under the initialled signature of Paul de Man, what we are doing here and now: to be sure, making a prosopopoeia, sacrificing to fiction – and what he reminds us is that prosopopoeia remains a fictive voice, although I believe that this voice already haunts any said real or present voice.' Jacques Derrida, *Mémoires: For Paul de Man* (New York: Columbia Press, 1986) p. 24.
26. Ibn Rāddas, *Shā'irāt min al-Bādīyah*, pp. 322–3.
27. In the context of this discussion it is necessary to propose a question of address. It is also relevant to introduce this trope when reading an elegy. In 'Apostrophe, Animation, and Abortion', Johnson suggests that when a poet apostrophizes, he is not only giving voice and animation to an object, but he is also implying 'that a poet has animation to give'. See Barbara Johnson, *A World of Difference* (Baltimore, MD: Johns Hopkins University Press, 1987) p. 188.

28. Ibn Rāddas, *Shāʿirāt min al-Bādīyah*, p. 319.
29. Ibid., p. 50
30. Ibid., p. 229.
31. Ibid., p. 29.
32. Ibid., p. 18.
33. There are textual affinities between the elegy we are reading and a Greek lament in which the speaker apostrophizes by addressing the deceased: 'Stretch out your hand, and take my hand in yours/Clasp me, as I clasp you, so as not to part/For once we part we'll never meet again.' For further discussion of women's laments and ritual, see Alexiou, *The Ritual Lament in Greek Tradition*, pp. 103 and 43. See also Holst-Warhaft, *Dangerous Voices*, p. 40.
34. Jacques Derrida, 'My Chances/Mes Chances: A Rendezvous with some Epicurean Stereophies', in Joseph H. Smith and William Kerrigan (eds) *Taking Chances, Psychoanalysis, and Literature* (Baltimore, MD: Johns Hopkins University Press, 1985) pp. 1–2.
35. Ibid., p. 2.
36. Culler, 'Deconstruction and the Lyric', p. 45.
37. De Man, *The Rhetoric of Romanticism*, p. 80.
38. In his deconstructive reading of the lyric, de Man questions generic naming in a negation of assigning it such a name. He writes, in *The Rhetoric of Romanticism*, p. 261, that 'the lyric is not a genre, but one name among several to designate a defensive motion of understanding.'
39. De Man, *The Rhetoric of Romanticism*, p. 78.
40. Chase, *Decomposing Figures*, p. 70.
41. Ibid., p. 68.
42. In her discussing death and deconstruction, Johnson raises another question: 'What is the connection between personification and death?' I would ask if we are dealing with personification or prosopopoeia? See Barbara Johnson, *The Wake of Deconstruction* (Oxford: Blackwell, 1994) p. 17.
43. Chase, *Decomposing Figures*, pp. 68–9.
44. For a thorough account of the term 'speculation', see Rodolphe Gasché, *The Tain of the Mirror: Derrida and the Philosophy of Reflection* (Cambridge, MA: Harvard University Press, 1986). Gasché shows how speculative thinking resides in a reflective mirroring. He unfolds a subtle analysis of the word 'speculation', demonstrating that 'it is rooted in the Latin *specio*, "to look," "to behold".' He proposes that since Kant we have regarded speculative knowledge as manifested in self-reflection. He states that 'speculative has meant a process of constant exchange between a mirror and its mirror image' (p. 43). The word *speculum*, then, suggests among other things, a mirror, whereas 'spectre' is related to its Latin root *spectrum*, which connotes 'appearance' or 'form'. It is also equivalent to *specere*, 'to look', 'to regard'. But 'spectral' pertains to a spectre and phantom. In this context it is important to note that de Man does not limit the effects of prosopopoeia to a specular

movement, but demonstrates how this trope has spectral effects as well. For him, the movement of tropes posits both specular and spectral effects. Thus, in both cases we are dealing with illusions of the trope of prosopopoeia, since it always propagates what contradicts itself.

45. De Man, *The Rhetoric of Romanticism*, p. 71.
46. See de Man's discussion of the absence of face in this figure: 'But *prosopon-poiein* means to give a face and therefore implies that the original face can be missing or nonexistent. The trope, which coins a name for a still unnamed entity, which gives face to the faceless, is, of course, catachresis. That a catachresis can be a prosopopoeia, in the etymological sense of "giving face", is clear from such ordinary instances as the face of a mountain or the eye of a hurricane' (de Man, *The Resistance to Theory*, p. 44).
47. Frey comments on this paradoxical effect of prosopopoeia in relation to bestowing face and decomposing it: 'In order to re-establish itself as the hypothetical figure it is, the face must decompose itself again. This removal of the face is the second form of defacement, and serves the disillusioning function of recalling the substitutive character of the face and the forgotten fictivity of the system.' See Hans-Jost Frey, 'Undecidability', *Yale French Studies*, no. 69, *The Lesson of Paul de Man* (1985) pp. 124–33.
48. Chase, *Decomposing Figures*, p. 74.
49. De Man, *The Rhetoric of Romanticism*, p. 75.
50. De Man extends Genette's observation that metaphor is like a revolving door to the nature of tropes in general. He writes: 'Genette's metaphor of a revolving door helps us to understand why this connotes the turning motion of tropes and confirms that the specular moment is not primarily a situation or an event that can be located in a history, but that it is the manifestation, on the level of the referent, of a linguistic structure. The specular moment that is part of all understanding reveals the tropological structure that underlies all cognition', *The Rhetoric of Romanticism*, pp. 70–2.
51. De Man, *The Rhetoric of Romanticism*, p. 122.
52. De Man, *The Resistance to Theory*, p. 45.
53. See J. Hillis Miller, 'Prosopopeia in Hardy and Stevens', in Lance St John Butler (ed.) *Alternative Hardy* (London: Macmillan, 1989) p. 134.
54. De Man (*The Rhetoric of Romanticism*, p. 285) remarks: 'such is language: it is always thrusts but never scores. It always refers but never to the right referent.'
55. De Man, *The Rhetoric of Romanticism*, p. 80.
56. Even though Miller cannot differentiate between personification and prosopopoeia, he still argues that texts are dependent on the latter: 'Prosopopoeia, it may be, is the one trope no poet or writer, however strong-minded and literal, can efface from his language … because personification is so intrinsic a part of language [that] no writing, however resolutely literal, can avoid it.' J. Hillis Miller, 'Catachresis, Prosopopoeia, and the Pathetic Fallacy:

The Rhetoric of Ruskin', in Roland Hagenbuchle and Laura Skandera (eds) *Poetry and Epistemology: Turning Points in the History of Poetic Knowledge* (Regensburg: Verlag Friedrich Pustet, 1986) pp. 402–3.

Chapter 5: Technology and Postcoloniality: Algeria and Arabia

1. Conley sheds light on this dissociation between the sciences and humanities and presents a variety of approaches to technology that do not support this separation. In the same anthology, Guattari points out that 'The relation between human and the machine has been a source of reflection since the beginning of philosophy. Aristotle considers that the goal of *techné* is to create what nature finds impossible to achieve, so that *techné* sets itself up between nature and humanity as a creative mediation.' See Félix Guattari, 'Machinic Heterogenesis', translated by James Creech, in Verena Andermatt Conley (ed.) *Rethinking Technologies*, (Minneapolis: University of Minnesota Press, 1993) p. 13.
2. Verena Andermatt Conley, 'Preface', in Verena Andermatt Conley (ed.) *Rethinking Technologies* (Minneapolis: University of Minnesota Press, 1993) p. x.
3. Martin Heidegger, *Basic Writings*, edited by David Farrell Krell (New York: Harper & Row, 1977) p. 287.
4. Conley, 'Preface', p. ix.
5. Frantz Fanon, 'Ici la Voix de l'Algérie', in Frantz Fanon, *L'an V de la Révolution algérienne* (Paris: François Maspero, 1962) p. 57. The same essay appears in English as 'This Is the Voice of Algeria, in Frantz Fanon, *A Dying Colonialism* (New York: Grove Press, 1965) pp. 69–97. See also, Munif, *Cities of Salt.*
6. See L. Kris Hardin and Mary Jo Arnoldi, 'Introduction', in M. J. Arnoldi, C. M. Geary and K. L. Hardin (eds) *African Material Culture* (Indiana: Indiana University Press, 1996).
7. The only book devoted to examining technology and Latin American literature is Jane Roinett, *This Rough Magic: Technology in Latin American Fiction* (New York: Peter Lang, 1994). A more recent essay by Parla examines Turkish novels and motorcars: 'As a setting from which the authors debated the issues of modernization, the car epitomizes the mental and psychic confusion of the novels' characters. That confusion ranges from stupid ignorance to suicidal defiance'. See Jale Parla, 'Car Narratives: A Subgenre in Turkish Novel Writing', *South Atlantic Quarterly*, vol. 102, nos 2/3 (2003) pp. 535–50. However, both studies affirm notions of ambivalence and resistance to technology.
8. Even critics who interrogate the encounter between East and West resist reading technology without attaching it to the notion of the foreign. Fourny, for example, presents an argument about 'laziness and technology' in the Egyptian writer Albert Cossery's francophone texts. He analyses Cossery's treatment of technology as being caught in the dichotomy of relations

between East and West. See Jean-François Fourny, 'Post/Colonial Conditions: Exiles, Migrations, and Nomadisms', *Yale French Studies*, Part 2 (1993) pp. 158–71.

9. In her discussion of Victorian poetry and technology, Linley refers to how 'the Victorians themselves developed the anti-technology narrative encapsulated in the definition of culture as the opposite of industry.' See Margaret Linley, 'Conjuring the Spirit: Victorian Poetry, Culture, and Technology', *Victorian Poetry*, vol. 41, no. 4 (2003) pp. 536–44.
10. 'A precise technical instrument: the radio'. Frantz Fanon, *L'an V de la Révolution algérienne* (Paris: François Maspero, 1962) p. 57 (in French); or Frantz Fanon, *A Dying Colonialism* (New York: Grove Press, 1965) p. 69 (in English).
11. 'There was no organized resistance to this device. No real lines of counter-acculturation, such as are described in certain monographs devoted to underdeveloped regions, have shown to exist, even after extensive surveys.' Fanon, *L'an V de la Révolution algérienne*, p. 58; Fanon, *A Dying Colonialism*, pp. 69–70.
12. Fanon shows the difference in the way that European farmers and Algerians related to the radio. The Algerians 'hesitate' to perceive it as anything other than a French presence: 'Chez l'algérien, par contre, la situation est totalement différente. Nous avons vu que la famille aisée hésite à acquérir un poste. Toutefois, il n'est pas constaté de résistance explicite, ordonnée et fondée, mais plutôt un désintérêt morne pour ce morceau de présence française' (Fanon, *L'an V de la Révolution algérienne*, p. 60). 'For the Algerian, however, the situation was totally different. We have seen that the more well-to-do family hesitated to buy a radio set. Yet no explicit, organized and motivated resistance was observed, but rather a dull absence of interest in that piece of French presence' (Fanon, *A Dying Colonialism*, p. 72).
13. 'Here, then, at a certain explicit level, is the apprehension of a fact: receiving sets are not readily adopted by Algerian society. By and large, it refuses this technique that threatens its stability and the traditional types of sociality' (Fanon, *L'an V de la Révolution algérienne*, p. 60; Fanon, *A Dying Colonialism*, p. 70).
14. 'The radio, as a symbol of French presence, as a material representation of the colonial configuration, is characterized by an extremely important negative valence.' Fanon, *L'an V de la Révolution algérienne*, p. 61; *A Dying Colonialism*, p. 73.
15. 'Before 1954, in the psychopathological realm, the radio was an evil object, creating anxiety and accursed.' Fanon, *L'an V de la Révolution algérienne*, p. 79; *A Dying Colonialism*, p. 89.
16. Fanon tends to conflate Algeria with inscriptions of femininity in his discussion of women and the veil, as is clearly shown in his essay's title. See Frantz Fanon, 'Algeria, Unveiled', in Frantz Fanon, *A Dying Colonialism* (New York: Grove Press, 1965) p. 35.

17. 'Radio-Alger, the voice of France in Algeria constitutes the sole centre of reference at the level of news.' Fanon, *L'an V de la révolution algérienne*, p. 60 (my emphasis); Fanon, *A Dying Colonialism*, p. 71.
18. 'An invitation not to "go native", not to forget the rightfulness of his culture.' Fanon, *L'an V de la Révolution algérienne*, p. 60; *A Dying Colonialism*, p. 71.
19. 'At the end of the evening, not hearing *the Voice*, the listener would sometimes leave the needle on a jammed wave length or one that simply produced static, and would announce that the voice of the combatants was here. For an hour the room would be filled with the piercing, excruciating din of the jamming. Behind each modulation, each active crackling, the Algerian would imagine not only words, but concrete battles. The war of the sound waves, in the *gourbi*, re-enacts for the benefit of the citizen the army's clash of his people and colonialism.' Fanon, *L'an V de la Révolution algérienne*, p. 78; *A Dying Colonialism*, p. 88.
20. Jacques Derrida, 'Voice II', *Boundary 2*, vol. 12, no. 2 (1984) p. 79.
21. 'The infidels' radio'. Fanon, *L'an V de la Révolution algérienne*, p. 84; *A Dying Colonialism*, p. 93.
22. 'An enemy object'. Fanon, *L'an V de la Révolution algérienne*, p. 73; *A Dying Colonialism*, p. 84.
23. 'In the colonial situation, the radio did not satisfy any need of the Algerian people.' Fanon, *L'an V de la Révolution algérienne*, p. 87; *A Dying Colonialism*, p. 96.
24. Jacques Derrida and Bernard Stiegler, *Echographies of Television* (Cambridge: Polity Press, 2002) p. 63.
25. Abdelrahman Munif was born in Amman, Jordan, in 1933 and died in 2004. His father was from Arabia and his mother from Iraq. He studied petroleum economics and gained a Ph.D. from the University of Belgrade in 1961. His oil industry career included working for the Syrian Oil Company in 1973. In 1975 he travelled to Iraq, where he edited a monthly periodical, *Al-Nifṭ wa-al-Tanmīyah (Oil and Development)*. See Al-Rashīd Bū Shaʿīr, *Musāʾalat al-Naṣ al-Riwāʾī fī ʿAmāl ʿAbd al-Raḥman Munīf* (Damascus: Manshūrāt Wizārat al-Thaqāfah, 2004) p. 7.
26. Edward Said, 'Embargoed Literature', *The Nation*, vol. 251, 17 September 1990.
27. Abdelrahman Munif, *Variations on Night and Day*, translated by Peter Theroux (New York: Vintage, 1994). Perhaps one could say that Munif explored his birth year of 1933, when the king of Arabia signed the first contract with the California Standard Oil Company to search for oil. Munif's novel was banned in Saudi Arabia and other Arab countries and he was stripped of his Saudi citizenship.
28. The discovery of oil in Arabia was widely publicized: 'Last week, however, Ibn Saud granted Standard Oil an oil concession covering his entire 912,500-square-mile Kingdom.' See Anon., 'Astute Ibn Saud', *Newsweek*, 21 August 1939, p. 21. However, oil had been sought for almost sixteen years beforehand. In a long article, Da Cruz discussed the background of the discovery of oil. He writes: 'In May 1923 King 'Abd al-'Aziz signed an agreement with

Holmes which entitled the Eastern and General Syndicate to find a company to search for oil in eastern Saudi Arabia.' See Daniel Da Cruz, 'How They Find Oil', *Saudi Aramco World*, vol. 17, no. 1, January/February 1966. <http://www.saudiaramcoworld.com/issue/196601/default.htm> For historical documentation of the relationship between Aramco and the United States, see Irvine H. Anderson, *Aramco, the United States and Saudi Arabia* (Princeton, NJ: Princeton University Press, 1981). In this context, it should be emphasized how the West developed its technological power after the Second World War: 'The West had emerged from World War Two with a fistful of technological and scientific trump[s] for the game of global dominance that followed. Wartime research and development seemed to argue for giving experts as free a hand as possible to design immensely complex systems for domestic markets and national defense.' See John M. Staudenmaier, 'Rationality, Agency, Contingency: Recent Trends in the History of Technology', *Reviews in American History*, vol. 30, no. 1 (2002) pp. 168–81.

29. Ironically, Munif addresses colonialism in this interview, even though he does not deploy the word colonialist in his novel. See Bu Sh'air, *Musaala al-nass*, p. 175, my translation.
30. Munif, *Cities of Salt*, p. 1.
31. Ibid., p. 2.
32. The encounter with the West in the modern Arabic novel is often associated with fascination and ambivalence. In fact, *Cities of Salt* elaborates on the anxiety of foreignness, which characterizes the encounter between the Americans and the inhabitants of the wadi; each views the other's looks, habits and language with a sense of estrangement and immense anxiety. One could argue that the machine is not singled out as something uncanny and alien, but is part of the encounter between the Americans and the oasis people.
33. Munif, *Cities of Salt*, p. 68.
34. Ibid., p. 69.
35. Ibid., p. 69.
36. Ibid., p. 98.
37. Ibid., p. 98.
38. Given the lack of critical studies of instrumental technology in Arabic literature, it is helpful to cite an essay that discusses Turkish novels and motorcars and shows some similarity to Munif's account: 'As the car stories are plotted in different periods of the Turkish novel by different novelists, these stories, which begin with the seemingly innocent acquisition of cars, grow into enigmatic narratives of possession and dispossession, empowerment and loss of power, function and dysfunction, maturation and infantilism, narcissism and fetishism, fragmentation and self-destruction, not to mention a whole century of estrangement and a feeling of inferiority inspired by the contact with the West.' See Parla, 'Car Narratives'.
39. King Abdulaziz, or Ibn Saud as he was called, was surrounded by new

technologies during the opening of a 43-mile pipeline: 'On 28 April a caravan of 100 gleaming automobiles rolled smoothly up to the main gate of Al Khobar in the Arabian Desert near the Persian Gulf. … For three days the King lived in a duplex air-conditioned house in a specially built tent city.' See Anon., 'Astute Ibn Saud'.

40. Robert Vitalis, *America's Kingdom: Mythmaking on the Saudi Oil Frontiers* (Stanford, CA: Stanford University Press, 2007) p. xviii.
41. Lloyd Hamilton to Airy Hamilton, *Hufuf*, Sunday 30 December 1934, Folder 11, Lloyd Hamilton Letters, 1934–35, Box 28, Letters, Journals, Interviews, Wallace Earl Stregner Papers, MS 676, Special Collections, Marriott Library, University of Utah, Salt Lake City. Cited by Vitalis, *America's Kingdom*, p. 54.
42. Munif, *Cities of Salt*, p. 432.
43. Ibid., p. 432.
44. Ibid., p. 433.
45. Ibid., p. 433.
46. Ibid., p. 436.
47. Ibid., p. 434.
48. Ibid., p. 450.
49. An example of the staging of technology in Arab women's writing can be seen in Etel Adnan's poetry. More specifically, in her book, *The Spring Flowers Own and the Manifestations of the Voyage* (Sausalito, CA: Post-Apollo Press, 1990), she deploys numerous references to instrumental technology such as the radio, air conditioner and motorcars during a meditation on life and death.
50. In my extensive investigation of Bedouin oral poetry I have found insufficient examples of men's poems on technology to be able to generalize their approach. In one example that relates a car to its Western origin, the poet is clearly ambivalent, especially when he compares the car's driver with someone 'who is possessed by a demon' and slurs the Westerner who exported the car. In the latter part of a 13-line poem, he says: 'O rider of a vehicle roaring in the featureless waste,/Like one who is possessed by a demon,/A car fitted with brand-new tyres,/Selected from the dealer's showroom for forty thousand riyals./In the early morning he sets out from the land of our brothers/Driving his spanking new car, a recent import from the dogs./The crew on the board are all brash and jaunty youngsters,/Bold men who store in their marrow the seed of equally brave ancestors./A vehicle that suits the dreams of a man hankering to depart,/One deprived of sleep by separation from his love.' See Kurpershoek, *Oral Poetry and Narrative*, p. 151.
51. For example, the protest by women in Saudi Arabia during the Gulf War. If I may assign it a name, it was the automobile crisis. A car became a figure of another crisis. During this war, women in Riyadh got into their motorcars and went onto the city streets in spite of the prohibition against them. In this protest, a car was driven beyond both the political limit and the limit of the law, and was stopped below the speed of freedom. Women shifted gears

publicly for the first time and drove on a road that was full of political and traditional stops. They were arrested by the police. These women have been robbed of their right to drive, a 'convention' agreed to without their consent. After women went onto the road in this way, a law was passed to 'discipline' them, as the *New York Times* commented. It was an historical collision, and Arabian women may be regarded as the world's most political drivers. See AP, 'Saudi Women Disciplined', *New York Times*, 13 November 1990; and James Lemoyne, 'MIDEAST TENSIONS: Saudi Interior Minister Prohibits All Protests for Change by Women', *New York Times*, 18 November 1990.

52. The motorcar was first introduced in 1925, according to K. S. Twitchell, *Saudi Arabia* (Princeton, NJ: Princeton University Press, 1953) p. 49. In fact, by 1829, a century earlier, the motorcar was already running on the roads of Britain. See David Beasley, *The Suppression of the Automobile* (New York: Greenwood Press, 1988) p. xii.
53. Poetry in general has been fascinated by technology and techniques. Take for example early twentieth-century American poetry and its incorporation of these tropes: 'American verse written between 1910 and 1925 exhibits a persistent fascination with several types of modern great buildings – railroad stations, department stores, hotels, theaters, sports arenas – but most of all with the skyscraper.' See John Timberman Newcomb, 'The Footprint of the Twentieth Century: American Skyscrapers and Modernist Poems', *Modernism/Modernity*, vol. 10, no. 1 (2003) pp. 97–125.
54. A similar change from the camel to the car took place among Bedouin in the Anti-Lebanon Mountains. 'During the 1960s, trucks replaced camels. The expenditure involved was calculated by placing the value of one truck at approximately the value of fifteen or sixteen camels. … Over the past fifteen years, among Bedouin tribes in Syria, Iraq, Saudi Arabia, and Jordan, the Datsun and Toyota half-ton trucks have become a common sight. These vehicles serve basically to transport households and livestock from one camp to another and to carry water to the herds when deep in the Badia.' See Dawn Chatty, *From Camel to Truck: The Bedouin in the Modern World* (New York: Vintage, 1986) pp. 107, 142.
55. Cole, *The Nomads of the Nomads*, p. 24.
56. Ibid., p. 24.
57. Ibn Rāddas, *Shā'irāt min al-Bādīyah*, p. 48.
58. Ibid., p. 269.
59. Ibid., p. 205.
60. Ibid., p. 109. Consider another reference to a red camel in an elegy where the poet recalls her warrior brother who was riding a red camel. See ibid., vol. 2, p.70.
61. Scheibler notes that Heidegger, in fact, presents a critique of Western metaphysics in his essay. She writes: 'For Heidegger, then, this means that the question concerning technology cannot be thought apart from the critique of

Western metaphysics.' See Ingrid Scheibler, 'Heidegger and the Rhetoric of Submission', in Verena Andermatt Conley (ed.) *Rethinking Technologies* (Minneapolis: University of Minnesota Press, 1993) p. 116.

62. Heidegger, *Basic Writings*, p. 294.
63. Ibn Rāddas, *Shā'irāt min al-Bādīyah*, p. 108.
64. Ibid., p. 339.
65. Ibid., pp. 108–9.
66. Ibid., p. 108.
67. T. S. Eliot, *The Waste Land*, in T. S. Eliot, *Collected Poems, 1909–1962* (New York: Harcourt, Brace & World, 1936) p. 61.
68. Ibn Rāddas, *Shā'irāt min al-Bādīyah*, pp. 108–9.
69. Ibid., p. 171.
70. Ibid., p. 105.
71. The post-colonial assumption that there must be a cultural and political basis for employing technological tropes in literary texts often discards the rhetorical and linguistic aspects of this textual feature. For many post-colonial critics, however, the recurring reference to technology has a national and political bearing, which they locate in the historical formation of the nation. This tendency limits a reading of technology to instruments and tools that are culturally and politically appropriated. For instance, Dame Gillian Beer, in an essay 'The Island and the Aeroplane: The Case of Virginia Woolf', interprets the aeroplane as a topos of cultural and national modalities. Beer follows the figuration of the aeroplane in Woolf's writing and notes that, aside from her interest in air crashes, Woolf is preoccupied with the aeroplane. Beer points out that the aeroplane is a frequent figure in *Mrs Dalloway*, *Orlando* and *Between the Acts*. She views this 'flying-machine' as related to national and social paradigms, and affirms that Woolf's texts are 'concerned with the representation of England and with the difficult moments of historical national change' (p. 265). Beer offers another cultural and social interpretation of the car and the aeroplane without reading the rhetorical and discursive manifestations of these technological tropes that are clearly depicted in Woolf's novels. More interestingly, Beer cites many instances which suggest that Woolf writes about the interplay between the aeroplane and language. She cites a character in Woolf's novel *Between the Acts*, stating that 'if the spirit animates the whole, what about the aeroplane?' This statement aligns the machine with a possibility of animation rather than with a cultural signification, which I discussed in the context of prosopopoeia (see Chapter 4). Another textual instance arises in *Mrs Dalloway*, where an old woman utters a song in the Regent's Park that becomes indecipherable sounds: 'ee um fah um so foo swee too eem oo' (*Mrs Dalloway*, p. 90). See Gillian Beer, 'The Island and the Aeroplane: The Case of Virginia Woolf', in Homi Bhabha (ed.) *Nation and Narration* (London: Routledge, 1990) pp. 265–90.
72. Cole adds: 'Within the past ten years, the old labyrinthine mud-brick cities

have felt the tread of the bulldozer opening up broad, straight thoroughfares and are crumbling as the old houses are abandoned for modern air conditioned villas in the suburbs of high-rise apartment buildings.' See Cole, *The Nomads*, p. 16–17.

73. Ibn Rāddas, *Shāʿirāt min al-Bādīyah*, p. 269.
74. Ibid., vol. 2, p. 175.
75. Verene addresses technology in relation to desire in an elaborate philosophical discussion. He asserts that 'Technology is rooted in desire, in the primordial struggle of the self to be something.' See Donald Phillip Verene, *Philosophy and the Return to Self-Knowledge* (New Haven, CT: Yale University Press, 1997) p. 146.
76. Ibn Rāddas, *Shāʿirāt min al-Bādīyah*, p. 18.
77. Ibid., p. 155.
78. Ibid., p. 165.
79. Ibid., p. 105.
80. Ibid., p. 184.
81. Ibid., p. 243.
82. Ibid., p. 53.
83. Ibid., p. 296.
84. Elizabeth Grosz, *Jacques Lacan: A Feminist Introduction* (London: Routledge, 1990) p. 65.
85. Ibid., p. 64.
86. Ibid.
87. Jacques Lacan, *The Four Fundamental Concepts of Psycho-Analysis*, edited by Jacques-Alain Miller (New York: W. W. Norton & Company, 1981) p. 162.
88. Ibid., p. 165.
89. Grosz, *Jacques Lacan*, p. 75.
90. One could suggest that there is a link between the erogenous zones and the unconscious. Ronell remarks that 'as Lacan and others have indicated, analytic experience shows that the bodily orifices are linked to the opening/closing of the gap of the unconscious.' See Avital Ronell, *The Telephone Book* (Lincoln: University of Nebraska Press, 1989) p. 89.
91. Grosz, *Jacques Lacan*, p. 75
92. See Heidegger, *Basic Writings*, p. 317.

Chapter 6: The Translatability of the Nomadic

1. Spivak cites her own comment in the 'Translator's Preface' to her translation of late eighteenth-century Bengali poetry. See Spivak, 'The Politics of Translation', p. 370.
2. Ibid.
3. Ibid., p. 376.
4. Ibid., p. 377.
5. Ibid., p. 377.

6. Ibid., p. 377.
7. Paul de Man, 'Walter Benjamin's "Task of the Translator"', in Paul de Man, *The Resistance to Theory* (Minneapolis: University of Minnesota Press, 1993) pp. 73–105, and Walter Benjamin, 'The Task of the Translator', translated by Harry Zohn, in Hannah Arendt (ed.) *Illuminations* (New York: Schocken Book, 1969) pp. 69–82. Since Benjamin's essay in the 1920s, translation studies have developed to include other theoretical and pedagogical approaches to foreign languages and literature. During the last two decades translation has expanded to incorporate feminist theory as well as postcolonial and cultural studies. For a mapping of these interdisciplinary interpretations consider Lawrence Venuti, *Rethinking Translation* (London: Routledge, 1992); and Lawrence Venuti (ed.) *The Translation Studies Reader* (London: Routledge, 2000). See also Antoine Berman, *The Experience of the Foreign*, translated by S. Heyvaert (Albany: State University of New York, 1992). For a postcolonial analysis of translation, see Niranjana's two chapters examining the political and historical implications of Benjamin's essay as she reflects on de Man and Derrida's reading of it: Tejaswini Niranjana, *Siting Translation* (Berkeley: University of California Press, 1992). For a more recent theoretical and philosophical reflection on translation from Arabic, see ʿAbd al-Salām binʿAbd Al-ʿĀlī, *Fī al-Tarjamah* [On Translation] (Beirut: Dār al-Ṭalīʿah al-Ṭibāʿah wa-al-Nashr, 2001).
8. Spivak, 'The Politics of Translation', p. 269.
9. De Man, 'Walter Benjamin', p. 97. I referred to the notion of the authentic and inauthentic oral poem in Chapter 1 by showing that the source text is always dispersed and appropriated in a number of recitations.
10. This evokes Hussain and the debate about pre-Islamic poetry. See my discussion in Chapter 1.
11. The word 'original' is used here to refer to the Arabic texts in Ibn Rāddas's collection.
12. Benjamin, 'Task of the Translator', p. 70.
13. Ibid., p. 71.
14. Ibid.
15. Ibid., p. 72.
16. Ibid., p. 74.
17. De Man, 'Walter Benjamin', p. 83.
18. Ibid., p. 82.
19. Ibid., p. 83.
20. Benjamin, 'Task of the Translator', p. 73.
21. Ibid., p. 74.
22. Ibid.
23. Ibid., p. 75.
24. De Man, 'Walter Benjamin', p. 84.
25. Ibid., p. 90.
26. Benjamin, 'Task of the Translator', p. 75.

27. Ibid., p. 79.
28. De Man, 'Walter Benjamin', p. 80.
29. Ibid.
30. Ibid., p. 86.
31. In his discussion of Benjamin's essay Johnston writes: 'In his deconstructive reading, for example, de Man shows that Benjamin's essay is itself an example of what Benjamin's theory calls for, and in that sense is "untranslatable". Yet one can also argue, following Benjamin, that for that very reason it must be translated, and that in doing so one is not necessarily condemned merely to repeat and thereby remain trapped within the aporias of language to which de Man so well draws our attention.' See John Johnston, 'Translation as Simulacrum', in Lawrence Venuti (ed.) *Rethinking Translation* (London: Routledge, 1992) p. 42.
32. De Man, 'Walter Benjamin', p. 98.
33. Munir Ba'alabki, *Al-Mawrid: A Modern English-Arabic Dictionary* (Beirut: Dār El-Ilm Lil-Malayen, 1999).
34. In a fascinating account of the vocabulary of pre-Islamic poetry and a study of its meanings and origins, al-Shāyiʿ lists hundreds of words that were deployed in pre-Islamic odes related to transportation, especially with regard to horses and camels. See Nadā al-Shāyiʿ, *A Dictionary of the Language of the Mu'allakat Poets* (Beirut: Maktabat Lubnān Nāshrūn, 1993) pp. 179–97.
35. Cole, *The Nomads of the Nomads*, p. 36.
36. Musil, *The Manners and Customs of the Rwala*, p. 334. For a detailed illustration of animals, birds, camels and horses, see especially pp. 20–43 and 329–88.
37. Ibn Rāddas, *Shāʿirāt min al-Bādīyah*, p. 286.
38. Ibid., p. 23.
39. Ibid., 97.
40. See Kurpershoek, *Oral Poetry and Narrative from Central Arabia*, p. 282. The author mentions that the motif of *mahalah*, the water wheel, has remained uninterrupted since the time of the pre-Islamic poet Zuhayr ibn Abi Sulma. He cites a description of *maḥāllah*: 'As Ibn Junaydil explains, the noise made by the *mahalah* becomes louder as the bucket becomes heavier with water and the tension on the rope increases. Sometimes the driver of the camels on the tow path (*masna*) used to hammer a small, tapered piece of fig tree or desert plum (*sidr*) wood into one of the cracked ends of the axis on which the roller turns. As a result the *mahalah* did not turn as smoothly as before and a bucket of smaller size had to be attached to the rope. But the advantage gained was a sound that, though far from melodious, was regular enough that the labourer could tune into it with his own chanting and thus find some distraction from the boredom of his work.' Kurpershoek, *Oral Poetry and Narrative from Central Arabia*, p. 49.
41. Soraya Altorki and Donald P. Cole, *Arabian Oasis City: The Transformation of 'Unayzah* (Austin: University of Texas Press, 1989) p. 40.
42. Ibn Rāddas, *Shāʿirāt min al-Bādīyah*, p. 68.

43. Ibid., pp. 258–9.
44. Ibid., pp. 184–5.
45. Musil, *Manners and Customs*, p. 347.
46. Ibid., p. 339.
47. Ibid., p. 338.
48. Ibid., p. 156.
49. Ibn Rāddas, *Shā'irāt min al-Bādīyah*, p. 58.
50. Ibid., p. 70.
51. An example is Al-Sayyab's poem, 'Rain Song', an innovative composition that influenced modern Arabic poetry especially in its mediation on life and death and its mythical references. More importantly, its musical and rhetorical aspects show how the modern Arab poet sways back and forth between the old poetic tradition and the modernist mode. In its fine weaving of the old and new, rain becomes a mythical and lyrical force in the poem, staging the importance of this trope in Arabic poetic discourse. Al-Sayyab intensifies the melodic tone by repeating the refrain, 'Rain .../Drip, drop, the rain. .../Drip, drop.' See Badr Al-Sayyab, 'Rain Song', translated by Lena Jayyusi and Christopher Middleton, in Salma Khadra Jayyusi (ed.) *Modern Arabic Poetry: An Anthology* (New York: Columbia University Press, 1897) p. 427.
52. Arberry, *The Seven Odes*, p. 66.
53. Al-Fīfī addresses the significance of the imagery of rain and clouds in Imru' al-Qays's *mu'allaqah* and refers to the mythological and symbolic implications of the lines cited above in relation to pre-Islamic traditions and other ancient Middle Eastern cultures. He explains how rain is considered a sacred occurrence. Also, the scene of rain is associated with the hope of salvation after death, and with ruins in the elegiac opening of the poem. Al-Qays perceives nature as a female and the clouds represent her breasts. See Al-Fīfī, *Mafātīḥ al-Qaṣīdah al-Jāhilīyah*, pp. 200–15.
54. Ibn Rāddas, *Shā'irāt min al-Bādīyah*, pp. 339–40.
55. Ibid., p. 41.
56. Ibid., pp. 320–1.
57. Ibid., p. 70.
58. Ibid., p. 330.
59. Ibid., p. 165.
60. Ibid., p. 111.
61. Ibid., p. 330.
62. Ibid., p.180.
63. Ibid., vol. 2, p.47.
64. Ibid., p. 322.
65. Ibid., p. 369.
66. Ibid., vol. 2, p.46.
67. Ibid., p. 97.
68. Ibid., p, 116.

69. This poem is cited in Arabic by Al-Kamālī, *Al-Sh'ir 'inda Al-Badū*, p. 231. The English translation appeared in Jibrail S. Jabbur, *The Bedouins and the Desert*, translated by Lawrence I. Conrad (Albany: State University of New York, 1995) p. 402.
70. Ibn Rāddas, *Shā'irāt min al-Bādīyah*, p. 215.
71. Niranjana, *Siting Translation*, p. 133.
72. Spivak, 'The Politics of Translation', p. 372.
73. Ibid., p. 372. Spivak refers to Irigaray, who 'argues persuasively that Emmanuel Levinas to the contrary; within the ethics of sexual difference the erotic is ethical.' See Spivak, 'The Politics of Translation', p. 387, n. 6. See also Luce Irigaray, 'The Fecundity of the Caress', in Luce Irigaray, *An Ethics of Sexual Difference*, translated by Carolyn Burke and G. C. Gill (Ithaca, NY: Cornell University Press, 1993).
74. Ibn Rāddas, *Shā'irāt min al-Bādīyah*, p. 225.
75. Spivak stresses that cultural translators 'ask us to attend to the rhetoric which points to the limits of translations, in the creole's, the slave-daughter's, the Carib's use of "English." Let us learn the lesson of translation from these brilliant inside/outsiders and translate it into the situation of other languages.' See Spivak, 'The Politics of Translation', p. 383.
76. The custom of refuge and protection is one of the most highly regarded and unique Bedouin attributes practised both before and after Islam. Anyone who seeks protection, whether he has committed a deliberate or an unintentional act of violence or has violated tribal law would be granted refuge and safety by another tribe or leader. This custom lies in protecting the defenseless and oppressed. Musil devotes a section to explaining the different kinds of protection, in *Manners and Customs*, pp. 438–54.
77. Stetkevych, *The Zephyrs of Najd*, p. 114.
78. Ibid., p. 180.
79. Ibid., p. 181.
80. See Jacques Derrida, 'The Retrait of Metaphor', translated by F. Gasdner et al., *Enclitic*, vol. 2, no. 2 (Fall 1978) p. 6.
81. Ibid.
82. Ibid., p. 7.
83. Ibid.
84. Ibn Rāddas, *Shā'irāt min al-Bādīyah*, p. 296.
85. Ibid.
86. Ibid., p.108.
87. Ibid.
88. Ibid., p. 171.
89. Ibid., p. 105.
90. Ibid.
91. Ibid., p. 205
92. Ibid., p.108.

93. In these poems, the signifier presents itself as something other in Arabic, designating itself towards another language as it points to another technological event. One could also read this in an American context, where there was a displacement of the horse. When Americans began to adopt motorcars, there was a sense of fear that the horse was going to be dethroned. 'By the time the Ford Motor Company was organized in 1903, the belief was common that the automobile would soon replace the horse, and mass ownership of reliable motor vehicles seemed probable in the near future.' The motorcar industry registered its superiority in popular culture. Companies, stables and small businesses switched to motorcars in 1905. In the popular street, the horse was dethroned. Thomas A. Edison articulated this and the anticipation of modernity when he told a *New York Times* reporter: 'the horseless vehicle is the coming wonder. … It is only a question of time when the carriages and trucks in every large city will be run with motors.' See James Flink, *The Car Culture* (Cambridge, MA: MIT Press, 1975) pp. 14–15. See also James Flink, *America Adopts the Automobile, 1895–1910* (Cambridge, MA: MIT Press, 1970).
94. See Derrida, 'Retrait of Metaphor', p. 17.
95. Derrida performatively inscribes the effects of translation in his essay 'Living On' by intertextually analysing, grafting and referring to many of his own texts and to those of others. See Jacques Derrida, 'Living on: Border Lines', in Geoffrey Hartman (ed.) *Deconstruction and Criticism* (New York: Continuum Publishing Company, 1979) p. 102.

Bibliography

ʿAbbas, Iḥsān, *Tārīkh Dawlat al-Anbāṭ* (The History of al-Anbat) (Amman: Dār al-Shurūq lil-Nashr wa-al-Tawzīʿ).

Abraham, Nicolas and Maria Torok, *The Shell and the Kernel: Renewals of Psychoanalysis*, translated by Nicholas T. Rand (Chicago: University of Chicago Press, 1994).

Abu-Lughod, Lila, 'Honor and the Sentiments of Loss in a Bedouin Society', *American Ethnologist*, vol. 12, no. 2 (1985) pp. 245–61.

'Islam and Gendered Discourses of Death', *International Journal of Middle East Studies*, vol. 25, no. 2 (1993) pp. 187–205.

Veiled Sentiments: Honor and Poetry in a Bedouin Society (Berkeley: University of California Press, 1986).

Writing Women's Worlds (Berkeley: University of California Press, 1993).

Adnan, Etel, 'At Both Ends', *First Intensity*, no. 11 (Fall 1998) pp. 13–22.

The Spring Flowers Own and the Manifestations of the Voyage (Sausalito, CA: Post-Apollo Press, 1990).

Adūnīs, *Al-Thābit wa-al-Mutaḥawwal* (Beirut: Dār al-ʿAwdah, 1977).

An Introduction to Arab Poetics, translated Catherine Cobham (Austin: University of Texas Press, 1990).

Agamben, Giorgio, *The Open: Man and Animal*, translated by Kevin Attell (Stanford, CA: Stanford University Press, 2004).

Stanzas: Word and Phantasm in Western Culture (Minneapolis, MN: University of Minnesota Press, 1993).

Alexiou, Margaret, *The Ritual Lament in Greek Tradition* (Cambridge: Cambridge University Press, 1974).

Allen, Roger, *The Arabic Literary Heritage* (Cambridge, UK: Cambridge University Press, 1998).

Al-Ansary, Rahman, *Qaryat Al-Fau* (New York: Palgrave Macmillan, 1982).

Al-Faraj, Khālid, *Dīwān 'Abd Allāh al-Faraj* (Poetry Collection of ʿAbd Allāh al-Faraj) (Bombay: publisher unknown, 1920).

Al-Fīfī, ʿAbd Allāh, *Mafātīḥ al-Qaṣīdah al-Jāhilīyah* (Jeddah: al-Nādī Al-Adabī al-Thaqāfī, 2001).

Al-Ḥasan, Ghasān, *Al-Sh'ir al-Nabaṭī fī Minṭaqāt al-Khalīj wa-al-Jazīrah al-'Arabīyah* (The Nabaṭī Poetry in the Gulf and the Arabian Peninsula) (Dubai: Wizārat al-Iʿlām wa-al-Thaqāfah fī Dawlat al-Imārāt al-Mutaḥidah, 1998).

Al-Ḥātim, ʿAbd Allāh, *Khīyār mā yultiqaṭ min al-Shi'r al-Nabaṭ* (The Best of What is Collected from Nabaṭī Poetry) (Damascus: Al-Matbaʿah al-Umumīyah, 1952).

Al-Jabri, Muḥammad, *Binyat al-Aql al-Arabi* (The Structure of the Arab Mind) (Casablanca: Al-Markaz al-Thaqāfī al-ʿArabī, 1986).

Al-Juhany, Uwaidah, *Najd Before the Salafi Reform Movement* (Ithaca, NY: Ithaca Press, 2002).

Al-Kamālī, Shafīq, *Al-Sh'ir 'inda Al-Badū* (Poetry for the Bedouin) (Beirut: Kutub, 1964).

al-Khālidī, Ibrāhīm Ḥamid, *Al-Mu'allaqāt al-Nabaṭīyah* (Kuwait: Mānshīt lil-Diʿāya wa-al-Iʿalān, 2009).

Al-Muṣṭāwī, ʿAbd al-Raḥman (ed.) *Dīwān Imru' al-Qays* (Beirut: Dār al-Maʿrifah, 2003).

Al-Musawi, Muhsin, *Arabic Poetry: Trajectories of Modernity and Tradition* (London: Routledge, 2006).

Al-Ṣafā, Ikhwān *The Animals' Lawsuit against Humanity*, translated by Rabbi Anson Laytner (Louisville, KY: Fons Vitae, 2005).

Al-Saʿīd, Ṭalāl, *Al-Mūswa'ah al-Nabaṭīyah al-Kāmilah* (The Complete Nabati Encyclopedia) (Kuwait: Dhāt al-Sālasil, 1987).

Al-Sayyab, Badr, 'Rain Song', translated by Lena Jayyusi and Christopher Middleton, in Salma Khadra Jayyusi (ed.) *Modern Arabic Poetry: An Anthology* (New York: Columbia University Press, 1997).

Al-Shanqīṭī, Aḥmad (ed.) *Al-Mu'allaqāt al-'Ashr* (Dār al-Kutub al-ʿIlmīyah, 2002).

Al-Shurā, Muṣtafah, *Shi'r al-Rithā' fī al-'Aṣr al-Jāhilī* (Beirut: Maktabat Lubnān Nāshirūn, 1995).

Al-Sūdānī, ʿAbd Allāh, *Rithā' Ghayr al-Insān fī al-Shi'r al-'Abbāsī* (Abu-Dhabi: Al-Majmaʿ al-Thaqāfī, 1999).

Al-Thumayrī, Muḥammad ibn Aḥmad, *Al-Funūn al-Sha'abīyah fī al-Jazīrah al-'Arabīyah* (Damascus: no publisher, 1972).

Altorki, Soraya and Donald P. Cole, *Arabian Oasis City: The Transformation of 'Unayzah* (Austin: University of Texas Press, 1989).

Anderson, Irvine H., *Aramco, the United States and Saudi Arabia* (Princeton, NJ: Princeton University Press, 1981).

Anon., 'Astute Ibn Saud', *Newsweek*, 21 August 1939, p. 21.

AP, 'Saudi Women Disciplined', *New York Times*, 13 November 1990.

Arberry, A. J., *The Seven Odes* (New York: Macmillan, 1957).

Ash-Shaye', Nada, *A Dictionary of the Language of the Mu'allakat Poets* (Beirut: Maktabat Lubnān Nāshrūn, 1993).

Ba'albakī, Munir, *Al-Mawrid: A Modern English-Arabic Dictionary* (Beirut: Dār El-Ilm Lil-Malayen, 1999).

Bailey, Clinton, *Bedouin Poetry from Sinai and the Negev: Mirror of a Culture* (Oxford: Oxford University Press, 1991.

Bamia, Aida, *The Graying of the Raven* (Cairo: American University of Cairo Press, 2001).

Beasley, David, *The Suppression of the Automobile* (New York: Greenwood Press, 1988).

Beer, Gillian, 'The Island and the Aeroplane: The Case of Virginia Woolf', in Homi Bhabha (ed.) *Nation and Narration* (London: Routledge, 1990) pp. 265–90.

Benjamin, Walter, 'The Task of the Translator', translated by Harry Zohn, in Hannah Arendt (ed.) *Illuminations* (New York: Schocken Book, 1969) pp. 69–82.

The Origin of German Tragic Drama, translated by John Osborne (London: National Library Board, 1977).

Berman, Antoine, *The Experience of the Foreign*, translated by S. Heyvaert (Albany: State University of New York, 1992).

Bhabha, Homi K., 'Postcolonial Authority and Postmodern Guilt', in Lawrence Grossberg et al. (eds) *Cultural Studies: A Reader* (New York: Routledge, 1992).

Bin'Abd Al-'Ālī, 'Abd al-Salām, *Fi al-Tarjamah* [On Translation] (Beirut: Dār al-Ṭalī'ah al-Ṭibā'ah wa-al-Nashr, 2001).

Bloom, Harold, *The Anxiety of Influence: A Theory of Poetry* (London: Oxford University Press, 1997).

Bū Sha'īr, Al-Rashīd, *Musā'alat al-Naṣ al-Riwā'ī fī 'Amāl 'Abd al-Raḥman Munīf* (Examining the Narrative Voice in the Works of Abdelrahman Munif) (Damascus: Manshūrāt Wizārat al-Thaqāfah, 2004).

Burton, Robert, *The Anatomy of Melancholy*, edited by Thomas C. Faulkner, Nicolas K. Kiessling and Rhonda L. Blair, 3 vols (Oxford: Clarendon Press, 1989–94).

Butler, Judith, *Precarious Life: The Powers of Mourning and Violence* (London: Verso, 2004).

Subjects of Desire (New York: Columbia University Press, 1987).

The Psychic Life of Power: Theories in Subjection (Stanford, CA: Stanford University Press, 1997)

Chase, Cynthia, *Decomposing Figures* (Baltimore, MD: Johns Hopkins University Press, 1986).

Chatty, Dawn, *From Camel to Truck: The Bedouin in the Modern World* (New York: Vintage, 1996).

Cheng, Anne, *The Melancholy of Race* (Oxford: Oxford University Press, 2000).

Clymer, Lorna, 'Graved in Tropes: The Figural Logic of Epitaph and Elegies in Blair, Gray, Cowper, and Wordsworth', *English Literary History*, vol. 62, no. 2 (1995) pp. 347–86.

Cole, Donald P., *The Nomads of the Nomads* (Chicago, IL: Aldine Publishing Company, 1975.

'Where Have the Bedouin Gone?' *Anthropological Quarterly*, vol. 76, no. 2 (2003) pp. 235–67.

Conley, Verena Andermatt, 'Preface', in Verena Andermatt Conley (ed.) *Rethinking Technologies* (Minneapolis: University of Minnesota Press, 1993).

Culler, Jonathan, *The Pursuit of Signs* (Ithaca, NY: Cornell University Press, 1981)

'Deconstruction and the Lyric', in Anselm Haverkamp (ed.) *Deconstruction is/in America: A New Sense of the Political* (New York: New York University Press, 1995) pp. 41–51.

'Reading Lyric', *Yale French Studies*, vol. 69, *The Lesson of Paul de Man* (1985) pp. 98–106.

Da Cruz, Daniel, 'How They Find Oil', *Saudi Aramco World*, vol. 17, no. 1, January/February 1966. <http://www.saudiaramcoworld.com/issue/196601/default.htm>

Deleuze, Gilles, 'What is Desire?' in Constantine V. Boundas (ed.) *The Deleuze Reader* (New York: Columbia University Press, 1993).

Deleuze, Gilles and Félix Guattari, *A Thousand Plateaus* (Minneapolis: University of Minnesota Press, 1983).

de Man, Paul, 'Autobiography as De-Facement', in Paul de Man, *The Rhetoric of Romanticism* (New York: Columbia University Press, 1984) pp. 67–81.

The Resistance to Theory (Minneapolis: University of Minnesota Press, 1993)

'Hypogram and Inscription', in Paul de Man, *The Resistance to Theory* (Minneapolis: University of Minnesota Press, 1993) pp. 27–53, first published 1986.

'Walter Benjamin's "Task of the Translator"', in Paul de Man, *The Resistance to Theory* (Minneapolis: University of Minnesota Press, 1993) pp. 73–105.

Derrida, Jacques, *Of Grammatology*, translated by Gayatri Chakravorty Spivak (Baltimore, MD: Johns Hopkins University Press, 1976).

'The Retrait of Metaphor', translated F. Gasdner et al., *Enclitic*, vol. 2, no. 2 (1978) pp. 3–33.

'Living on: Border Lines', in Geoffrey Hartman (ed.) *Deconstruction and Criticism* (New York: Continuum Publishing Company, 1979).

'Voice II', *Boundary 2*, vol. 12, no. 2 (1984) p. 79.

'My Chances/Mes Chances: A Rendezvous with some Epicurean Stereophonies', in Joseph H. Smith and William Kerrigan (eds) *Taking*

Chances, Psychoanalysis, and Literature (Baltimore, MD: Johns Hopkins University Press, 1985).

Mémoires: For Paul de Man (New York: Columbia University Press, 1986).

'"Eating Well", or the Calculation of the Subject: An Interview with Jacques Derrida', in Eduardo Cadavo, Peter Connor and Jean-Luc Nancy (eds) *Who Comes after the Subject?* translated by Peter Connor and Avital Ronell (New York: Routledge, 1991).

'The Animal That Therefore I Am (More to Follow)', translated by David Wills, *Critical Inquiry*, vol. 28, no. 2 (Winter 2002).

Derrida, Jacques and Bernard Stiegler, *Echographies of Television* (Cambridge: Polity Press, 2002).

Eliot, T. S. *The Waste Land*, in T. S. Eliot, *Collected Poems, 1909–1962* (New York: Harcourt, Brace & World, 1936).

Fanon, Frantz, *L'an V de la Révolution algérienne* (Paris: François Maspero, 1962).

'Ici la Voix de l'Algérie', in Frantz Fanon, *L'an V de la Révolution algérienne* (Paris: François Maspero, 1962).

A Dying Colonialism (New York: Grove Press, 1965).

'Algeria, Unveiled', in Frantz Fanon, *A Dying Colonialism* (New York: Grove Press, 1965)

'This Is the Voice of Algeria', in Frantz Fanon, *A Dying Colonialism* (New York: Grove Press, 1965) pp. 69–97.

Fantham, E., 'The Role of Lament in the Growth and Eclipse of Roman Epic', in Margaret Beissinger, Jane Tylus and Susanne Wofford (eds) *Epic Traditions in the Contemporary World: The Poetics of Community* (Berkeley: University of California Press, 1999).

Finke, Laurie A., *Feminist Theory, Women's Writing* (Ithaca: Cornell University Press, 1992).

Flink, James, *America Adopts the Automobile: 1895–1910* (Cambridge, MA: MIT Press, 1970).

The Car Culture (Cambridge, MA: MIT Press, 1975).

Forter, Greg, 'Against Melancholia: Contemporary Mourning Theory, Fitzgerald's *The Great Gatsby* and the Politics of Unfinished Grief', *Differences: A Journal of Feminist Cultural Studies*, vol. 14, no. 2 (2003) pp. 134–70.

Foucault, Michel, *History of Sexuality*, vol. 1, *An Introduction* (New York: Vintage, 1980).

Fourny, Jean-François, 'Post-Colonial Conditions: Exiles, Migrations, and Nomadisms', *Yale French Studies*, vol. 82 (1993) pp. 158–71.

'Laziness and Technology according to a Storyteller of Cairo', *Yale French Studies*, vol. 82 (1993).

Freud, Sigmund, 'Mourning and Melancholia', in James Strachey (editor and translator) *The Standard Edition of the Complete Psychological Works of Sigmund Freud*, 24 vols (London: Hogarth, 1953–74).

Frey, Hans-Jost, 'Undecidability', *Yale French Studies*, no. 69, *The Lesson of Paul de Man* (1985) pp. 124–33.

Gasché, Rodolphe, *The Tain of the Mirror: Derrida and the Philosophy of Reflection* (Cambridge, MA: Harvard University Press, 1986).

Gilroy, Paul, *After Empire: Multiculture or Postcolonial Melancholia* (London: Routledge, 2004).

Grosz, Elizabeth, *Jacques Lacan: A Feminist Introduction* (London: Routledge, 1990).

Guattari, Félix, 'Machinic Heterogenesis', translated by James Creech, in Verena Andermatt Conley (ed.) *Rethinking Technologies* (Minneapolis: University of Minnesota Press, 1993).

Gutas, Dimitri, *Greek Thought, Arabic Culture: The Graeco-Arabic Translation Movement in Baghdad and Early Abbasid Society* (London: Routledge, 1998).

Hardin, L. Kris and Mary Jo Arnoldi, 'Introduction', in M. J. Arnoldi, C. M. Geary and K. L. Hardin (eds) *African Material Culture* (Bloomington: Indiana University Press, 1996).

Heidegger, Martin, *Basic Writings*, edited by David Farrell Krell (New York: Harper & Row, 1977).

Hitti, Philip K., *History of the Arabs* (New York: Macmillan, 1951).

Holst-Warhaft, Gail, *Dangerous Voices: Women's Laments and Greek Literature* (London: Routledge, 1992).

Ḥusayn, Ṭāhā, *Al-Ḥayāt al-Adabīyah fī Jazīrat al-'Arab* (Literary Life in the Arabian Peninsula) (Beirut: Dār al-Kitāb al-Lubnānī, 1973).

Ibn Junaydil, Saʿad, *'Ālīyat Najd* (Riyadh: Dār al-Yamāmah, 1978).

Ibn Khaldūn, *The Muqaddimah*, translated by F. Rosenthal (Princeton, NJ: Bollingen, 1967).

Al-Muqaddimah (Beirut: Dār al-Qalam, 1992).

Ibn Khamīs, ʿAbd Allāh, *Al-Adab al-Sha'bī fī Jazīrat al-'Arab* (Popular Literature in the Arabian Peninsula) (Riyadh: Maṭābiʿ al-Farazdaq al-Tijārīyah, 1982).

Ibn Rāddas, ʿAbd Allāh, *Shā'irāt min al-Bādīyah* (Riyadh: Dār al-Yamāmah, 1969).

Irigaray, Luce, 'The Fecundity of the Caress', in Luce Irigaray, *Ethics of Sexual Difference*, translated by Carolyn Burke and G. C. Gill (Ithaca, NY: Cornell University Press, 1993).

Jabbur, Jibrail S., *The Bedouins and the Desert*, translated by Lawrence I. Conrad (Albany: State University of New York, 1995).

Johnson, Barbara, *A World of Difference* (Baltimore, MD: Johns Hopkins University Press, 1987).

The Wake of Deconstruction (Oxford: Blackwell, 1994).

Johnston, John, 'Translation as Simulacrum', in Lawrence Venuti (ed.) *Rethinking Translation* (London: Routledge, 1992).

Kennedy, Hugh, *The Early Abbasid Caliphate* (London: Croom Helm, 1981).

Kristeva, Julia, *Black Sun* (New York: Columbia University Press, 1989).

Kurpershoek, Marcel P., *Oral Poetry and Narrative from Central Arabia* (Leiden: E. J. Brill, 1994).

Lacan, Jacques, *The Four Fundamental Concepts of Psycho-Analysis*, edited by Jacques-Alain Miller (New York: W. W. Norton, 1981).

Laplanche, Jean. and J. B. Pontalis, *The Language of Psychoanalysis* (New York: W. W. Norton, 1973).

Lemoyne, James, 'MIDEAST TENSIONS: Saudi Interior Minister Prohibits All Protests for Change by Women', *New York Times*, 18 November 1990.

Linley, Margaret, 'Conjuring the Spirit: Victorian Poetry, Culture, and Technology', *Victorian Poetry*, vol. 41, no. 4 (2003) pp. 536–44.

Lionnet, Françoise, 'Translating Grief', *The Romantic Review*, vol. 94, nos 3–4 (2003).

Lord, Albert, *The Singer of Tales* (Cambridge, MA: Harvard University Press, 1960).

Lutwack, Leonard, *Birds in Literature* (Gainesville: University of Florida Press, 1994).

McDonald, M. V., 'Animal-Books as a Genre in Arabic Literature', *Bulletin: British Society for Middle Eastern Studies*, vol. 15, nos 1/2 (1988) pp. 3–10.

Menocal, Maria Rosa, *The Arabic Role in Medieval Literary History: A Forgotten Heritage* (Philadelphia: University of Pennsylvania Press, 1987).

Miller, J. Hillis, 'Catachresis, Prosopopoeia, and the Pathetic Fallacy: The Rhetoric of Ruskin', in Roland Hagenbuchle and Laura Skandera (eds) *Poetry and Epistemology: Turning Points in the History of Poetic Knowledge* (Regensburg: Verlag Friedrich Pustet, 1986).

'Prosopopoeia and Praeterita', in Laurence Lockridge and John Maynard (eds) *Nineteenth-Century Lives* (Cambridge: Cambridge University Press, 1989).

'Prosopopoeia in Hardy and Stevens', in Lance St John Butler (ed.) *Alternative Hardy* (London: Macmillan, 1989).

Monroe, James T., 'Oral Composition in Pre-Islamic Poetry', *Journal of Arabic Literature*, vol. 3 (1972) pp. 1–53.

'Which came first, the *Zajal* or *Muwashshaḥah*? Some Evidence for the Oral Origin of Hispano-Arabic Strophic Poetry', *Oral Tradition*, vol. 4, nos. 1 and 2 (1989).

Monroe, James T. and Menjamin M. Liu, *Ten Hispano-Arabic Strophic Songs in the Modern Oral Tradition* (Berkeley: University of California Press, 1989).

Munif, Abdelrahman, *Cities of Salt*, translated by Peter Theroux (New York: Vintage International, 1987).

Variations on Night and Day, translated by Peter Theroux (New York: Vintage International, 1994).

Musil, Alois, *The Manners and Customs of the Rwala* (New York: American Geographical Society, 1998).

Newcomb, John Timberman, 'The Footprint of the Twentieth Century: American Skyscrapers and Modernist Poems', *Modernism/Modernity*, vol. 10, no. 1 (2003) pp. 97–125.

Niranjana, Tejaswini, *Siting Translation* (Berkeley: University of California Press, 1992).

Nicholson, Reynold A., *Eastern Poetry and Prose* (Cambridge: Cambridge University Press, 1922).

Parla, Jale, 'Car Narratives: A Subgenre in Turkish Novel Writing', *South Atlantic Quarterly*, vol. 102, nos 2/3 (2003) pp. 535–50.

Pensky, Max, *Melancholy Dialectics* (Amherst: University of Massachusetts Press, 1993).

Racy, Ali jihad, 'Heroes, Lovers and Poet-Singers: The Bedouin Ethos in the Music of the Arab Near-East', *Journal of American Folklore*, vol. 109, no. 434 (1996) pp. 404–24.

Radden, Jennifer (ed.) *The Nature of Melancholy: From Aristotle to Kristeva* (Oxford: Oxford University Press, 2000).

Riffaterre, Michael, *Semiotics of Poetry* (Bloomington: Indiana University Press, 1978).

Roinett, Jane, *This Rough Magic: Technology in Latin American Fiction* (New York: Peter Lang, 1994).

Ronell, Avital, *The Telephone Book* (Lincoln: University of Nebraska Press, 1989).

Royle, Nicholas, 'Nuclear Pieces: Memories of Hamlet and the Time to Come', *Diacritics*, vol. 20, no. 1 (spring 1990) pp. 37–55.

Sacks, Peter M., *The English Elegy* (Baltimore, MD: Johns Hopkins University Press, 1985).

Said, Edward, 'Embargoed Literature', *The Nation*, vol. 251, 17 September 1990.

Scheibler, Ingrid, 'Heidegger and the Rhetoric of Submission', in Verena Andermatt Conley (ed.) *Rethinking Technologies* (Minneapolis: University of Minnesota Press, 1993).

Schiesari, Juliana, *The Gendering of Melancholia: Feminism, Psychoanalysis, and the Symbolics of Loss in Renaissance Literature* (Ithaca, NY: Cornell University Press, 1992).

Sells, Michael, *Desert Tracings* (Middletown, CT: Wesleyan University Press, 1989).

Socin, Albert, *Diwan aus Centralarabien* (Diwan from central Arabia) published by Hans Stumme (ed.) (Leipzig: Abhandlungen der philologisch-historischen classe der Koniglich sachsischen *Gesellschaft der Wissenschaften*, no. 19, 1901/1).

Sowayan, Saad, *Nabati Poetry: The Oral Poetry of Arabia* (Berkeley: University of California Press, 1985).

Al-Shi'r Nabaṭī: Dhā'iqat al-Sha'ab wa-Sulṭat al-Naṣ (Nabati Poetry: The Public Taste and the Power of the Text) (London: Saqi, 2000).

Spivak, Gayatri Chakravorty, 'The Politics of Translation', in Lawrence Venuti (ed.) *The Translation Studies Reader* (London: Routledge, 2000).

Stamelman, Richard, *Lost Beyond Telling* (Ithaca, NY: Cornell University Press, 1990).

Staudenmaier, John M., 'Rationality, Agency, Contingency: Recent Trends in the History of Technology', *Reviews in American History*, vol. 30, no. 1 (2002) pp. 168–81.

Steeves, H. Peter and Tom Reagan (eds) *Animal Others: On Ethics, Ontology, and Animal Life* (Albany: State University of New York, 1999).

Stetkevych, Jaroslav, *The Zephyrs of Najd* (Chicago, IL: University of Chicago Press, 1993).

Stetkevych, Suzanne P., 'Archetype and Attribution in Early Arabic Poetry: Al-Shanfarā and the Lāmīyat al-ʿArab', *International Journal of Middle East Studies*, vol. 18 (1986) pp. 361–90.

Twitchell, K. S. *Saudi Arabia* (Princeton, NJ: Princeton University Press, 1953).

Venuti, Lawrence, *Rethinking Translation* (London: Routledge, 1992).

(ed.) *The Translation Studies Reader* (London: Routledge, 2000).

Verene, Donald Phillip, *Philosophy and the Return to Self-Knowledge* (New Haven, CT: Yale University Press, 1997).

Vitalis, Robert, *America's Kingdom: Mythmaking on the Saudi Oil Frontiers* (Stanford, CA: Stanford University Press, 2007).

Weber, Samuel, *Return to Freud: Jacques Lacan's Dislocation of Psychoanalysis*, translated by Michael Levine (New York: Cambridge University Press, 1991).

Weinbaum, Batya, 'Lament Ritual Transformed into Literature: Positing Women's Prayer as Cornerstone in Western Classical Literature', *Journal of American Folklore*, vol. 114, no. 451 (2001) pp. 20–39.

Williams, R. Grant, 'Disfiguring the Body of Knowledge: Anatomical Discourse and Robert Burton's *The Anatomy of Melancholy*', *English Literary History*, vol. 68, no. 3 (2001) pp. 593–613.

Wolfe, Cary, *Animal Rites: American Culture, the Discourse of Species, and Posthumanist Theory* (Chicago, IL: University of Chicago Press, 2003).

(ed.) *Zoontologies: The Question of the Animal* (Minneapolis: University of Minnesota Press, 2003).

Wormhoudt, Arthur, *Selections from the Diwan of Al-Khansa* (Oskaloosa, IA: William Penn College, 1973).

Yamamoto, Kejji and Charles Burnett (eds) *Abu Ma'Sar on Historical Astrology: The Book of Religions and Dynasties (On the Great Conjunctions)*, 2 vols (Leiden: Brill, 2000).

Zumthor, Paul, *Introduction à la Poésie orale* (Paris: Éditions du Seuil, 1983).

Index

www.ingramcontent.com/pod-product-compliance
Lightning Source LLC
Chambersburg PA
CBHW070521100726
47907CB00004B/929

* 9 7 8 0 7 5 5 6 5 2 9 9 0 *